Italian Politics

DATE DUE

DE 2'97			
DE19'97			

Italian Politics

Ending the First Republic

EDITED BY

Carol Mershon
and Gianfranco Pasquino

A Publication of the Istituto Cattaneo

Westview Press

BOULDER • SAN FRANCISCO • OXFORD

Italian Politics: A Review, Volume 9

This Westview softcover edition is printed on acid-free paper and bound in library-quality, coated covers that carry the highest rating of the National Association of State Textbook Administrators, in consultation with the Association of American Publishers and the Book Manufacturers' Institute.

Published in 1995 in the United States of America by Westview Press, Inc., 5500 Central Avenue, Boulder, Colorado 80301-2877, and in the United Kingdom by Westview Press, 12 Hids Copse Road, Cumnor Hill, Oxford OX2 9JJ

Library of Congress Cataloging-in-Publication Data
Italian politics : ending the First Republic / Carol Mershon and
    Gianfranco Pasquino, eds.
    p. cm.
    Includes bibliographical references and index.
    ISBN 0-8133-8893-7
    1. Italy—Politics and government—1976– 2. Political corruption—
Italy. 3. Elections—Italy. I. Mershon, Carol. II. Pasquino,
Gianfranco.
JN5451.I835   1995
320.945'09'049—dc20   94-36048
                                                                           CIP

The Istituto Cattaneo, founded in 1965, is a private, nonprofit organization. It aims to promote, finance, and conduct research, studies, and other activities that contribute to the knowledge of contemporary Italian society and, especially, of the Italian political system.

Istituto Carlo Cattaneo, Via Santo Stefano 11, 40125 Bologna, Italy

Printed and bound in the United States of America

Contents

Foreword

This is the ninth volume in the series *Italian Politics*, edited by the Cattaneo Institute.

The series, which began in 1986, remains faithful to its original intention: the thorough examination and analysis of the facts and events that, each year, mark trends and continuities in the Italian political system. This volume provides a chronicle and analysis of the events of 1993.

When the project *Italian Politics* began, thirty years of scholarship had focused on the stability of Italian political life. In contrast to the situation of other countries, where the shifting electoral fates of politicians gave the appearance, if not the reality, of political change, the persistence of political leadership in Italy from the post-war period until the 1980s was taken as proof of the absence of political change in general. Nevertheless, during the long period that followed post-war democratic consolidation, Italian politics *was* changing, though at a pace much slower than changes in the economy and society. There were no grand transformations like those that elsewhere announced a restructuring, true or presumed, between politics and society. Rather, political change was subtly manifested in a multitude of everyday events: interviews, manifestos, demonstrations, and partial elections. To inventory these events, to weigh their significance and to analyze their meanings, were the goals of the *Italian Politics* project at its inception in 1986 and remain our guiding principles in this volume.

The Italian politics of the present has lost every trace of stability. For Italy, the passage from the 1980s to the 1990s has signaled deep transformations in the main components of the political system: in political parties and institutions, in the orientation of public opinion, and in the mechanics of the electoral system. In the eyes of the international media, Italy has become a "laboratory" for the observation of the dynamics of democratic regimes. Scholars now debate whether this transformation constitutes a new regime and if it is legitimate to speak of a "Second Republic."

In a certain sense, the acceleration of change in Italian politics has made it easier to single out, from the multitude of chronicled facts, those events that most contributed to the destruction of the political equilibrium. The following examples, themes dealt with in this volume, are worth mentioning — the end of the Christian Democrats, the referendum of April 18th, and the new electoral law.

Nevertheless, the goal of our series remains the same: to bring together Italian and foreign researchers who recount and interpret the tempestuous events of the year. The entire series is an archive, which the passing of the years renders a precious tool for reconstructing the circumstances of these events and their deeper motivations. In this sense, *Italian Politics* is not only an authoritative interpretation of the present but, above all, our memory.

Roberto Cartocci

Chronology of Italian
Political Events, 1993

January

1 Mafia boss Aldo Madonia is arrested after new revelations from State's witnesses.
As usual, accidents causing deaths and injuries follow the celebration of the New Year.

2 The OECD predicts a further rise in unemployment in Italy.
A cautionary warrant (*avviso di garanzia*, which notifies the recipient that he or she is under judicial investigation) is issued to DC Senator Lello Lombardi for charges related to a business office development in L'Aquila.
Giulio Andreotti replies that he is "surprised and indignant" at a *New York Times* story, according to which the ex-Premier had contacts with Mafia figures.

4 Storm hits the lira: The US dollar rises to 1512 lire and the D-mark to 924.
As "Clean Hands" (*Mani pulite*) investigations into corruption unfold, Roberto Spallarossa of the San Matteo Hospital in Pavia commits suicide. This is the sixth suicide since the investigations started.
Minister of the Interior Nicola Mancino announces that the Mafia had planned an attempt on the life of Rete leader Leoluca Orlando.

5 The dollar closes at 1534 lire and the mark reaches 938.
Anti-Mafia summit is held at the Quirinale, the President's residence.
Minister of the Treasury Barucci refers to the interest that several Arab countries have in the privatization of Italian state-held industries.

7 A select committee of the Senate begins discussing the reform of public financing of political parties.
State's witness Leonardo Messina names Andreotti as a politician with Mafia ties.

8   A second cautionary warrant is issued to PSI secretary Bettino Craxi for corruption and violation of the law on party financing. Craxi declares, "they want to eliminate me from the political scene."
    The lira gains ground against the dollar and the mark.
    Beppe Alfano, journalist for the newspaper La Sicilia, is assassinated by the Mafia.

9   "Clean Hands" comes to Rome and investigations focus on a contract for cleaning services at the EUR Agency.
    Minister of the Treasury Barucci declares that the public deficit will reach 163,000 billion lire (US$107 billion) instead of the target of 155,000 billion lire.

10 Traffic is restricted in eleven Italian cities suffocating from smog.
    The PDS no-confidence motion sets the stage for discussions on a post-Amato phase.

11 Minister Barucci outlines a Euro-loan plan and the lira gains ground.

12 The cabinet abolishes the Ministry of State Holdings and modifies the law on illicit drugs, allowing for the decriminalization of the possession of small amounts.
    The Euro-loan succeeds but gives no boost to the lira.
    Minister Barucci announces the definitive start of the privatization of the Credit Bank, INA (National Insurance Institute), SME (food products holding company), and the Nuovo Pignone metalworking concern.

13 Forty-one separate charges in 122 pages detail the request for authorization to proceed in investigations against Craxi.
    The Constitutional Court meets to judge the admissibility of 13 referendum proposals.
    Roberto Boemio, Air Force General, is killed in Brussels. He is considered one of the most important witnesses in the investigations into the Ustica disaster.
    The Confindustria expresses support for the Amato government, calling those who threaten the stability of the executive "insane."

14 Parliament grants 12 authorizations to proceed in investigations. Among those under investigation are ex-Minister of Transportation Carlo Bernini (DC), DC administrative secretary Severino Citaristi, and PSI parliamentarian Sisinio Zito.
    A suitcase containing computer diskettes with data on the Ustica disaster is stolen from Swedish engineer Gunno Gunnval.

15 Salvatore Riina, considered the number-one man in the Mafia, is captured in downtown Palermo after more than a decade at large.

16 The Constitutional Court declares ten referendum items admissible, among which are those proposed by Mario Segni, Massimo Severo Giannini, and Marco Pannella.

17 Baldassarre Di Maggio, ex-chauffeur for the "boss of bosses," is revealed as the State's witness whose testimony allowed Riina to be captured.

18 Riina denies all accusations.
The EC grants a maxi-loan to the Italian government.
Giuseppe Carbone and Emidio Di Giambattista, the President and the Chief Prosecutor of the Court of Accounts, respectively, come under investigation, accused of abuse of office and forgery.

19 In protest, MSI secretary Gianfranco Fini and League ideologue Gianfranco Miglio quit the Bicameral Committee on Electoral Reform.

20 Carlo Azeglio Ciampi, Governor of the Bank of Italy, does not deny the possibility of departures from current economic policy.
Mario Segni resigns from the Bicameral Committee. Cesare Salvi (PDS) resigns as rapporteur on the electoral law and is replaced by Sergio Mattarella (DC).
Investigations into the ENI-Montedison affair (ENI's purchase of Montedison's stake in Enimont) are started after a declaration by Giacomo Mancini about PSI involvement.
The Bank of Italy and ABI (Italian Banking Association) declare a liquidity crisis in the banking system.

21 Gambardella resigns as chief executive officer of ILVA after the company registers serious losses.
The Confindustria and unions reach an agreement on special contracts for youth, which combine training and employment.

22 Alarming statistics on unemployment: 40% of young people are unemployed in the South and 15% in the North and Center.
Ciampi proposes readying Italy to rejoin the European Monetary System (EMS), since membership affords more flexibility in battling inflation.
The government approves a decree privatizing public employment, making mobility, subsidized layoffs and dismissal possible for state employees, and abolishing "double salaries" for members of parliament who are state employees.
An account is discovered at the Lugano branch of the Unione delle Banche Svizzere. According to a Swiss magistrate, the account served to finance the PSI.
Suspicions grow about the ENI-Montedison affair.

23 Socialist Giovanni Manzi, ex-head of SEA (Airport Management Author-

ity), is expelled from Santo Domingo after 8 months as a fugitive and returns to Italy.

Raimondo Fassa, the first mayor in Varese from the League, takes office thanks to support from the PDS and the PRI.

24 Craxi asks that Parliament start investigating the financing of all parties.

25 The Swiss Court of Appeals decides to waive rules on bank secrecy for the Lugano account allegedly financing the PSI.

26 Magistrates order a search of the home and office of ex-Montedison chairman Giuseppe Garofano.
   Inflation stands at 4.3%, the lowest rate in 5 years.
   Claudio Martelli declines the position of PSI secretary after Craxi's departure.

27 The Confindustria asks for a significant reduction in the discount rate to fight unemployment.
   There are new worries about exchange rates.
   Investigations of Enimont and ANAS (National Roads and Highways Agency) begin.

28 FIAT chairman Giovanni Agnelli calls for political renewal to restore economic health.
   The Chamber approves a new law on the direct election of mayors.
   Ex-Minister of Public Works Giovanni Prandini (DC) is investigated in the ANAS case.
   New evidence against Craxi emerges.

29 The PSI's administrative offices are searched in Rome. In Milan Giovanni Manzi tells of the division of bribes among the PSI, DC, PRI, and PSDI.
   A third cautionary warrant is issued to Craxi, a second to Gianni De Michelis (PSI), and a seventh to Citaristi.
   The accusations against Craxi center on illicit funds diverted to several foreign accounts.

30 Judge Gerardo Colombo describes the heavy work load at the Palazzo di Giustizia, saying "everyone questioned here talks."
   Giorgio Casadei, secretary to De Michelis, turns himself in. Craxi declares, "this is not an atmosphere of renewal, but of the undoing of democracy."
   The City Council of Milan approves (42 votes for, 33 against) the city's candidacy for the Olympics in the year 2000.

31 Socialist Valerio Bitetto, ex-Director of ENEL (National Electrical Energy Agency), gives himself up. His is the 110th arrest by "Clean Hands."

February

1 The EC reminds the Italian government that it should immediately take action to spur economic recovery.
The PSI secretariat cannot agree on who should be named new party secretary.

2 Top management in the food products holding company under IRI (Institute for Industrial Reconstruction) approve the division of the SME into three companies, soon to be privatized.

3 An eighth cautionary warrant is issued to Citaristi, a fourth to Craxi, and a second to Paolo Pillitteri (PSI).
Republican Regional Councillor Antonio Savoia attempts suicide in Milan, fearing that he will be involved in the corruption scandal.
Achille Occhetto (PDS secretary general) outlines to the Chamber his no-confidence motion against Amato's government.
Albino Longhi is nominated to the management of Tg1, the RAI-1 news program. RAI-1 is one of three channels in the state-held television system.

4 Milan Public Prosecutor Francesco Saverio Borrelli declares that the raid in the Chamber of Deputies carried out by Finance Guards in search of PSI budgets was only a misunderstanding.
Italy's trade balance is positive.

5 The Amato government wins the vote of confidence (321 to 255).
The Court of Cassation denies the request to release SISDE (Information and Security Service) executive Bruno Contrada, who is accused by four State's witnesses of collusion with the Mafia.

6 President Oscar Luigi Scalfaro asks the government to continue its investigations into reconstruction efforts in Irpinia.
State's witness Francesco Mannoia will receive protection and financial support in the United States, as did Tommaso Buscetta, in exchange for his collaboration.

7 Silvano Larini, in hiding for 8 months, turns himself in. He is believed to be the key man needed to retrace the path of PSI illicit funds.

8 In Isernia, a joint list of the Left and lay parties defeats the DC, which plummets from 61% to 39% of the vote.
Ciampi, who wanted to resign from the Bank of Italy in September 1992, has the full support of Premier Amato. Speculation about Ciampi's successor begins.
A second cautionary warrant is issued to Antonio Del Pennino and a first to Italico Santoro (both PRI), as part of the ENEL case.

A cautionary warrant is issued to Vittorio Sbardella (DC), for kickbacks on contracts for the extension of the Roman subway system.

Rosetta Cutolo, sister of Mafia boss Ottaviano Cutolo, is arrested after 13 years in hiding.

9 Silvano Larin (PSI) reveals that he holds the Lugano account in his name and claims that Craxi and Martelli are involved.

Ex-DC secretary Arnaldo Forlani appears to be involved in the ENEL case.

10 After receiving a cautionary warrant for fraudulent bankruptcy, Minister of Justice Claudio Martelli resigns from the government and from the PSI.

11 Overwhelmed by the "Clean Hands" investigations, Craxi resigns as PSI secretary after over 16 years in the post. Valdo Spini and Giorgio Benvenuto seem to be the only candidates to replace him.

12 The Socialist Assembly elects Benvenuto as party secretary (56% of the votes). Valdo Spini receives 41%.

Giovanni Conso, ex-President of the Constitutional Court, is named Minister of Justice. Three ministers who are under investigation (Carmelo Conte, Giovanni Goria, and Francesco De Lorenzo) retain their posts.

Judge Antonio Di Pietro calls for new rules to strengthen morals in the country.

13 A cautionary warrant is issued to' Gabriele Cagliari, president of ENI (National Hydrocarbons Agency), for falsification of company reports and embezzlement.

A cautionary warrant goes to ex-Minister of the Budget Paolo Cirino Pomicino, accused of accepting bribes.

Other cautionary warrants are issued in cases regarding the Roman subway system, ANAS, and Irpinia reconstruction funds.

Segni declares that he wants to create a new political party.

15 Cautionary warrants are imminent for the entire ex-board of ENI and for Raul Gardini, ex-chief executive officer of the Ferruzzi Group.

Ugo Zilletti, ex-President of the Superior Council of the Judiciary (CSM) is arrested for fraudulent bankruptcy.

16 From 1970 to 1980 ENI maintained illicit funds (*fondi neri*) to finance parties: 40% each to the DC and PSI, 10% each to the PSDI and PRI.

Cautionary warrants are issued to Undersecretaries Vito Bonsignore (DC) and Claudio Lenoci (PSI).

After 395 days in office, Giampiero Borghini (ex-PCI/PDS) resigns as mayor of Milan.

17 Licio Gelli, the head of the P2, is interrogated for seven hours in Milan on the

Lugano bank account.

Craxi's loyal secretary, Vincenza Tomaselli, is jailed for complicity in corruption. Two more cautionary warrants go to De Michelis (the ENEL case and funds diverted from aid for developing countries).

The lira falls to 949 against the mark.

Ciampi urges banks to lower interest rates by two points.

18 Economic forecast is bleak.

The government is shaky after the DC and PLI oppose a reshuffle desired by Amato and after Minister of Health Francesco De Lorenzo refuses to resign. Jacques Delors of the EC praises the Amato government and speaks of the risks of unemployment.

19 Minister of Finance Goria and Minister of Health De Lorenzo resign. De Lorenzo's resignation follows the house arrest of his father, who is accused of having pocketed a 1.7 billion lire bribe ($1.1 million).

A thirteenth cautionary warrant is issued to Severino Citaristi and a first to Giusi La Ganga for corruption relating to the Asti hospital. La Ganga resigns as head of the PSI delegation in the Chamber.

Enzo Carra, ex-spokesman for Forlani, is arrested for false declarations and failure to cooperate in the Enimont case.

20 Carra's arrest is justified as a measure to prevent any tampering with evidence.

A cautionary warrant is issued to PSDI president Antonio Cariglia, accused of complicity in corruption.

21 Government reshuffle: Raffaele Costa (PLI) becomes Minister of Health; Franco Reviglio (PSI), Minister of Finance; Nino Andreatta (DC), Minister of the Budget; and Gianfranco Ciaurro (PLI), Minister of EC Policies. The Ministry of Privatizations is established and entrusted to the non-party expert Paolo Baratta.

Giorgio Medri, ex-head of the PRI secretariat's office, is arrested on charges of corruption and violation of the law on party financing.

22 Francesco Mattioli, finance director of FIAT, and Antonio Mosconi, chief executive officer of Toro Assicurazioni, are arrested. Both are accused of aggravated corruption and of violation of the law on party financing.

Amato declares that he does not want to force the resignation of the many undersecretaries who have received cautionary warrants.

23 The government says it will ask for a vote of confidence on its reshuffle.

The lira falls further against the mark, reaching a low of 970.

In the Veneto, the entire regional administration resigns due to the corruption scandal. Sergio Castellari, ex-administrative director of the Ministry of State Holdings, disappears.

24 The mark gains against the lira, closing at 983.
Justice Minister Conso outlines a political solution to *Tangentopoli* (Italy's corruption scandal): plea bargaining for the accused in exchange for confession, return of funds and disqualification from holding public office.

25 The lira recovers slightly. Ciampi states that in the crisis of the preceding autumn, Italy risked financial ruin.
Having received a cautionary warrant for violation of the law on party financing, Giorgio La Malfa resigns as PRI secretary.
A cautionary warrant is issued to Lorenzo Necci, chief executive officer of the State Railways and 1989-90 chairman of Enimont. Financier Gianpiero Pesenti is placed under house arrest.
Sergio Castellari, ex-administrative director of the Ministry of State Holdings, is found dead in the Roman countryside.
The government sets a date for the referenda: April 18.

26 Cautionary warrants are issued to Raul Gardini and Sergio Cragnotti for involvement in the Enimont affair.

27 The PDS seems also to have a Swiss bank account in which illicit funds were deposited.
In Rome 300,000 workers, acting independently of the CGIL, CISL, and UIL, demonstrate in defense of employment and against the Amato government.

28 Umberto Ortolani, the financier and P2 member already sentenced to nineteen years in prison for his role in the Banco Ambrosiano affair, is interrogated about the Lugano account and the relationships between the PSI and the Banco Ambrosiano.

March

1 Primo Greganti, PCI functionary, is arrested and accused of having accepted on behalf of his party a bribe of 621 million lire, which he later deposited in a Swiss account.
Michele De Mita, brother of Ciriaco, is arrested and accused of criminal association, fraud, and forgery in the Irpinia affair.

2 Ciriaco De Mita (DC) resigns as President of the Bicameral Committee.
Craxi declares before the Chamber Committee on Authorizations to Proceed that he is the victim of a plot.
Despite downgrading by Moody's, the lira maintains its value.

3 Disputes continue over a political solution to *Tangentopoli*.
De Mita resubmits to the Bicameral Committee his resignation, which had been refused and is now accepted.

It is found that reconstruction in Valtellina went forward thanks to bribes and kickbacks.

4   Ex-Forlani spokesman Enzo Carra is brought into court in handcuffs. Forlani speaks of "Gestapo methods."
A bank account in the name of Enza Tomaselli, Craxi's secretary, is discovered.

5   The cabinet approves the political solution to *Tangentopoli*, decriminalizing the offense of illicit party financing and establishing administrative sanctions (the trebled restitution of bribes and disqualification from holding public office for from three to five years).

6   Conso's solution to *Tangentopoli* generates controversy.
Another cautionary warrant is issued to ex-Minister of Public Works Giovanni Prandini.

7   President Scalfaro refuses to sign the cabinet's decrees on *Tangentopoli*.
Milan Public Prosecutor Borrelli speaks for all "Clean Hands" judges, expressing clear dissent from the decisions on *Tangentopoli*.
Carlo Ripa di Meana, Minister of the Environment, disagrees with the government's decisions on *Tangentopoli* and resigns from his post.

8   Students at Bocconi University boo Amato and shout encouraging slogans to "Clean Hands" magistrates.
Giuseppe Ciarrapico is sentenced to two years in prison without possibility of parole for the acquisition of Casina Valadier.

9   Gabriele Cagliari, president of ENI, is arrested for having paid a bribe of 4 billion lire ($2.5 million) to the PSI.
Enzo Carra is sentenced to two years in prison for a bribe of 5 billion lire in the Enimont affair.
The Chamber Committee on Authorizations to Proceed approves the requests from Milan judges to investigate Craxi for receipt of stolen goods, corruption, and violation of the law on party financing.
Primo Greganti maintains that the 621 million lire are his own, as is the Gabbietta account.
Valdo Spini (PSI) is named the new Minister of the Environment.

10 In a tumultuous Senate session on the Conso decree, confidence in the Amato government is reaffirmed.
The lira falls to 967 against the mark and to 1611 against the dollar.

11 "Clean Hands" magistrates consider charging Craxi and Martelli with fraud in the Banco Ambrosiano affair.
The Chamber rejects the cabinet decree that would have lifted the freeze on

public contracts and that had been urged by the National Builders' Association.

12 Scalfaro declares that whoever breaks the law must be punished.
   Unemployment continues to rise.

13 Antonio Crespo, ex-general manager of ANAS, describes businessmen lining up to pay bribes to ex-Minister Prandini, bringing their money in big boxes and shopping bags.
   Budget Minister Andreatta favors privatizing ENEL, INA, ENI, and STET (the IRI telecommunications holding company).

14 The campaign for the April 18 referenda opens. The Rete, MSI, and Communist Refoundation champion a "no" vote. A segment of the PDS founds the "Committee for a No."

15 Cautionary warrants are issued to Renato Altissimo, PLI secretary, and Antonio Cariglia, PSDI president, in the ENEL case.
   A request is made for authorization to proceed against the ex-Minister for the South, Riccardo Misasi (DC), accused of criminal association with the Mafia and extortion.
   New PSI secretary Benvenuto reveals the party's deficit of 180 billion lire ($112 million).

16 PLI secretary Altissimo resigns.
   In resigning, ENI president Cagliari declares that he inherited the system of illicit funds for party financing, thus involving Finance Minister Reviglio, ex-president of ENI, in the scandal.
   IRI closes 1992 with losses of 4,400 billion lire ($2.7 billion) and accumulated debts of 74,000 billion lire ($46 billion).

17 Reviglio denies any involvement in the management of illicit funds at ENI.
   Roman magistrates discover that bribes paid to ex-Minister Prandini were deposited in a Swiss bank account.

18 A cautionary warrant is issued to Vincenzo Muccioli, founder of the Community of San Patrignano.
   Giuseppe Ciarrapico and Mauro Leone are accused of criminal association for purposes of fraud and false reporting in the SAFIM Italsanità scandal.
   The Chamber grants authorization to proceed in investigations for vote buying against Francesco De Lorenzo (PLI), Giulio Di Donato (PSI), and Alfredo Vito (DC).

19 Attilio Bastianini, PLI vice secretary, is arrested and accused of aggravated corruption and violation of the law on party financing.
   The Confindustria asks that the discount rate be lowered; the Governor of

the Bank of Italy denies the request.

21 Minister of Agriculture Gianni Fontana resigns, accused of receipt of stolen goods and violation of the law on party financing. He is the sixth minister to resign from the Amato government.
Ciarrapico, accused in the SAFIM Italsanità case, gives himself up.

22 The projected annual rate of inflation holds at 4.2%, while the German inflation rate is 4.4%.
Alfredo Luigi Diana, ex-president of Confagricoltura, is named Minister of Agriculture.
Renato Altissimo and Egidio Sterpa (PLI) as well as Antonio Del Pennino and Girolamo Pellicano (PRI) are investigated regarding illicit funds at Assolombarda.

23 Industrial production declines by 3.4%.
Public accounts show a deficit 18,000 billion lire greater than the previous estimate.

24 Investigation of *Tangentopoli* begins in Naples. The headquarters of all parties (except the Greens and Radicals) are searched.
Vito Ciancimino, ex-mayor of Palermo, begins to collaborate with magistrates.
The abolition of special aid to the South is included as a referendum item.

25 Parliament approves the majoritarian system for municipalities under 15,000 inhabitants and provides for direct mayoral elections. It reserves 30% of candidacies for women.
Ambassador Giuseppe Santoro is arrested as part of the investigation into the diversion of aid for developing countries.
The lira reaches 982 against the mark and 1604 against the dollar.

26 Seventeen parliamentarians from Naples are under investigation, including Vincenzo Scotti (DC), Cirino Pomicino (DC), De Lorenzo (PLI), and Giuseppe Galasso (PRI), for bribes related to post-earthquake reconstruction efforts and the 1990 World Cup.

27 A sensational cautionary warrant is issued to Giulio Andreotti, accused by six State's witnesses of association with the Mafia. The DC leader is said to have guaranteed the respect of a pact between politicians and the Mafia.
Nello Polese, mayor of Naples, ends up in handcuffs. State's witness Pasquale Galasso accuses Antonio Gava, ex-Minister of the Interior, of belonging to the Camorra (Campania organized crime).

28 Neapolitan magistrates accuse Antonio Gava of association with the Camorra.

29 Mario Segni quits the DC, declaring that "it is hopeless to attempt to reform this party from the inside." DC secretary Mino Martinazzoli replies, "the great torment is over."
    Corrado Carnevale, ex-president of the First Penal Section of the Court of Cassation, is accused of Mafia association by some State's witnesses for having overturned sentences of Mafia bosses.
    PSDI secretary Carlo Vizzini resigns: He no longer has the resources to provide for the daily needs of the party (from rent to salaries).

30 Minister of Finance Franco Reviglio resigns after receiving a cautionary warrant as part of the investigation into ENI illicit funds.

31 Amato worries about the risk of early elections held before the approval of new electoral laws.
    Francesco Paolo Mattioli, the number-three man at FIAT, is granted house arrest after 38 days of imprisonment.

April

2   The DC asks for investigations of mysterious persons who "might have contacted Mafia and Camorra State's witnesses" in order to damage the DC with false evidence.
    The Court of Cassation decides that legislation on mayoral elections should not be submitted to a referendum because the new law "has innovatively superseded the [previous] rule."

3   The Roman Public Prosecutor asks for authorization to arrest ex-Minister of Public Works Prandini, accused of pocketing bribes of over 25 billion lire ($15.6 million) in the awarding of ANAS contracts.
    Budget Minister Andreatta intends to float 51% of SIP's shares on the market.
    Francesco Tagliamonte (DC) becomes mayor of Naples, backed by a majority made up of the DC, PSI and PLI.

4   Francesco Carraro (PSI) is elected as mayor of Rome for the third time, backed by a majority in the city council that includes many politicians under investigation.

5   Cautionary warrants go to Giulio Andreotti for violation of the law on public financing of parties and to Arnaldo Forlani for receipt of stolen property in the ANAS case.
    Roman vice-mayors Oscar Mammì and Enzo Forcella resign.

6   The report of the Parliamentary Anti-Mafia Committee reveals links between Salvo Lima and the Cosa Nostra and casts suspicions on Giulio Andreotti, the head of Lima's faction in the DC.

7   Another celebrated "Clean Hands" arrest: Giorgio Garuzzo, general manager of FIAT-Auto.
    Gaetano Amendola, secretary to Arnaldo Forlani, confesses to judges that he delivered bribes received from Antonio Crespo, general manager of ANAS, to Forlani.
    The Court of Cassation declares that the referendum on special aid to the South is inadmissable.
    Day liberty is granted to Renato Curcio, leader of the Red Brigades, who had served 17 years of a 28-year sentence.

8   Neapolitan judges issue accusations against ex-Minister of the Interior Antonio Gava, alleged to have reached agreement with the Camorra to free ex-Regional Councillor Ciro Cirillo, kidnapped by the Red Brigades. Ex-Budget Minister Paolo Cirino Pomicino and parliamentarians Alfredo Vito (DC), Vincenzo Meo (DC), and Raffaele Mastrantuono (PSI) are also accused of ties with organized crime.
    Ambassador to Argentina Claudio Moreno is jailed as part of the investigation into diversion of aid for developing countries.

9   Ex-Minister Prandini faces further accusations of corruption and Ambassador Santoro is arrested.

10 A new request for authorization to proceed against ex-Minister of Justice Claudio Martelli, accused of profiting from stolen certificates of deposit, is issued.
    Roberto D'Alessandro, chairman of Agusta, is arrested, accused of extorting bribes of 2.5 billion lire.

11 State's witnesses Tommaso Buscetta and Marino Mannoia accuse Giulio Andreotti of having personal ties with Mafia boss Stefano Bontade.

12 Mannoia states that Andreotti met Bontade in 1979 to plan the elimination of journalist Mino Pecorelli and General Carlo Alberto Dalla Chiesa.
    Segni asks the electorate to approve, by at least 60% of the vote, the referendum on the Senate electoral laws.

13 Ex-Board member of ENEL, Valerio Bitetto, describes "red cooperatives" as the channel through which illegal funds went to the ex-PCI.
    Vito Bonsignore (DC) resigns as Budget Undersecretary after receiving his third cautionary warrant.

14 For over two hours Andreotti defends himself before the Senate Committee on Authorizations to Proceed.
    Preventative custody is ordered for financier Ferdinando Mach di Palmstein, close to the PSI, accused of extortion in the scandal surrounding diversion of aid for developing countries.

Ottaviano Del Turco resigns as adjunct secretary general of the CGIL and is replaced by Guglielmo Epifani.

15 Senator Francesco Forte (PSI) is implicated for accepting bribes.
The City of Naples registers a budget deficit of 746 billion lire ($470 million). The CSM censures Martelli, telling him to contest the accusations brought against him, not attack the accusers.

16 Giuliano Di Bernardo, Grand Master of the Masons of the Great Orient in Italy, resigns.
Antonio Salomone, noted Sicilian Mafia Boss, is arrested in Brazil. He had been a fugitive since the early 1980s.

17 Giovanni Agnelli acknowledges the existence of "improper episodes" in relations between FIAT and Italian politicians, and announces his full collaboration with Milanese judges.
Amato announces his intention to go to the President immediately after the referendum vote in order to decide the timing and means of his government's resignation.

18 Initial data on turnout for the referenda show it is the highest since the 1985 referendum.

19 The "yes" wins in all eight referenda. The referendum on the Senate electoral laws is approved with 83% of the votes. The referendum decriminalizing possession of small amounts of drugs wins with 55%.
Positive response in financial markets following the referendum outcomes. The Roman municipal administration (*giunta*) and the Lazio regional administration resign.

20 Baldassare Di Maggio, ex-chauffeur of Mafia "boss of bosses" Totò Riina, states that in September 1988 he drove Riina, who was still a fugitive at the time, to a meeting with Giulio Andreotti.
The city council in Rome is dismissed and an emergency administrator is named under the authority of the Ministry of the Interior.
Claudio Burlando (PDS) is reconfirmed as mayor of Genoa, supported by a majority made up of the PDS, PSI, PSDI, PRI, Greens, and Antiprohibitionists.

21 "Clean Hands" magistrates have a long conversation with Cesare Romiti, chief executive officer of FIAT.
A cautionary warrant is issued to Minister of Defense Salvo Andò, under investigation for vote buying and for ties to Nitto Santapaola's Mafia clan. Claudio Martelli receives another cautionary warrant for corruption.
In Italy's largest cities inflation falls to an annual rate of 4.0%.

22 After a lengthy debate in Parliament, Premier Giuliano Amato resigns.
The Bank of Italy reduces the discount rate by one-half percentage point, to 11%.
Ex-Minister of Public Works, Emilio De Rose (PSDI), is arrested and accused of extortion.

23 In a long letter to the *Corriere della Sera*, Cesare Romiti of FIAT urges industrialists to bring to light the web of bribes and kickbacks: Businessmen should "go to magistrates and confess all."
Guido Carli, ex-Minister of the Treasury and Governor of the Bank of Italy for nearly 15 years, dies in Rome at the age of 79.
The lira rises to 1483 against the dollar and 935 against the mark.
The CSM suspends Corrado Carnevale from his post (and his salary) at the Court of Cassation.

25 The President of the Republic urges political forces to work toward the creation of a new government not linked to parties, in order to realize electoral reform and promote economic recovery.

26 President Scalfaro entrusts Carlo Azeglio Ciampi, Governor of the Bank of Italy, with the task of forming the new government.
The Public Prosecutor of Palermo decides to hand over to the Senate Committee on Parliamentary Immunity previously omitted sections of interrogations of the State's witnesses accusing Andreotti.

27 The Senate Committee on Parliamentary Immunity favors granting authorization to proceed against Andreotti.
Gabriele Cagliari, ex-president of ENI, confesses to Milan judges that he paid bribes of 26 billion lire ($17 million) to the DC and PSI.

28 Carlo Azeglio Ciampi, the first Premier in the history of the Republic who is not a member of parliament, presents the list of ministers of his cabinet.
The 24 ministers include 9 non-party technicians and 3 PDS ministers. The governing majority also includes the PRI and Greens.
Renato Pollini, ex-administrative secretary of the PCI, is implicated in investigations into bribes at the State Railways.
In the ongoing scandal surrounding diversion of development aid, the Court of Accounts condemns decisions made by the Ministry of Foreign Affairs between 1982 and 1987.
The IRI Board of Directors approves a restructuring plan for ILVA.

29 The Chamber of Deputies denies four requests for authorization to proceed against Craxi and authorizes investigation only of violation of the law on party financing and corruption; the two requests approved had been advanced by the Rome Public Prosecutor. Milan judges decide to appeal to the Constitutional Court.

After the Chamber's vote, Francesco Rutelli (Greens), Minister of the Environment, and the three PDS ministers resign. The opposition calls for early elections.

Giorgio Garuzzo, general manager of FIAT-Auto, and Paolo Torricelli, chief executive officer of FIAT-Avio, turn themselves in.

A cautionary warrant is issued to parliamentarian Giuseppe Santonastaso (DC), accused of extortion related to contracts for the Capodichino airport.

30 Demonstrations throughout Italy protest the Chamber's vote on Bettino Craxi.

The effects of the Craxi case are felt even in the stock and financial markets.

Mauro Bertini, manager of FIAT-Avio, gives himself up. He was the last of four FIAT executives still in hiding.

May

1 The leaders of the CGIL, CISL and UIL celebrate May Day and urge the government to approve electoral reforms as soon as possible so as to usher in early elections.

3 Andreotti announces that he will give up parliamentary immunity, inviting Palermo judges to investigate him. Only Parliament, however, can grant authorization.

A cautionary warrant is issued to ex-Minister Rino Formica (PSI), accused of having accepted bribes for contracts at the port of Manfredonia.

Andrea Manzella, professor of constitutional law at LUISS in Rome, is named general secretary in the Premier's office, the post he held in the Spadolini and De Mita governments.

4 Prime Minister Ciampi replaces the four ministers who resigned, naming PaoloBarile to the Ministry for Relations with Parliament, Livio Paladin to European Community Policy, Franco Gallo to Finance, and Umberto Colombo to Scientific Research; Valdo Spini returns to the Ministry of the Environment.

The Superior Council of the Bank of Italy names Antonio Fazio as the new Governor.

The PSI replaces the members of its directorate who are under investigation.

5 The Premier names 36 undersecretaries (20 DC, 10 PSI, 3 PSDI, and 3 PLI), completing his cabinet.

The Senate and Chamber modify their rules on open voting for all authorizations to proceed.

The IRI Board of Directors approves the plan for the sale of SME.

6 Ciampi declares that electoral reform is the first priority of his government.

He rejects a freezing of government bonds (BOT) and state bonds and endorses privatization.

Antonio and Lucio Cirino Pomicino, brothers of ex-Minister of the Budget Paolo Cirino Pomicino, are arrested in Naples for corruption.

Unions and the iron and steel concern Falck agree on a solution for the loss of over 1,000 jobs, forecast for 1993.

7 The Chamber votes its confidence in the Ciampi government (309 in favor from the DC, PSI, PSDI, and PLI; 185 abstaining from the PDS, Greens, PRI, and Northern League; 60 against from the MSI and Communist Refoundation).

Franco Nobili, president of IRI, is formally investigated for abuse of office.

8 Mario Segni announces that the Democratic Alliance will run a slate of candidates in the next parliamentary elections.

As part of investigations into diversion of development aid, a cautionary warrant goes to Giuseppe Balboni Acqua, Ambassador to Poland, for abuse of office.

9 Massimo D'Alema, on behalf of the PDS, refuses Segni's invitation to join the Democratic Alliance.

10 Multiple arrests are made in Milan and Rome for bribery at the State Railways.

At Enichem, the chemical concern under ENI, the deficit rises.

11 Renato Pollini, ex-administrative secretary of the PCI, is arrested for corruption and violation of the law on party financing.

The FIAT Board of Directors approves a new code of ethics to regulate relationships between FIAT employees and public officials.

La Sapienza University in Rome is also investigated as part of Tangentopoli.

12 Franco Nobili, president of IRI, is arrested for corruption and violation of the law on party financing.

The Ciampi government passes the vote of investiture in the Senate (162 in favor, 50 abstaining, 36 against).

13 The Senate grants authorization to proceed in an investigation of Giulio Andreotti, on the charge of criminal association with the Mafia.

Cautionary warrants are issued to Valdo Spini (PSI), Minister of the Environment, and Claudio Vitalone (DC), ex-Minister of Foreign Trade, as part of the investigation into aid for developing countries.

14 A bomb in the Parioli district of Rome: Dozens are wounded and damages amount to billions of lire.

A cautionary warrant goes to ex-secretary of the PSDI, Carlo Vizzini, accused of having pocketed 3.5 billion lire to facilitate the granting of contracts at the State Telephone Services Company (ASST).

15 The cabinet names Romano Prodi as president of IRI, a post he had held from 1982 to 1989.
   Pietro Ingrao, long-standing leader in the PCI/PDS left wing, leaves the party.

17 Carlo De Benedetti, chairman of Olivetti, admits that he had to pay bribes and kickbacks totaling tens of billions of lire to the DC and PSI to obtain orders from the Ministry of Posts and Telecommuncations and from ASST. Top managers at the Monte dei Paschi di Siena bank are arrested for having received bribes from a businessman in exchange for granting financing.

18 In Catania the police arrests Nitto Santapaola, the "number-two man" in the Cosa Nostra who had been at large for 11 years.

19 FIAT acquires a 51% interest in Maserati.
   The Public Prosecutor of Verona issues 15 orders of preventative custody against local politicians and administrators of local health units (USL).

20 Giorgio Benvenuto resigns as PSI secretary after disputes with the old-guard leadership of the party.
   Cautionary warrants go to deputies Bruno Landi, Raffaele Rotiroti, Agostino Marianetti (all PSI) and to Senator Giorgio Moschetti (DC), in the La Sapienza scandal.
   Nine Neapolitan magistrates are under investigation for handing down judgments favorable to the Camorra.

21 The government launches an economic package to reduce the deficit by 12,500 billion lire.
   Cautionary warrants are issued to Oscar Mammì (PRI), ex-Minister of Posts and Telecommunications, and to Vincenza Bono Parino (PSDI), ex-Minister of Culture. Both are accused of receipt of stolen goods and violation of the law on party financing.
   Monthly inflation reaches 4.0%, the lowest rate since October 1969.

22 A cautionary warrant goes to Giorgio La Malfa, ex-secretary of the PRI, for receipt of stolen goods and violation of the law on party financing.

23 In Palermo 100,000 people commemorate the tragic deaths of magistrate Giovanni Falcone, his wife, and bodyguards, who were murdered one year earlier.

24 Cesare Romiti, FIAT's chief executive officer, is under investigatation for complicity in corruption and violation of the law on party financing.

Two cautionary warrants are issued to Giusi La Ganga (PSI) for extortion. Industrial production falls further.

25 Cautionary warrants reach Ciriaco De Mita (DC) and Elveno Pastorelli, administrative director of the Ministry for Civil Protection, for aggravated extortion in reconstruction efforts in Campania.
Corrado Ferlaino, president of Napoli Calcio, is arrested for having paid bribes to win contracts connected with the 1990 World Cup.
FIAT-Auto faces severe economic difficulties.

26 Giulio Andreotti is investigated for complicity in the murder of journalist Mino Pecorelli, killed in 1979.

27 A car bomb kills five people in Florence near the Uffizi Museum.
The rapporteur of the Bicameral Committee, Sergio Mattarella (DC), presents the Chamber with the bill that will serve as the basis for electoral law reform.
Luigi Abete, president of Confindustria, proposes a "social contract" to create 500,000 new jobs over the next two years.

28 The PSI directorate elects Ottaviano Del Turco as secretary. Raffaele Costa, Minister of Transportation, becomes PLI secretary.
The hypothesis gains ground that the Mafia organized the bombings in Rome and Florence with the help of segments of the secret services.

29 Matteo Cinque, the *Questore* of Palermo (province-level chief of police) who is accused by State's witness Pasquale Galasso of complicity with the Camorra, is transferred.

31 The DC and PSI suffer severe losses in elections in Valle d'Aosta.
A cautionary warrant for extortion is issued to ex-Minister of Labor Franco Marini (DC).
Antonio Fazio, the new Governor of the Bank of Italy, gives his first report on the state of the Italian economy.

June

1 Offices at the Ministry of Posts and Telecommunications are sealed up due to the scandal surrounding the assignment of TV frequencies.
Orders go out to arrest for extortion all members of a previous provincial cabinet in Catania.
The 1992 budget for the State Railways Agency shows a deficit of 4,146 billion lire ($2.8 billion).

2 The *carabinieri* discover and disarm a bomb in Rome's historic center.

Gianluigi Gabetti, chief executive officer of IFI (Italian Financial Institute), is under investigation.

The *carabinieri* arrest Mafia boss Giuseppe Pulvirenti in Catania, at large for eleven years and believed to be the successor to Nitto Santapaola.

Carlo Zini, general administrator of the Monte dei Paschi di Siena bank, resigns after receiving a cautionary warrant for corruption.

3   Salvatore Randi, chief executive officer of Italtel, turns himself in. He is accused of corruption.

A second cautionary warrant goes to deputy Giuseppe Garesio (PSI), accused of extortion.

After eight years of profits, ENI's accounts are in the red.

4   Prime Minister Ciampi names a committee of ministers to reform the Mammì law on Italian television.

Mediobanca, Comit, Credit, Banco di Roma and San Paolo di Torino take responsibility for defining and implementing the financial restructuring of the Ferruzzi Group.

Changes are made in the top management of the secret services.

6   The governing parties meet defeat in the first round of local elections, involving 11 million voters.

7   The DC collapses everywhere except the South and the PSI is decimated. The PDS and *Rete* perform well and the League triumphs in the first direct mayoral elections.

8   Disputes over the cost of labor follow Luigi Abete's rejection of two-level bargaining (at both national and factory levels).

The number of jobholders drops by 6.5%.

A cautionary warrant reaches Fabiano Fabiani, chief executive officer of Finmeccanica.

9   A new request for authorization to proceed against Andreotti carries the accusation that he instigated the murder of Pecorelli, killed because he knew too much about the Moro case.

The value of Ferfin stocks plummets.

10 The Chamber Committee on Constitutional Affairs rejects the plan for a two-round electoral system advanced by Mario Segni, PDS, PRI and PLI. The single-round system prevails, supported by the DC, most of the PSI, the League, MSI, *Rete*, and Pannella List.

At the congress of the National Association of Magistrates, Di Pietro proposes "incentives" to collaborate with magistrates and "provisions that would allow companies to resume [aboveboard] activity."

11 Ciampi transfers responsibility for assigning television frequencies from Maurizio Pagani (PSDI), Minister of Posts and Telecommunications, to undersecretary to the Prime Minister, Antonio Maccanico (PRI).

12 The Young Entrepreneurs call for immediate electoral reform, reject the "gerontocracy," endorse the return of morality to politics, and back the privatization of state-held firms.
The due date for personal income tax returns (Forms 740) is deferred to July 15, but June 18 remains the deadline for payment.

14 The Northern League asks that the second round of mayoral elections be suspended in Turin due to electoral fraud.
In the stock market, the price of Ferruzzi shares plummets and the sale of Fondiaria is announced.

15 Controversy continues on the complexity of Form 740.

16 The Chamber rejects amendments to the parliamentary electoral laws that would have introduced a two-round system.
Banks rescue Ferruzzi.

17 Scalfaro affirms that the complexity of Form 740 is due to the "skill of four technicians from the moon." Parliament approves the extension to July 15 for the filing date of Forms 740 and reduces penalties for unintentional errors by 90%.
The Senate also opts for single-round parliamentary elections. The Chamber sets at 25% the portion of seats to be assigned by proportional representation.

18 League leader Bossi declares that Nando Della Chiesa is "a man of the Cosa Nostra" and that Turin judges are "delinquents."
Ferfin property is transferred to banks.

19 Guido Rossi, ex-president of the CONSOB (Stock Market Oversight Commission), is named president of Ferfin and Montedison.
Abete declares that he accepts a two-level bargaining structure.

20 In the Milan mayoral race, Marco Formentini (Northern League) wins over Nando Dalla Chiesa (supported by PDS, Communist Refoundation, Greens, Rete, and Milan List). In Turin, Valentino Castellani (PDS, Greens, Turin Alliance) defeats Diego Novelli (*Rete*, Green Turin Alliance, Pensioners, Communist Refoundation).
Fininvest is also involved in the corruption scandal; bribes changed hands as part of an anti-AIDS campaign.

21 Enzo Bianco (backed by the Pact for Catania) is elected mayor of Catania,

narrowly beating Claudio Fava (*Rete* and Communist Refoundation). The League obtains fifteen mayors in the North. The PDS wins 72 of 145 municipalities. The DC is badly beaten: only 7 mayors in 61 races. Inflation rises to 4.2%.

22 Fininvest chief executive officer Fedele Confalonieri is accused of illicit financing of parties (several hundred million lire paid to *Avanti*, the PSI newspaper).
Paolo Cirino Pomicino's house in Naples is seized; it may have been bought with a 4 billion lire bribe ($2.7 million).

23 Builder Vincenzo Lodigiani reveals that he paid 100 million lire to a CISL unionist and agreed to a contribution with a UIL functionary.

24 The Senate approves the reform of the RAI.
Ciampi admonishes those who wish to impede the accord between Confindustria and unions on the cost of labor.

25 Rosy Bindi, DC regional secretary in the Veneto, officially opens the renewal phase of the DC.

26 Minister of Foreign Affairs Nino Andreatta announces inspections of funds assigned by the Ministry to Bettino Craxi in 1990-1991 for his activities as United Nations representative.
Two SISDE executives are arrested and accused of embezzlement of public funds.

27 A chorus of criticism greets the slow progress of privatization.

28 At the start of the CISL National Congress, secretary general Sergio D'Antoni declares that he was not involved with the bribes that Lodigiani claims to have paid to the CISL and UIL.
In the Cirillo kidnapping case, Raffaele Cutolo speaks of links among the Camorra, politicians, and secret services.
A shortfall of 320 billion lire ($208 million) is discovered in Montedison accounts.

29 The Presidents of the Chamber and Senate name the new Board of Directors for the RAI: Claudio Demattè, acting rector of Bocconi University; Feliciano Benvenuti, president of the Palazzo Grassi Foundation; editor Elvira Sellerio; Paolo Murialdi, ex-president of the National Federation of the Italian Press; and Tullio Gregory, board member of the Italian Encyclopedia.
The arrest of Vittorio Ghidella, ex-chief executive officer of FIAT-Auto and now chairman of Graziano Trasmissioni, is ordered.
Another shortfall of 118 billion is found in Montedison accounts.

30 A directive from the Prime Minister establishes that within a month the calendar for the privatization of state firms must be ready.

The Chamber approves electoral law reform with a surprise amendment proposed by Mirko Tramaglia (MSI) on granting the vote to Italians abroad.

July

1 With an amendment introduced by Angelo Scivoletto (PDS), the Senate limits parliamentarians' terms to three legislatures or fifteen years.

The new mayor of Milan, Marco Formentini (League), inaugurates his first City Council meeting.

2 Record revenues from income taxes (IRPEF), show an increase of 37.7% on the year before.

3 The Confindustria and unions agree on the abolition of wage indexation (the *scala mobile*), the maintenance of two levels of bargaining, youth contracts for training and employment up to the age of 32, and temporary employment.

5 The Bank of Italy lowers the discount rate from 10% to 9%.

A pharmaceutical pricing scandal brings seven new arrests, although 5 fugitives remain, including the brother of ex-Minister of Health De Lorenzo. New order of preventative custody given for Salvatore Ligresti.

6 The president of the Confindustria asks that banks' interest rates be lowered.

7 Romiti is interrogated for three hours by Turin magistrates.

Minister of Finance Franco Gallo announces that non-self-employed workers will be refunded the additional taxes they paid in 1992 because wage indexation had placed them in a higher tax bracket.

8 Francesco Sisinni, second in command at the Ministry of Culture, is arrested for fraud against the State, corruption, and falsification of documents.

9 The yield on three-month government bonds (BOT) falls below 8%.

10 Rosy Bindi launches the *"Cosa Bianca,"* the project for a new, as yet un-renamed DC.

11 Bossi announces a tax strike if Scalfaro does not dissolve Parliament immediately after the approval of the budget.

12 Economic recovery without inflation is predicted for 1994.

The government will attempt to reduce the State deficit by 32,000 billion lire.

13 Claudio Demattè, acting rector of Bocconi University, is named the new President of the RAI.
Surveys of ISCO and ISTAT furnish bleak data on employment, domestic demand, and investment.

14 CONSOB declares that Ferruzzi accounts are false.
Giuseppe Garofano, ex-chairman of Montedison, is arrested in Geneva.
Consideration of the government's 1994 economic package is postponed until after the August vacation.

15 The government makes the decrees on employment and on urgent measures to boost the economy votes of confidence.
Romano Prodi declares that the IRI Group has 32,000 excess employees, 10% of all employees.

16 The Court of Accounts denounces: the failure of privatizations and of the plan to sell State real estate; the hundreds of incomplete public works projects, "authentic monuments to waste and inefficiency;" and the thousands of irregular State concessions.

17 Minister Sabino Cassese announces important reforms in public administration.

18 Garofano confesses at length.

19 Four arrest orders are issued for high officials of SISDE.
Pensions for those who retire before 60 years of age will be reduced by up to 50%, depending on income level.

20 Ex-president of ENI Gabriele Cagliari commits suicide at the San Vittorio-Prison, where he had been held since March 9. Judge Di Pietro declares, "this is a defeat."
Agostino Cordova is named the new Chief Public Prosecutor of Naples.

21 Minister of Finance Gallo declares that tax brackets and the definitions of taxable income and property will not be modified.

22 Minister of Justice Conso and Milanese judges disagree on preventative imprisonment.

23 Raul Gardini commits suicide at his home in Milan.
The DC Constituent Assembly opens in Rome.

24 Unemployment reaches 10.5% in April.

25 The entire DC is converted to the Popular Party.

Garofano confesses to having paid 280 billion lire ($175 million) to the DC and PSI.

26 Raul Gardini's funeral is held in Ravenna.

27 Bombs kill five people and injure three in Milan and injure four in Rome. Garofano, ex-chairman of Montedison, and Carlo Sama, formerly of the Ferruzzi Group, name the politicians who collected the "super-*tangente*" of 150 billion lire ($94 million) for Enimont.

28 Head of SISDE Angelo Finocchiaro is dismissed, another casualty of "Clean Hands."
    Bruno Pazzi, ex-president of CONSOB, is placed under house arrest for his involvement in the Enimont affair.

29 Cautionary warrants go to Craxi, Forlani, Cirino Pomicino, Martelli, and Citaristi for their roles in the Enimont affair.
    Cautionary warrants are issued to La Malfa, Vizzini, and Altissimo.

30 Craxi announces that he wishes to leave Italy. Martelli writes to the President of the Chamber that he wants to leave the political stage.
    The Prime Minister announces that parliamentary elections will be held in spring 1994.

31 The Minister of the Interior sounds the alarm: "Authoritarian outcomes are possible."
    The Regional Adminstrative Court (TAR) upholds the appeal of the Northern League on irregularities in the Turin mayoral election.

August

1 Controversy continues over the health tax, which applies even to the dead.

2 Ciampi announces his intention to reform totally the secret services.

3 The Senate approves the new electoral law for the Chamber (128 for, 29 against, and 59 abstaining).
   According to Mediobanca, Italy's major companies lost 11,000 billion lire and eliminated 80,000 jobs in 1992.

4 The Chamber approves the new electoral law for the Senate (287 for, 78 against, and 153 abstaining).

6 The government refuses to accept the resignation of the Head of Police, Vincenzo Parisi.

Sergio Mattarella resigns as vice president of the Bicameral Committee for Institutional Reforms after he is accused of having received 50 million lire in illicit financing for his electoral campaign.

7 The Minister of the Interior decides to dissolve the Naples City Council.

8 In the first six months of 1993, 47,681 billion lire in government bonds were acquired abroad.

10 The value of Ferfin shares sinks from 1,000 to 5 lire.
  Health services are now free for those over 65, for children up to age 12, for pregnant women, and for the chronically ill.

11 The decree law enters into effect that puts off until September 1 the removal of 56,000 school classes and the use of tenured inactive teachers (instead of aspiring teachers) as substitutes.

13 Diego Curtò, acting president of the Milan Tribunal, is accused of aiding and abetting those under investigation in the Enimont case.
  The public deficit falls by 6.2% on the preceeding year.

16 Minister of the Interior Mancino announces success in the fight against organized crime.
  The Ferruzzi family blames the late Raul Gardini for the Ferruzzi Group's financial problems.

17 The unemployment rate in the South is triple that in the Center and North: 21.3% as compared to 7.9%.
  Interest rates fall, the stock market gains.
  Federfarma has gathered 5 billion lire from pharmacists to influence legislative decisions; the minimum contribution was 150,000 lire.

18 Minister Cassese outlines his policy for public administration: mobility for public employees, demotion of those promoted outside the system of competitive examinations, restucturing of the top management in government ministries.

19 The public debt rises further: 1,727 billion lire.
  Ex-Minister of Health De Lorenzo promises to repay the 4 billion lire ($2.5 million) in illegal contributions that he received for his party.

20 Businessman Lodigiani asserts that he bribed several unionists, in particular those of the CISL.

23 Martinazzoli says "no" to cooperation with the League and to early elections in spring 1994.

Finance Minister Gallo urges top fiscal inspectors to carry out more thorough audits.

24 Minister of the Interior Mancino fears that the employment crisis is raising serious risks for public order.
A cautionary warrant for corruption and violation of the law on party financing is issued to Marcello Stefanini, PDS administrative secretary.

25 Ciampi presents his plan to create new jobs.
Stefano Micossi, director of the Confindustria's Research Center, labels Mancino's declarations "unjustified and irresponsible."
The PDS rallies around Stefanini.

26 Payment of municipal real property taxes exceeds forecasts by the Ministry of Finance.
"Clean Hands" magistrates disagree on the cautionary warrant issued to Stefanini.

27 The labor confederations are not convinced of the effectiveness of the Ciampi employment plan.

28 Controversy continues among Milan magistrates regarding the Stefanini cautionary warrant.

30 The government announces the enlistment of 4,000 volunteers who will serve in U.N. peace-keeping missions.
The top administrators of the Ferruzzi Group are all guilty of extremely poor management, according to Guido Rossi, new chairman of Montedison.

31 A prescription will now be necessary for nearly all drugs. Protests by Federfarma and the Federative Democratic Movement follow.
The cabinet approves a decree that revolutionizes the traffic code that had been in effect for only eight months.

September

1 Obligatory prescriptions for pharmaceuticals are delayed; basic drugs will continue to be free.

2 Labor confederations reject the Ciampi plan, maintaining that the investments intended to generate new employment are insufficient.

3 Magistrate Curtò is arrested for having collected a 320 million lire payment ($200,000) for ordering the seizure and precautionary custody of Enimont shares.
A modification in the minimum tax is considered.

5 Budget legislation is needed to resolve the problem of INPS (National Institute for Social Security), where a deficit of roughly 10,000 billion lire is foreseen.

6 Diego Curtò admits to having pocketed the bribe.
   Workers at the Enichem plant in Crotone protest the decision to place 333 employees on *cassa integrazione* (state-subsidized layoffs).
   "Baby pensions" are at risk (pensions paid after 20 years of state employment, 15 for women, regardless of age).

7 Minister of Labor Giugni condemns the demonstration at Enichem in Crotone.
   The mystery of "Clean Pens" continues: Journalists are said to have been instructed by Sama to clean up the image of Montedison.
   The Board of IRI announces the immediate sale of controlling interest in two banks, Comit and Credit.

8 Relations improve between Segni and Martinazzoli, who meet at Andreatta's office.

9 The budget is approved, with spending cuts of 28,000 billion lire and additional taxes and fees of 3,000 billion lire. Early pensions for state employees are lowered and people with medium-to-high incomes will pay more for health services.

11 Municipal governments will receive 1,000 billion lire less from the State compared to 1993. Municipal fees for electricity, gas, water, and garbage collection could rise.

12 President Scalfaro defends magistrates against the generic accusations directed at them by Andreotti's U.S. lawyer.

13 An agreement is reached on the Enichem-Crotone employees slated to be put on *cassa integrazione*.
   MSI secretary Fini will run for mayor in Rome.

14 In a controversial vote, the Chamber Committee for Authorizations to Proceed decides to refuse the request for arrest of ex-Minister De Lorenzo.

15 Payment of regional taxes covering visits to family doctors is postponed to October 31.

16 Giuseppe Puglisi, priest in a Palermo parish, is assassinated by the Mafia.
   Pietro Barilla dies, leaving a firm with 10,000 employees, 3,700 billion lire in total sales, and the production of 35% of the pasta consumed in Italy.

17 Antonia Di Pietro, the wife of Magistrate Curtò, is arrested and accused of corruption.
State's witness Pasquale Galasso accuses Gava, Scotti, and Cirino Pomicino of collusion with the Camorra.

18 Marco Fredda, in charge of PDS real estate, is arrested; a new order for preventative custody is issued for Primo Greganti.
Minister of Justice Conso asks the CSM for the precautionary suspension of Claudio Vitalone, magistrate and ex-Minister.

20 The Premier indicates to Parliament and the President that he is willing to resign.
Wilfredo and Claudio Vitalone are accused of fraudulent bankruptcy and extortion for having collected a bribe of 2.5 billion lire ($1.6 million) from an agricultural cooperative.

21 A second warrant for the arrest of Primo Greganti is issued, for corruption and violation of the law on party financing.
Andreotti admits that he gave 170 million lire to Radaelli as part of his electoral campaign and that he asked Radaelli not to tell judges about the payment.
The annual inflation rate falls to 4%.

22 Arrests are ordered for Roberto Cappellini, ex-secretary of the Milan PDS, and for Giovanni Donegaglia, chairman of the Argenta cooperative, regarding contracts at Malpensa, the Milan airport.
Tax revenues rose by 9.8% in the first six months of 1993.

23 By only two votes, the full Chamber rejects the request to arrest ex-Minister De Lorenzo. It grants authorization to proceed against ex-Interior Minister Gava, accused of associating with the Mafia. Ex-Public Works Minister Giovanni Prandini is sent to trial.

24 The cabinet approves a bill that would modify the minimum tax.

25 Swiss bank accounts attributed to the PDS actually belonged to two Verona Christian Democrats.

26 Bossi throws down the gauntlet: tax revolt in November; plebiscite in April on federalism; creation of a parliament for the Northern Republic.

27 An account in the name of the wife of Duilio Poggiolini, ex-director of pharmaceutical services in the Ministry of Health, contains 15 billion lire ($9.6 million).
"Clean Hands" magistrates defer a decision on the request for authorization to proceed against Marcello Stefanini of the PDS.

A Bahrain holding company buys the Gucci fashion house for 270 billion lire.

28 FIAT proposes to double its capitalization; Giovanni Agnelli will continue as chairman and Cesare Romiti as chief executive officer.
Mario Segni officially abandons the Democratic Alliance, refusing any agreement with the PDS.
Confcommercio and Confesercenti ask for a complete abolition of the minimum tax.
Minister of Labor Giugni estimates that 250,000 Italians are unemployed in 1993, against a figure of 500,000 given by the Governor of the Bank of Italy.

29 Gold bullion, jewels, antique coins, and paintings: These treasures were accumulated by Duilio Poggiolini and his wife in their Naples home.
A cautionary warrant for complicity in corruption is issued to Barbara Pollastrini, ex-secretary of the Milan PDS.
The Milan stock market rejects FIAT's maxi-proposal.

October

1 Scalfaro declares that after the vote on De Lorenzo, had all other responsibilities been met, he would have dissolved Parliament.
Arrested for bribery: Alberto Grotti, ex-vice president of ENI; Daniel Kraus, director of Assolombarda; Vittorio Barattieri, director of the Ministry of Industry; and Ruggero Ravenna, ex-adjunct secretary of the UIL.

2 The Minister of Finance plans compensatory revenues of 1,000–2,000 billion lire to make up for the lower revenues stemming from the modification of the minimum tax.

4 The Milan Public Prosecutor closes the case against PDS treasurer Stefanini without trial.
Grain magnate Francesco Ambrosio is arrested for laundering money.
In August 1993 the use of *cassa integrazione* saw an increase of 43% on August 1992.

5 Several parliamentarians protest that Scalfaro has too often expressed support for early elections.
Tax returns: De Lorenzo 336 million lire ($213,000), Cirino Pomicino 219 million lire, Citaristi 129 million lire. These are among the lowest incomes claimed by parliamentarians under investigation for corruption.

6 Parliament begins to consider the cabinet's bill for reform of the minimum tax.
Fifteen more accounts in the name of Duilio Poggiolini and his wife are

discovered, containing at least 10 billion lire ($6.3 million).

7 Italo Ghitti, judge overseeing preliminary investigations (GIP), rejects the "Clean Hands" magistrates' decision to close the case against Stefanini without trial.

8 The Ministry of Defense replaces 300 SISME (Military Information and Security Service) agents.
Ciampi threatens that any additional budget deficit caused by the cancellation of the minimum tax would be covered by new taxes on self-employed workers.

9 Minister of Industry Paolo Savona and IRI President Romano Prodi disagree on privatization; Prodi would follow a "public company formula" for privatization.
Head of the Joint Chiefs of Staff General Goffredo Canino declares, in an open controversy with Gianfranco Miglio (League), that whoever attacks the unitary State is a traitor.

10 Minister of Industry Savona resigns over the dispute with Prodi, and with Ciampi, who had expressed confidence in Prodi's formula for privatization.

11 Savona withdraws his resignation.
Discord among the "Clean Hands" magistrates: Tiziana Parenti wants more thorough investigations of the PDS.
Defense Minister Fabio Fabbri defends General Canino but asks him to abstain from further polemics.

12 Twelve high-ranking military officers are under investigation for allegedly plotting a coup.

13 The Chamber limits the instances in which parliamentary immunity applies: Requests for authorizations to proceed will be required only when magistrates anticipate arrests, searches, and wire-tapping.

14 The Rights and Freedoms Tribunal orders the release of Primo Greganti (PCI/PDS).
A Mediobanca analysis reveals record debt for public and private firms.
A 'Ndrangheta (Calabria organized crime) boss is reputed to have been part of the Red Brigades commando unit during the kidnapping of Aldo Moro.

15 A request is made for authorization to proceed against Marcello Stefanini, accused of tax fraud and violation of the law on party financing.
The Senate Budget Committee proposes that pensions of up to one million lire ($629) be indexed by the inflation rate.

16 Liguria SISDE head Augusto Maria Citanna is accused of having organized the bomb threat on the Siracusa-Turin train of September 21.
Minister of Public Administration Cassese adds to budget legislation a three-year freeze on pay raises for state employees.

18 The cabinet approves a reform of the secret services, creating a unified command directly under the Premier's control.
Five magistrates are under investigation in Palermo for criminal association with the Mafia.
In Milan 100,000 artisans demonstrate against changes in the minimum tax.

19 Three more Palermo magistrates are investigated for alleged ties to Mafia bands.
GIP Italo Ghitti orders a new investigation of the relationship between PDS treasurer Marcello Stefanini and Primo Greganti.
For the first time in 22 years, national savings in Italy fall.

20 In the Senate, Ciampi explains his plans and timetables for privatization, and maintains that the public company formula is most suitable for public services.
The Chamber approves the reform of the minimum tax. Confcommercio objects and advocates a tax strike.

21 Confcommercio president Francesco Colucci and his assistant Aldo Antoniozzi receive cautionary warrants for fraud, budget falsification, and embezzlement.
The Bank of Italy reduces the discount rate from 8.5% to 8%, the lowest since 1986.
Adriana Faranda states that Moro was killed not by Prospero Gallinari but by "the fourth man," Germano Maccari, and Mario Moretti.

22 Head of the Joint Chiefs of Staff General Goffredo Canino resigns in protest and is immediately replaced by Army Corps General Bonifazio Incisa di Camerana.
Bomb at the Palazzo di Giustizia in Padua.
FIAT declares its interest in French privatizations and acquires a stake in Rhône Poulenc.

23 The Governor of the Bank of Italy urges industrialists to invest in Italy following the reduction in the discount rate.

24 Minister of Industry Savona declares that organized crime is prepared to buy shares in firms undergoing privatization.

25 Data from income tax returns: In 1990 non-self-employed workers declared average incomes of 23 million lire ($14,000) as compared to an average of

15.5 million lire for entrepreneurs, artisans, and shopkeepers. Professionals declared an average income of 31.2 million lire.

Ciampi, seeking to calm savers, declares that the sale of state-held firms will be subject to the scrutiny of the Bank of Italy, CONSOB, and anti-trust authorities.

26 Senators attack the provision for pension cuts included in the 1994 budget bill.

27 There are 12,000 superfluous workers at Alfa plants in Arese and Mirafiore, while FIAT's recapitalization announced on September 28 has not yet been realized.

28 The Senate also approves the limiting of parliamentary immunity.

CGIL, CISL and UIL call a four-hour general strike to protest the measures on employment and taxation included in budget legislation.

The in absentia trial of Sergio Cusani, linked to the PSI and financial adviser to Raul Gardini, opens.

Donatella Di Rosa and her husband, Lieutenant Colonel Aldo Michittu, are arrested in connection with the alleged coup.

29 Riccardo Malpica, ex-director of SISDE, is arrested and accused of managing illicit funds. According to Maurizio Broccoletti, ex-treasurer of SISDE, the ex-Minister of Defense Salvo Andò and Head of Police Vincenzo Parisi were aware of the management of illicit funds. Scalfaro is alleged to have been involved as well.

The government wins a vote of confidence on the reform of the minimum tax, which then becomes law.

30 The Public Prosecutor of Rome exonerates President Scalfaro from Broccoletti's accusations.

The Public Prosecutor of Rome issues a warrant for the arrest of Carlo De Benedetti, the chairman of Olivetti.

November

1 Riccardo Malpica, ex-director of SISDE, asserts that all Ministers of the Interior were aware of the management of illicit funds.

2 De Benedetti, accused of having paid a bribe of 10 billion lire ($6.2 million) to the Ministry of Posts and Telecommunications, turns himself in and is put under house arrest.

Gianni Letta, vice president of Fininvest, and Adriano Galliani, chairman of Rete Italia, are accused of having paid bribes to the Ministry of Posts and Telecommunications for the assignment of television frequencies.

Craxi maintains that entrepreneurs wanted the system of corruption and that their participation in it was "conscious, voluntary, and self-interested" and very often "organized and planned."
Health care taxes were paid by only 67% of Italians.

3 President Scalfaro rejects the accusations that when he served as Minister of the Interior he knew about the SISDE illicit funds.
Arturo, Franca, and Alessandra Ferruzzi ask their sister Idina, wife of Raul Gardini, to pay 3,000 billion lire ($1.8 billion) as compensation for losses incurred as a result of Gardini's management.

4 The Bank of Italy denies Andreotti's claim that the Bank had for five days withheld information about the FBI's raid on the BNL (Banca Nazionale del Lavoro) branch in Atlanta.
Carlo Sama states that 93 billion lire ($57 million) in bribes paid by Montedison in the Enimont affair were deposited in the IOR, the Vatican bank.
Ex-director of SISDE Riccardo Malpica insists, "I paid Scalfaro."

5 The Public Prosecutor of Rome charges that SISDE agents assaulted the Constitution when they accused the President of condoning illicit funds.
The Senate approves mobility for state employees and for the first time *cassa integrazione* becomes possible in public employment. State workers who refuse to be transferred will be dismissed.

6 Rosa Maria Sorrentino, ex-vice director of a SISDE division, is arrested and charged with embezzlement of public funds and criminal association.

7 An order for the arrest of Matilde Paola Martucci, secretary to Riccardo Malpica, is issued. She is alleged to have deposited roughly 12 billion lire ($7.3 million) in Italian and foreign banks.

8 Prefect Alessandro Voci, ex-director of SISDE and Provisional Administrator (*Commissario straordinario*) of Rome, is under investigation for embezzlement of public funds.
Children under 10 years of age and adults over 60 will be exempt from co-payments on pharmaceuticals.

9 After a flurry of sell-offs, SIP, STET and Italcable shares lose 4.47%, 4.09%, and 3.88%, respectively.
The Senate approves a bill to expose anyone receiving undeserved civilian disability pensions. All will be required to return to the State the funds received.

10 With deliberate absences from the ranks of the governing majority and the abstention of the PDS and the League, the Senate fails to pass the bill that

would have granted the vote to Italians abroad.

Pensions are increased slightly to keep up with inflation.

Naples magistrates issue 14 warrants for preventative custody to representatives of the major pharmaceutical industries in Italy. The accusation is corruption.

Adriano Galliani, member of the Board of Fininvest, receives a cautionary warrant.

11 Totò Riina and 17 other mafiosi are believed to be responsible for the assassination of Giovanni Falcone, a renowned magistrate in the fight against crime.

Public Prosecutors in Rome continue investigations of Vincenzo Scotti and Antonio Gava for complicity in embezzlement at SISDE; they ask that the case against Minister of the Interior Nicola Mancino be closed without trial.

12 Two State's witnesses describe Falcone's murder. According to them, the order to kill came from Totò Riina in the name of all Corleone Mafia families.

Umberto Agnelli takes over the leadership of IFI, leaving the Board of Directors of FIAT, where he is replaced by his son Giovanni Alberto. Gianluigi Gabetti becomes vice president of FIAT.

13 Industrial production fell by 3.8% in the first nine months of 1993.

It is rumored that the Public Prosecutor of Florence has opened an investigation of a few Milanese magistrates in connection with the so-called "Mafia parking lot" case.

15 A wave of speculation further lowers the lira's value, even though experts state that the lira is undervalued.

Occhetto announces a signature-gathering effort for early elections.

The "boss of Corleone," Luciano Loggio, dies in the Nuoro prison at age 68.

16 The Milan Court of Appeals exonerates De Benedetti, who for 65 days served as Banco Ambrosiano vice president. He is not required to repay the 81 billion lire ($49 million) he received from stock transactions.

17 A warrant is issued for the arrest of Sergio Cragnotti, financier and president of the Lazio soccer team, who is accused of falsifying accounts while he was on the Board of Montedison and chief executive officer of Enimont.

ABI decries the burden on the banking system represented by 50,000 billion lire ($30.2 billion) in loans, which must be restructured.

18 Top management at RAI asks for the immediate intervention of the government and IRI, to restore liquidity.

Italian investors hold fewer government bonds and more stock.

19 Buscetta charges, "There is no Mafia crime that was not ordered by Riina."

Riina replies that Buscetta is immoral: "He's had too many wives."
The cabinet approves the refunding of the additional taxes (due to bracket creep caused by wage indexation) paid by non-self-employed workers and pensioners with a gross annual income of up to 60 million lire.

20 Minister of Finance Franco Gallo announces a simplified 740 Form for personal income tax returns.

22 Local elections: *Rete* leader Orlando wins in Palermo with 75% of the vote. All Progressive candidates proceed to the second round in other large cities. In Rome and Naples, MSI candidates Fini and Mussolini come in second. League candidates are second in Genoa and Venice. The center disappears. It is revealed that Gardini paid 100 billion lire ($60 million) to governing parties in order to win influence.

23 FIAT has 5,000 superfluous workers.
In the Enimont case, Cragnotti confesses that he paid 10 billion lire to the Craxi-Andreotti-Forlani trio for tax relief.

24 Local health units (USL) will become autonomous agencies.
During the inauguration of his Shopville supermarket in Casalecchio (Bologna), Silvio Berlusconi announces that he intends to enter politics. He says that if he lived in Rome, he would vote for Fini.

25 Demand for government bonds remains strong.
In the Chamber, the four-party coalition (DC-PSI-PSDI-PLI) continues to seek approval of a bill that would silence journalists and hamper magistrates.

26 Director of the Bank of Italy Lamberto Dini accuses Italian banks of inefficiency, waste, and exorbitant salaries.

28 Controversy continues over Berlusconi's political moves.

29 Cossiga reveals that a plan existed to isolate and confine Aldo Moro in a nursing home, if he had been liberated.

30 In a long interrogation session, Severino Citaristi, DC administrative secretary, states that both Forlani and De Mita were aware of bribery.
24,500 workers in 282 companies are put on *cassa integrazione*.

December

1 The Public Prosecutor of Rome denies Cossiga's revelations on the plans to neutralize Moro. Cossiga replies that he has documentary evidence of the plans.

Ex-Minister of the Budget Paolo Cirino Pomicino confirms that he received 5 billion lire ($3 million) in the Enimont affair, as a contribution to his electoral campaign. He also implicates Giuliano Amato, who was then vice secretary of the PSI.

2 The lira tumbles: The dollar rises above 1,700 and the mark above 1,000 lire.
The RAI announces that it cannot pay year-end bonuses in December.
La Malfa admits that he accepted 300 million lire from Sama.
Maurizio Broccoletti, key man in the SISDE illicit funds scandal, is arrested.

3 Excitement grows about the second-round elections in Italy's major cities.
Agreement on budget legislation: The PDS announces its firm commitment to a rapid approval.
The cabinet approves a simplification of the 740 Form.
Craxi announces that, for "reasons of public order," he cannot testify at Socialist financier Cusani's trial.
Forlani maintains that he never received cautionary warrants.

5 Cities vote Progressive: The five candidates from Progressive Alliances win on the second round, against MSI and League candidates. Rutelli is mayor of Rome with 53.1% of the vote; Bassolini wins 55.6% of the vote in Naples; Sansa 59.2% in Genoa; Cacciari 55.4% in Venice; and Illy 53% in Trieste.
The lira regains ground against the dollar and the mark. The Milan stock market rebounds. Credito Italiano stock is in great demand.

6 Massimo D'Alema, leader of the PDS in the Chamber of Deputies, states that Ciampi could continue to head the government after the upcoming parliamentary elections.
Criticisms of Bossi's strategy emerge within the League.
The *Osservatore Romano*, the official Vatican daily, gives a positive report on the outcomes of the municipal elections.

7 Ex-administrative secretary of the League Alessandro Patelli is accused of having received 200 million lire from Montedison. He confesses that money exchanged hands.

8 The costly recount in Turin, requested by the League for the mayoral race, confirms Castellani's victory.

9 The Confindustria frames a ten-part questionnaire on the economy, to be presented to parties and candidates.

10 An unexpected and lengthy meeting between Di Pietro and Occhetto: "It was cordial, very important, useful, and positive," according to the PDS secretary.

11 At the League's Congress, Bossi relaunches the idea of dividing Italy into three: Padania, Etruria, and the South.
Ex-parliamentarian Alfredo Vito (DC) is sentenced to a two-year suspended prison term as a result of plea bargaining and the restitution of 5 billion lire ($2.9 million).

12 Bossi welcomes discussion with Berlusconi, who says he is interested but does not exclude an alliance with Fini.

13 Segni is also willing to negotiate with Bossi, while Scalfaro defends as sacred the principle of national unity.
Martelli confesses to having received 500 million lire ($293,000) for his electoral campaign from Sama. Did 5 or 7 billion lire go to Craxi?

14 The government postpones its plan to restore financial health to RAI. Tensions mount in the state radio and television system.
Andreotti is interrogated for 12 hours by the Chief Public Prosecutor of Palermo, Giancarlo Caselli, who brings Andreotti face to face with his accuser.

15 Ciampi declares that, with the approval of the budget, his government will have completed its program.
Bossi takes a small step back from federalism and Segni applauds.

16 The PSI splits: Del Turco wins against Craxi's loyalists and convenes an assembly to join the Progressives.
The DC divides on alliance alternatives, as neo-centrists push for an agreement with Berlusconi.

17 At the trial on the Enimont maxi-bribes, Forlani claims no knowledge. Craxi counter-attacks, "everyone acted that way and everyone knew it." Craxi states that from 1987 to 1990 the PSI collected "contributions" of 186 billion lire ($110 million).

18 The Chamber approves the budget with support from the PDS.
A whirl of meetings among centrists: Martinazzoli receives Berlusconi and Segni calls on Agnelli.

19 President Scalfaro, a member of Parliament without interruption since 1946, hopes that the next Parliament will contain few professional politicians.

20 Bossi goes to Di Pietro and pays back the bribe of 200 million lire he received from Sama. He then urges a drive for contributions to contest the law on party financing.

21 Inflation stands at 4%.

Carlo Sama maintains that he knew that the PCI took contributions from Gardini. Di Pietro asks that D'Alema (PDS) be called as a witness.

22 The Senate approves the budget and the League walks out of Parliament.General Electric wins the bidding for the acquisition of Nuovo Pignone.
Berlusconi attacks Scalfaro for saying that Italian democracy is capable of facing change. Berlusconi hears a pro-PDS tone in Scalfaro's words.
Ex-Radical Marco Pannella gathers signatures to force debate on a no-confidence motion, which would postpone elections.

23 In Florence workers and local government officials demonstrate against the privatization of Nuovo Pignone.
Socialist financier Cusani is released from prison after five months.
Unemployment continues to rise: 11.3% in October. The yield on government bonds continues to decline: 7%, but demand for them exceeds supply.
In Parliament 350 members ask Scalfaro to schedule the parliamentary elections to coincide with the European Parliament elections, to be held on June 12, 1994. This step, they claim, will save 100 billion lire ($60 million); it will also give them more time in office.

24 The President of the Chamber sets January 12 as the date for parliamentary debate of the motion of no-confidence in the Ciampi government.

25 In his Christmas greetings, the Pope calls for a united Italy that, on "strong and deep foundations," will "construct its future with courage, hope, and determination."
In his Christmas sermon, a parish priest in Palermo, Don Paolo Turturro, reveals that he was told in the confessional who killed Judge Falcone.

27 State bonds valued at 16.5 billion lire ($9.8 million) are seized from Licio Gelli, the head of the P2; he is accused of laundering dirty money.
According to the *Sole-24 Ore*, Aosta, then Parma, are the cities that offer the best quality of life. Emilia Romagna leads the list with four cities: Parma, Piacenza, Reggio Emilia and Bologna are among the top ten.

28 In the traditional year-end press conference, Ciampi reviews the achievements of his "transition government," which are all positive, except unemployment, which remains a "distressing" problem. Ciampi announces that he wants to "conclude methodically the mission assumed."
Ten arrests in Sicily for the co-conspiracy of the Mafia and Masons to "adjust" trials.
Franco Bernabè, chief executive officer of ENI, announces that in February the daily *Il Giorno* will be sold.

29 Fiscal package of 70,000 billion lire: Gasoline and value-added tax increase.
Martinazzoli makes a lengthy visit to Berlusconi's villa in Arcore.

The government raises antenna fees and reduces RAI license fees, which remain forty times greater than the fees paid by Berlusconi's frequencies. A cabinet representative is named to the RAI Board of Directors.

30 Ninth Italian victim in Somalia: The death was caused by an overturned vehicle.
Francesco Saverio Borrelli applies for the position of President of the Milan Court of Appeals. He will leave the "Clean Hands" pool of magistrates.
IRI's debt amounts to 75,000 billion lire ($44.5 billion).
Pannella travels to Arcore, seeking "an understanding on values and goals with Berlusconi," against the "PDS shop."

31 In his year-end message Scalfaro declares that "Italy is rising again." He emphasizes the importance of his role as designator of the Premier.

1

Introduction

Carol Mershon and Gianfranco Pasquino

"The Second Republic Is Under Way" (*Seconda Repubblica, si parte*): This headline appeared on the front page of *L'Unità* on August 5, 1993. It accompanied a malicious juxtaposition, a story on the final approval of Italy's new electoral laws, "The Great Reform," and a subtitle depicting the exit of the political protagonist of the 1980s, an erstwhile champion of reform: "Craxi defends himself in Parliament: `Leave me to my destiny.'"

Much of the political year is captured in these titles, which neatly convey the two most important events of 1993: the approval of electoral reforms in the wake of popular referenda and the unfolding of *Tangentopoli* (or Bribe City, as Italy's vast corruption scandal has come to be known). And since that front page was published in the newspaper identified with the Democratic Party of the Left (PDS), it offers an especially telling illustration of how the referenda, the debates on electoral laws, and investigations into corruption have transformed party competition in Italy. The party system that defined the postwar Republic no longer exists. Moreover, in highlighting Craxi's strenuous self-defense, *L'Unità* pointed to the desperate attempt of one of Italy's most powerful politicans to save himself, to stay afloat at least, or to drag everyone with him to jail. Yet not all old-school politicians wanted to be left to their destinies, like Craxi or, even worse, together with him. For some, it was a question of remaining free rather than going to prison. Others, more presumptuous, were probably thinking of those few pages of Italy's national history that would not compare them with Craxi for their shrewdness or decisiveness but instead would criticize and blame them or neglect them altogether. Still others — to date, nineteen politicians, entrepreneurs, and managers — chose suicide.

What many observers and protagonists of Italian politics see as the transition to the Second Republic does not mark a sharp, clear break with the past. In this and several other aspects, the current Italian experience resembles that of Spain in the mid-1970s. An obvious difference separates the Spanish and Italian cases, of course. Spain after Franco underwent a change *of* regime type, a transition from authoritarian rule to democracy, whereas the events of 1993 in Italy signaled a change *within* one regime type: a transition from one democratic regime, now worn-out and unable to renew itself, to a different democratic regime.[1] Furthermore, in contemporary Italy, as in the Spanish transition, the old political class has fought — and is fighting — to remain on the scene; and yet, paradoxically, the veterans have been forced to introduce institutional reforms that are likely to deprive most of them of political power.

In Italy, the passage from one regime to another — a passage ordered by, but altering, democratic rules of the game — consists of subtle, overlapping changes that will yield some settlement only with time and repeated elections.

Precisely because these changes continue, because their outcomes are unknown, they are difficult to analyze and interpret. Yet it is possible to isolate four dimensions or aspects of change that need to be considered in any assessment of contemporary Italian politics.

Perhaps the most striking mutation, as already suggested, is in the structure of the *party system*. The redrawing of the party system seems likely to lead soon to a epoch-making shift in the *party composition of the government*. Christian Democracy's permanent incumbency is near its end and the DC's function as a Catholic party may well be exhausted. The DC's finish heralds the start of alternation in government. Third, a new set of local and national institutions is gradually replacing the political institutions characteristic of the postwar Republic. In other words, a *regime* transition is under way that is reshaping both the formal rules and procedures directing political life and the actual behavior that long bent and subverted those rules.

The three aspects of change just described — involving which parties compete, which parties govern, and which institutions regulate parties' competition and modes of governance — contribute to a fourth: a redefinition of *the sociopolitical system*, that is, a change in the nature of relationships between civil society, on the one hand, and political forces and institutions, on the other.

Due to ongoing — though still incomplete — developments along all of these dimensions, Italian political life has been transformed in ways that would have been unimaginable only a short while ago. And yet the journey towards the Second Republic has only just begun. To show why, we discuss the governments headed by Giuliano Amato and Carlo Azeglio Ciampi.

From Amato to Ciampi:
Two Anomalous Governments

In 1993, Prime Minister Giuliano Amato walked off the political stage. It is difficult to say how definitive his departure really was, given Amato's continued visibility as "statesman in reserve," thanks to his collaboration with *Panorama*, one of Italy's leading newsweeklies. At any rate, his government attained the average duration of postwar Italian governments, about 10.5 months. Amato's coup de théâtre, a voluntary resignation, did not quite live up to expectations but the moment was well chosen: immediately after the April referendum on the Senate electoral laws. Indeed, when Amato was vice-secretary of the Socialist Party (PSI), he had argued, exploiting his fame as an expert on constitutional law, that the electoral referenda were "unconstitutional in the highest degree."[2] Even though the Constitutional Court was brimming with Socialists chosen by Amato, the Court proved him wrong and the electorate then buried Italy's proportional electoral laws under an avalanche of votes for reform.

Whereas Amato simply left the stage, the entire Craxi-Andreotti-Forlani alliance (the "CAF" in Italian political jargon) was overwhelmed by requests for authorizations to proceed in criminal investigations.[3] Particularly devastating were the charges against Giulio Andreotti, who was accused of collusion with the Mafia and of having ordered the murder of the journalist Mino Pecorelli. Perhaps now even Amato would find it difficult to justify his statement of May 1992, made during the election of the President of the Republic, "Better [Arnaldo] Forlani than [life senator and eminent political philosopher Norberto] Bobbio." Any justification would become more elusive after the formation of the Ciampi government, which was influenced by the President to an unusual degree and saw the entrance of a substantial number of professors, evidently preferred over the Forlanis of the day. A regime transition and a shift in the sociopolitical system are facilitated, if not made, by governments composed of ministers who are not professional politicians and who, at least temporarily, push professional politicians out of the game. The contribution of Gianfranco Pasquino and Salvatore Vassallo to this volume details policies and accomplishments under Ciampi. Here it suffices to emphasize that the Ciampi government took on the institutional task of translating into new electoral laws the citizens' response in the electoral referendum. The political novelty of 1993 was Ciampi, Italy's first non-party premier, and the institutional novelty was the adoption of predominantly majoritarian electoral laws.

The main players of the First Republic were all strong advocates of proportionalism. Even the opposition adhered to proportionalism, as demonstrated by the unsuccessful experience of the "Committee for a

No," made up exclusively of exponents of the Left, campaigning in the referendum on the Senate electoral laws. Communist Pietro Ingrao, who had tenaciously fought for radical positions during the PCI's evolution into the Democratic Party of the Left, lost this final battle both inside and outside the PDS and took his leave. This is yet another sign that all components of the Italian party system are engaged in a profound redefinition of symbols, identities, programs, and strategies. It also confirms that rules for proportional representation had constituted a splendid and comfortable bog in which movements were few and difficult and all players could, and indeed had to, maintain their positions. If the environment changed, obsolete parties and coalitions cemented only by systemic corruption would collapse resoundingly. Proportional representation created, perpetuated, and undermined the Italian party system. Once proportional representation was questioned, the entire party system began to founder.

Toward a New Party System

The upheaval in the old party system had dramatic consequences for Italy's traditional governing parties. Some have probably disappeared for good (the case of the Liberals [PLI] and the Social Democrats [PSDI]), due to a lack of bribes as well as a lack of votes, which were usually delivered in exchange for bribes. Other parties were divided over a crucial decision: whether to align with the progressives or to stay with some group of moderates. This dilemma confronted the Republicans (PRI), many of whom moved toward the Progressive Alliance, which would be inaugurated in February 1994. Still other parties attempted reconstruction.

At first, the Socialist Party seemed to desire dissolution more than reconstruction. The PSI was forced to seek a new secretary among the ranks of the union leaders of proven Socialist loyalty, who were no less professionalized, no less bureaucratized, and no less partisan than other party leaders. In rapid succession two candidates were found. Within a few months the party consumed the first: Giorgio Benvenuto, the ex-secretary general of the UIL (Italian Union of Labor), who was under the illusion that he could promote rapid and far-reaching renewal. The party came to an agreement on the second, Ottaviano Del Turco, ex-adjunct secretary general of the CGIL (Italian General Confederation of Labor), who was much more thoroughly versed in the arcane rules of the party that sponsored his component in the CGIL. But the electoral results were unrelentingly harsh. In municipal elections in Milan and Turin, in Rome and Naples, cities with solid, even if differing, Socialist histories, voters now completely rejected PSI candidates, who struggled just to obtain symbolic representation in city councils. Nationwide, public opinion surveys showed that support for the PSI fluctuated around the four percent threshold, which, if not exceeded, would under the new electoral laws mean the near-complete disappearance of the PSI from the Chamber of Deputies.

Developments were almost as threatening for Christian Democracy, even though the DC started from a better position than the PSI: The DC had more real power, a firmer grounding in society, a greater role in government, and the backing of the Catholic Church. The hemorrhage of support that brought the Christian Democrats below 20% in opinion surveys seemed slower than that of the PSI, but not any more easily checked. At the same time, the old-guard DC mayors were losing office, ousted by the continuing investigations into *Tangentopoli*; and very few of the new mayors belonged to the DC. The DC was once the major pole of attraction in Italian politics, reassuring to voters, receptive to interest groups, and generous to allies. It now labored to find candidates, allies, sponsors, and voters. Faced with unpleasant realities and sustained pressures from Veneto regional secretary Rosy Bindi, DC secretary Mino Martinazzoli finally convened a Constituent Assembly in July 1993. Without further ado, one and all in the DC were converted to the new Popular Center. The DC thus intentionally postponed the choice between the moderate and the progressive camps. Some Christian Democrats did not know which choice to make and others did not want to make any choice. Indeed, most hoped — and some prayed — that they would never be forced to choose. Sergio Mattarella, rapporteur for the reform of electoral laws, worked towards this goal and from one point of view he achieved it: The new electoral laws did not "bipolarize" in principle and offered voters a broad menu of candidates and parties. Mattarella was quickly punished, however, presumably by his Sicilian "friends" in the DC, for having acted as a too rigorous emergency administrator and as a too straightforward innovator.

A cautionary warrant (*avviso di garanzia*) for breaking the law on public financing of parties, which Mattarella probably did not violate, was ready for him in early August. With great propriety and admirable dignity, Mattarella immediately resigned from his parliamentary and political positions. DC centrists rejoiced and were reinvigorated. But in early 1994, theirs would turn out to be a Pyrrhic victory, a prelude to the party's renaming, split, and further weakening. Douglas Wertman's chapter further examines the final months of the Christian Democratic Party.

The Northern League was bursting with health and continued to amaze the party-ocracy and the public at large, for it was probably more forthright than the old parties, suffered no guilt, and had nothing to hide. In June, the League won in Milan but lost in Turin. In December it lost in other large cities: Genoa, Venice, Trieste. Overall the League performed well in the North, above all in Lombardy. However, it could not penetrate south

of the "Gothic Line" (the shifting front in the Appenines dividing northern
Nazi-occupied Italy from liberated Italy between late 1943 and early 1945).
In proposing federalism, the League reinforced its protest against the
status quo. There was still much to protest in the Italy of *Tangentopoli*,
which was in the process of liberating itself from the Craxi-Andreotti-
Forlani alliance and perhaps from the grip of organized crime. The League
challenged its potential and actual rivals and thus shaped the future of the
party and political systems.

With all the traditional parties disintegrating, the League decided that
its only true opponent was the Democratic Party of the Left. For its part, the
PDS recognized both the honor and the onus of this challenge. Opinion
polls uniformly identified the PDS as the party most preferred by Italian
voters, and yet its support stood at only 20%. Unlike the League, the PDS
was a national party, that is, it won votes throughout Italy. More than the
old Christian Democrats, though, the PDS displayed pockets of weakness,
especially in the South but also in the Northeast. The PDS could hope to
inherit Socialist votes, to recover votes from Communist Refoundation,
and to elicit a youth vote for a Left that was renewed and prepared to
govern. The true strength of the PDS, a product of that mix of fortune and
virtue that Machiavelli considered indispensable, lay in its willingness to
forge alliances, to build progressive coalitions, and to back even non-PDS
mayoral candidates. The success of the united progressives, proven above
all in the December local elections, was preceded in late April 1993 by the
breakdown of the *conventio ad excludendum* (agreement to exclude) that had
operated against the PCI/PDS since 1947. For eleven hours the PDS lent
three ministers to the nascent Ciampi government: Augusto Barbera, Luigi
Berlinguer, and Vincenzo Visco. The vote in the Chamber to save Craxi and
a hurried decision on the part of the PDS secretariat forced their resignations. The role of the PDS as a governing party, however, will be played not
on the basis of that brief presence in government but as part of a more
ambitious, complex, and controversial project: the drive for the electoral
victory of a progressive coalition, the springboard to alternation in government. The many positive results of the June and November-December
local elections narrowed the options from which the PDS could, and had
to, choose. Politically and strategically the winning alternative was that of
the Democratic Alliance, even though it was imperfectly pursued. Large
cities saw victories of progressive coalitions of various types, which all
included the PDS and at times, together with the Republicans, the Greens
and the *Rete* (Network), also contained Segni's *Popolari per la riforma* or
Communist Refoundation. Since the *Popolari* traveled down the centrist
road, together with Segni, who in his moment of greatest weakness came
forward as a candidate for the premiership, it seemed likely that Communist Refoundation would become an integral part of the progressive

coalition. But if the coalition's program had as its core the conscious and complete acceptance of the challenge of governing the country, in the end Communist Refoundation would probably withdraw. In any case, the progressive alliance had already attracted the "social Christians" Ermanno Gorrieri and Pierre Carniti.

A progressive alliance thus emerged nationwide as the only coalition able to rival the League in the North and the MSI in the South, even though the MSI made a strong showing in Rome and Naples and scored several victories in smaller communities (yielding a total of forty-four MSI mayors). The progressive coalition drew confidence from the news that the lira had stabilized, and had even gained against the U.S. dollar and the German mark, immediately after progressive mayors were elected in large cities. The international economic community cancelled its *conventio ad excludendum*, in other words, and some Italian industrialists voiced their approval. But media magnate Silvio Berlusconi did not share this opinion, and in a televised address he announced his plan to enter the political arena and found a centrist party able to defeat the Left and assure good government — a party named *Forza Italia* (Go, Italy). None of the centrists — the center-right Christian Democrats, Berlusconi's followers, Segni's *Popolari*, or even the League — seemed to realize that the more closely competitors crowded into the same political area, the more easily progressive candidates could win the race. Habits of thought born under proportional rules were slow to die. On the other hand, what might have appeared to be examples of the classic maneuvers for advantage that for too long had plagued Italian political life were instead steps in the necessary process of alliance-building, now more important than in the past due to the new electoral laws.

Electoral Laws and Election Outcomes: A Bipolar Confrontation or a Reconstructed Center?

Even though the electoral laws approved in August 1993 could be criticized for several reasons, many observers greeted them as a sign that Parliament, with roughly one third of its members under investigation,[4] was still able to enact legislation and to respond to voters' preferences as expressed in the referendum. Here we need not explore the mechanisms and workings of the new electoral laws, which Richard S. Katz ably analyzes in his chapter. Instead we evaluate their probable consequences: in particular, whether and how they might promote alternation in government, contribute to the regime transition, and help to redefine relationships between civil society and the political sphere. To be sure, much depends on the goals and resources of the actors making the decisions that will introduce change along these dimensions. But beyond the specific objectives of different actors, the fundamental task is to design and install a political and institutional system that permits alternation in government.

Many of Italy's political problems have been caused by the lack of alternation in government. Was alternation unwelcome? dangerous? impossible? These questions could be debated at length and an Italian variant of consociationalism could also be discussed as the product and reflection of the absence of alternation, of its many vices and its very few virtues.[5] Without taking up such debates, we emphasize that the lack of alternation has given rise to almost all of those defects in the Italian political system that require immediate remedy: inadequate turnover in, and thus the aging of, the political class; insufficient circulation of ideas and programs and thus ineffective public policies; and a crystallization of relationships between members of government and interest groups and hence systemic corruption. The solution to these problems would consist of electoral rules and institutional mechanisms that can guarantee turnover, circulation, alternation, and integrity. The battle over the electoral laws pitted those who consciously aimed for a system that could foster alternation against those who, equally consciously, wished to defer or at least attenuate the impact of majoritarian principles. The predominantly majoritarian laws that were enacted would aid Martinazzoli, Segni or Berlusconi if any one of them tried to save a political center. But if all three made separate attempts at the same time, the laws would exact some punishment.

Almost all of the old political class agreed on the attempt to recreate and refurbish a center. Many Christian Democrats in 1993 deliberately moved toward that end, as an automatic reflex after years of reaping benefits from centrist positions. The Liberals and Social Democrats who were still presentable — and they were quite few — worked in the same direction. They hoped to enlist the Socialists, who for their part still wanted to weaken the PDS, and Giuliano Amato meant to guide the effort and even coined a name for the new center: Eta Beta. An anti-PDS center pleased the ex-Radical Marco Pannella as well. If the center were recomposed, however, the logic of bipolar competition, which alone would allow voters to view alternative blocs and opt for alternation, would be destroyed. The Mattarella electoral laws, in particular those framed for the Chamber, seemed to offer some opportunity to salvage and reinstate not "many centers," but one center alone, and thus only some centrist politicians. These centrists would quite probably constitute a minority in a tripolar party system. Some centrists hoped that their numbers would be great enough to make them indispensable to the formation of a parliamentary majority, so that they could ally, according to their pleasure and/or payment, either with the LeagueLeague or with the PDS (and the Progressive Alliance). Since it was unlikely that the League and the PDS would join in a governing coalition, only two options remained. The first option (and the most likely as of late January 1994) was that the Progressive Alliance would capture a narrow parliamentary majority on its own. The second was that the Progressive Alliance would emerge as the largest group in the new Parliament, but that it would need additional votes for a majority. The centrists would then exert their power. Blackmail, veto, threat, coalition: All have already appeared in Italian politics, with devastating effects.

The Redefinition of Relationships
Between Politics and Society

Despite the uncertainty surrounding electoral outcomes, the renewal of the political system proceeded. Understandably, counter-reactions occurred. At long last, the war against the Mafia and the Camorra was being waged seriously.[6] After more than a decade at large, Salvatore Riina, considered by many to be the "boss of all bosses" in the Mafia, was arrested in January in the center of Palermo. Other celebrated arrests followed periodically and almost systematically. Repentant *mafiosi* were talking, magistrates were interrogating, and the police forces were investigating. But the head of the New Organized Camorra, Raffaele Cutolo, continued to refuse to reveal — and yet continued to claim that he knew — the names of politicians who, thanks to his intervention, had negotiated in 1981 with the Red Brigades and the Camorra to free Ciro Cirillo of the DC, then Councillor of Urban Planning for Campania. Even the secret services felt threatened.

The political battle was thus fought not only in the electoral arena. Not surprisingly, some opponents of renewal decided to resort to bombings in 1993, convinced that such messages would be clearly understood. From Rome to Florence to Milan, the strategy was the same, even if the hands and heads behind the crimes, so to speak, might have differed. Finally under vigorous attack, organized crime, sectors of the secret services, and pieces of the political world decided to counterattack and to negotiate. They counterattacked to show that they were not tamed, finished, or gone. On the contrary, they were still politically and technically able to generate destruction and death. They negotiated to communicate that their continued silence on the many mysteries of Italian political life could be bought and that they were able to blackmail and slander their opponents. Their price was impunity. Broadly construed, their silence would mean a smooth exit from the political system, with no loss of acquired privileges, status, or liberty — or, at worst, a postponement of any formal accusation.

These violent groups would be very comfortable with a flourishing electoral center, combative and able to bargain for itself and for them. If any alliance between such groups and an electoral center were ever to materialize, the burden weighing on the various Italian transitions, including the one leading to the Second Republic, would be heavy indeed and would perhaps even halt them. A democratic pursuit of the transitions instead requires the victory of a coalition brave enough to open closets, bring out skeletons, and send culprits to prison or at least return them to private life. The success or failure of political renewal in Italy does not hinge on total change — a revolution is neither in progress nor on the horizon — but on the extent and types of discontinuity that punctuate an inevitable and perhaps indispensable continuity.

All the same, and despite the loud calls for the renewal of politics and politicians, two questions remain that no one has yet convincingly addressed. First, is a renewal of civil society required as well, beginning with businessmen and, to a different degree and for different reasons, union leaders — or will it suffice to replace the politicians? Second, if replacing politicians across the board were indeed to suffice, where would the new political personnel come from? Can a new political class be recruited entirely and exclusively from a civil society that sees itself as not responsible for, and inured to, *Tangentopoli*, but that has for too long tolerated — and often participated in — corruption for personal advantage?

Entrepreneurs have reacted to *Tangentopoli* in two ways. At first, with some justification, they put all the blame on the politicians. After all, if politicians had not asked for, and often extorted, bribes and kickbacks, then (most) businessmen would not have volunteered them. Nonetheless, more than a few entrepreneurs, individually and grouped into employers' associations, have given some large contributions or paid illicit funds to governing parties and politicians. Moreover, honest businessmen have rarely expelled corrupt ones from employers' associations. This is all the more disturbing since, as della Porta and Vannucci document, corrupt entrepreneurs broke the principle of market competition: Their generous contributions and payments benefitted them in the assignment of public contracts, to the detriment of their honest rivals. Occasional corruption is one thing, systemic corruption is quite another. Later, in a second stage, Italian businessmen acknowledged responsibility for their actions, thanks to the (rather tardy) admissions of Cesare Romiti of FIAT and then Carlo De Benedetti of Olivetti. Both men justified themselves by pointing to the need to obtain public contracts, subcontracts, and work orders, citing the noble end of keeping their companies alive and thus creating or preserving jobs. Whoever refused to pay, they said, was cut out of the bidding and failed; the employer lost the company, and employees, their jobs. The politicians' threats were impossible to ignore. This was all or almost all true, but it would have been more persuasive if it had been presented not only as economic blackmail but also as a political bargain.

At bottom, the five-party coalition that governed Italy for much of the 1980s and early 1990s could improve its standing and boost its power in businessmen's eyes by stressing its determination to keep the Communists out of government, to wear them out once and for all.[7] Many entrepreneurs found the deal acceptable and not at all unfair. Then, the Berlin Wall fell, the PCI was transformed into the PDS, and some businessmen began to wonder if the five-party coalition had become too greedy, since the principal danger had receded. Some of them turned to the LeagueLeague, which promised to free them from the old politicians and the old parties. Of course, the governing politicians were more guilty and probably more corrupt than the businessmen. But there were probably few businessmen who could honestly say that they were completely outside the network of corruption. Not by chance, when government by politicians gave way to government by professors (and not government by technicians and managers), the business world greeted it with applause. At least some businessmen, then, wanted a pause for reflection and may have been meditating on their responsibilities. A few, overwhelmed by their responsibilities, committed suicide. Even so, it is not clear to what extent this important sector of civil society was — and is — aware of its past and present inadequacies, including its role in sustaining not only the old political system but also *Tangentopoli*.

The Transition to the Second Republic

If almost all the old political world is to be purged, as it must be, how will the new political class be recruited, in the absence of an incisive and decisive commitment to renewal on the part of civil society? The simplest response is that not all of the current political class will disappear immediately. As in the Spanish transition, in Italy too, some segment of the old political world will survive, in part because it deserves survival and in part because it will earn the right to survival (which will be facilitated by the new electoral laws). Indeed, the new electoral rules allow for a filtered opening to some sectors of civil society that will yield change and turnover of notable dimensions — even generational turnover. This implies that the transition to the Second Republic will not be rapid. On the contrary, it will continue for at least a few rounds of elections. A protracted transition, however, could increase the risk of struggles for power, attempts at revenge, and violence.

The success of the regime transition — the establishment and consolidation of the political institutions constituting the Second Republic — depends on transition in the sociopolitical system, on the remaking, on new grounds, of relationships between society and politics. This is so because all the major social and political actors, willingly or not, to a greater or lesser degree (and the differences are crucial) have been involved in the degeneration of the preceding system and of the First Republic. In other words, the distinction between politics and civil society, which is so often drawn, had vanished in Italy. Politics had penetrated deep into society, and society had carved comfortable niches in politics, often simply for survival, at times to acquire political privileges. If this past is to be overcome, the transition to the Second Republic must continue for some time — despite the risks noted above.

Readers of this introduction will know the results of the 1994 parliamentary elections. Obviously, the new elections will have important consequences for the balance of power among what is left of the old parties and among party alliances, for turnover in Parliament, for the formation of the government, and for the future of institutional reform. Nonetheless, the March 1994 elections will not suffice to consolidate the Second Republic. A regime is replaced only when its successor is built; and this construction requires imagination and time, consensus and competence, all scarce resources. A corrupted system is corrected only when its structure and the relationships and actors within it are redefined. The transitions will thus continue for several years. The party system is still quite fluid, alternation in government is still a novelty, political institutions are still being redesigned, and the relations between the political arena and civil society are still being renegotiated. The results of all these aspects of the transition remain uncertain, indeterminate, and in the hands of Italian citizens and their representatives.

Notes

1. Here we understand a "regime transition" in the terms set forth by O'Donnell and Schmitter in their classic study: "[T]he 'transition' is the interval between one political regime and another. ...[D]uring it the rules of the political game are not defined. Not only are they in constant flux, but they are usually arduously contested; actors struggle not just to satisfy their immediate interests and/or the interests of those whom they purport to represent, but also to define rules and procedures whose configuration will determine likely winners and losers in the future." Guillermo O'Donnell and Philippe C. Schmitter, *Transitions from Authoritarian Rule: Tentative Conclusions about Uncertain Democracies* (Baltimore and London: The Johns Hopkins University Press, 1986), p. 6. Whereas O'Donnell and Schmitter consider changes of regime type, we examine a transition from one democratic regime to another.

2. The gap between Amato as party leader and Amato as professor of constitutional law could not be bridged. In the latter role, in more or less the same period,

Amato reached a rather different conclusion: "We confirmed the choice in favor of the proportional [electoral law] (without including it in the Costitution, though, which left greater freedom for any future change)." G. Amato, "Le istituzioni: figlie della politica," in G. Urbani, ed., *Dentro la politica. Come funzionano il governo e le istituzioni* (Milano: Edizioni Il Sole 24 Ore, 1992), pp. 181-182.

3. As Martin Rhodes explains in his contribution to this volume, the informal alliance bringing together Bettino Craxi, Giulio Andreotti and Arnaldo Forlani originated in spring 1989 and served to benefit both the DC's center and right (as Andreotti and Forlani aimed) and Craxi's PSI. In order to proceed in investigations involving parliamentarians, Italian magistrates have had to request that Parliament vote authorization of the investigation. For further discussion of these rules, see the chapter by Gianfranco Pasquino and Salvatore Vassallo.

4. "Parlamento e Tangentopoli: Sono 325 gli `indagati' il 30% degli onorevoli," *L'Unità*, August 12, 1993, p. 6.

5. Alternation (Japan, Sweden and Israel), see T. J. Pempel, ed., *Uncommon Democracies: The One-Party Dominant Regimes* (Ithaca and London, Cornell University Press, 1990). A classic analysis of the search for consensus in Italian politics — which does not, however, identify Italy as consociational democracy — is G. Di Palma, *Surviving without Governing: The Italian Parties in Parliament* (Berkeley: University of California, 1977). Arend Lijphart defines consociationalism in *Democracy in Plural Societies: A Comparative Exploration* (New Haven and London: Yale University Press, 1977).

6. As explained in the chapter by della Porta and Vannucci, the Camorra refers to organized crime in the region of Campania.

7. For further discussion of the five-party (DC-PSI-PSDI-PLI-PRI) coalition, see the chapter by Gianfranco Pasquino and Salvatore Vassallo.

2

The Government of
Carlo Azeglio Ciampi

Gianfranco Pasquino and Salvatore Vassallo

The April Referendum
and the Fall of the Amato Government

It was both inevitable and opportune that Prime Minister Giuliano Amato announced in advance that he would resign immediately after the referendum had been held on the electoral law for the Senate. And it was only proper that Amato kept his word. In fact, as vice-secretary of the Socialist Party (PSI), Amato had repeatedly and vigorously affirmed that electoral referenda were "unconstitutional in the highest degree" — despite his juridical expertise, which had led him for more than a decade to argue for the necessity and propitiousness of incisive electoral reform.[1]

The electoral referenda were judged constitutional by the Constitutional Court, though not all were admissible due to their formulation. The first referendum, which in June 1991 established the single preference vote, undermined the power of the Socialist Party. Then, a new gathering of signatures obliged the Parliament to enact legislation in March 1993 on the direct election of mayors; the legislation avoided a referendum on the issue, which, given the way it was framed, would have produced an even more strongly majoritarian law. The last remaining referendum, held on April 18-19, went straight to the heart of electoral reform for the Parliament, which the Socialist Party continued to oppose, albeit with diminished powers. On April 19, 1993, Amato's brief experience as prime minister ended. After a fierce parliamentary debate, Amato's resignation became effective on April 22. On the one hand, Amato — a professor of constitutional law turned subtle, extremely skillful politician — had little cause to complain. He had obtained the post on June 18, 1992, and the confidence of the Senate and Chamber on July 2 and 4, 1992, respectively.[2]

Amato's government had reached the average duration of Italian postwar governments, about 10.5 months.[3] On the other hand, Amato had been forced to endure a stream of resignations from fully seven of his cabinet ministers.

The Minister of Foreign Affairs, Vincenzo Scotti, resigned on July 29, 1992, in order to avoid the new rule imposed by the Christian Democratic leadership, which required DC ministers to give up their parliamentary seats. Between March 10 and March 30, 1993, other resignations followed, all in the wake of official notifications that investigations were under way on crimes of political corruption. Those who relinquished their ministerial posts were Claudio Martelli at Justice, Francesco de Lorenzo at Health, Giovanni Goria at Finance (who was replaced by Franco Reviglio, who in turn would resign after only thirty-seven days in office), and Gianni Fontana at Agriculture. In addition, the Minister of the Environment, Carlo Ripa di Meana, resigned on March 7, due to his dissent on the decree depenalizing crimes of illicit financing for parties.

These resignations offered Premier Amato the opportunity to fill the open positions with ministers who in many cases were not professional politicians, were new nominees, and were substantially better than their predecessors. Amato signed an important accord on the cost of labor on July 31, 1992, and started the difficult and hard-fought process of privatizing public companies. Amato was constrained by the past, however. Thus, in the end, and this is perhaps the greatest stain on his reputation, his recognition of debt to his political sponsor, Bettino Craxi, probably forced Amato to try to ensure the passage of a blanket decree on the crimes of "Tangentopoli" (Bribe City, as the corruption scandal came to be known). Nonetheless, after solemnly announcing in a turbulent Senate session his return to university life, Amato left the premier's office with his head held high, even though he may have been somewhat subdued.[4] Amato neither had known how, nor had wanted, nor had perhaps been able to, exploit all the opportunities that this particular phase of the political system seemed to give him. In fact, Amato was rooted and anchored, inevitably, in the old system.[5] With Amato's resignation, the transition towards a new political system that had been launched by the electoral referenda could proceed further.

The Formation of the Ciampi Government

After Amato, it was to clear to all observers that it was best not to entrust the transitional period again to a professional politician. The outcome of the electoral referendum, along with the outcomes of the referenda on the abolition of certain ministries and on public financing of parties, pointed to a new and different institutional era in the history of the Republic. The old four-party governing majority (of the DC, PSI, Social Democrats, and Liberals) appeared to be shaken by scandal, worn-out in its programs, unpresentable in its personnel, and ill suited for the task of directing whatever transition might occur. Appeals and pressures for the creation of a "presidential government" (strongly influenced by the President rather than by party executive organs), which were animated by divisiveness and anti-party sentiment and had often been deployed inappropriately for at least fifteen years, had by this time become quite strong and widespread. What was wanted, in effect, was that the President of the Republic apply Article 92 of the Constitution to the letter and in its entirety: "The President of the Republic shall nominate the Prime Minister."

In contrast to the appeals of the past, which were often self-serving, now both the political and institutional conditions were such that it might be possible to truly return to the Constitution, advantageously and without compulsion, looking to the future and at the same time responding to the demands of a solid portion of the electorate. The political conditions were rooted in the terminal crisis of both the four-party coalition and the internal organizations of those parties, which were weakened by scandal and weighted down by the corruption of their leaders. The institutional conditions had been produced by the electoral referendum, which, correctly interpreted, signaled not only the demand for a majoritarian reform of electoral laws, but also highlighted the need for citizens to have greater influence on the formation of the executive, from mayors to prime ministers. If party secretaries were no longer to have the task of making and unmaking governments, and this could not yet be the task of the voting citizenry, then the President of the Republic, who "represents national unity" (Article 87 of the Constitution), might assume this duty and its corresponding responsibilities. From the very start the names that circulated as potential premiers were relatively few, and in large part they were the same players as always: the ex-Presidents of the Constitutional Court, the Presidents of the Chamber and Senate, some authoritative national figures, and, naturally, the Governor of the Bank of Italy. In addition, on the one hand, there were those proposing Mario Segni, the leader of the referendum movement, in order that he might take up the mandate he had received and form a government that would carry to completion the complex process of electoral and institutional reform. Segni appeared undecided, probably making a political mistake, but perhaps he felt it would be difficult to transpose into a governing majority the inevitably heterogeneous referendum majority. In any case, the candidacy of Segni, who certainly did not enjoy the support of the four-party majority, was vetoed by the Christian Democrats and in particular by the DC secretary, Martinazzoli.

On the other hand, there were those who advanced the candidacy of a technician, preferably one who was not a complete stranger to Roman political circles so that he would not be an impotent premier, and preferably one who embodied the new in Italian politics and who at the same time would be able to take charge of the old politics as well. The ex-President of IRI (the Institute for Industrial Reconstruction), Professor Romano Prodi, was among those thought to meet these requirements. Prodi's candidacy, which at one point seemed about to succeed, was almost certainly blocked both by the PDS's less than enthusiastic reaction to a man considered too close to the Christian Democrats and by feeble support from Segni himself, who was not inclined to accept the post of vice premier in a Prodi government.

The Governor of the Bank of Italy, Carlo Azeglio Ciampi, had already been suggested as a potential candidate during the election of the President of the Republic. This time Ciampi had the advantage over other candidates for two fundamental reasons. First, the press and informed public opinion seemed to agree on a specific point: the absolute necessity that the parties step back from the government and that the new premier thus not be a professional politician. The second reason was that, given Italy's enduring economic difficulties, the government needed to be headed by a person capable of winning the confidence of the international economic community. The Governor of the Bank of Italy met both of these conditions, which were not only useful but indispensable in the exceptional context in which the fifty-second government of the Italian Republic formed. Born in 1920, in Livorno, Ciampi had fcught in the Resistance as a young man and became Governor of the Bank of Italy in 1979. Ciampi knows the Italian political world well. He is highly regarded in Italy and abroad. He has never been touched by suspicion or scandal.

The governmental crisis that preceded Ciampi's appointment was quite brief. The parliamentary acceptance of Amato's resignation took place on Thursday, April 22. Ciampi was named as premier-designate on Monday, April 26. His nomination was unanimously received with approval. Ciampi immediately announced his intention not to engage in formal consultations with party leaders. This was an encouraging sign since the long and wearisome consultations held by preceding premiers-designate had essentially served to guarantee the subdivision of positions in the government and the public sector (the *sottogoverno*, or subgovernment) among parties, factions, and lobbies and to assure, more or less directly, the opportunity of gaining access to the market of illicit public and private funds. By avoiding the consultations, Ciampi could immediately go to work in choosing ministers, with the additional objective of enlarging the parliamentary base of his government, which could not rely exclusively on the four-party alliance, shaken as it was by the authorizations to proceed (*autorizzazioni a procedere*) requested for many of its parliamentarians and for the majority of its ministers from the 1980s and early 1990s, the years of the five- and four-party coalition.[6] And Ciampi could not have only the President of the Republic on his side, even though the President's support was authoritative and constant. An advance towards the Northern League was impracticable not only because of its federalist stance, which was marked by bombastic and repeated secessionist impulses, but above all because such a move would prevent Ciampi from receiving appreciation and support from progressive forces, in particular the Democratic Party of the Left (PDS). For its part, the League was still determined to present itself as a movement of adamant purity and toughness, which refused to be involved in the system. Moreover, Ciampi had to take into account the President's request (which the President had earlier issued to Amato as well) that a "lean" cabinet be formed, with a limited number of ministers and undersecretaries.

It was not very difficult for the Amato government to trim its numbers in comparison with Andreotti's last government, which had been full to overflowing with over 100 members: 32 ministers of various sorts and 69 undersecretaries. Under Ciampi there were 24 ministers (with Andrea Maccanico designated to take over as Minister of Tourism, held in the interim by Ciampi himself), the same number as in the Amato government (although under Amato the 24 became 25 when Paolo Baratta was named to oversee privatizations); and the Ciampi government included 37 undersecretaries, as compared to 35 under Amato. It should be noted that three ministries were abolished in the case of the Ciampi government (Civil Protection, Urban Areas and Privatization). The responsibilities attached to the first two ministries were assigned to the two additional undersecretaries, Vito Riggio and Roberto Formigoni. Three ministries gained autonomy under Ciampi: Public Administration, Relations with Parliament, and Institutional Reform.

Ciampi was also well placed to effect significant change in the quality of the ministers. Ciampi had the opportunity to innovate since the most embarrassing representatives of the old politics had fallen by the wayside under Amato. Indeed, few ministers in the preceding government — which was still in effect an appendix to the story of the four-party coalition, however redesigned it might be — could hope for, or deserve, a reappointment. For the sake of continuity, particularly in the fight against organized crime, and, obviously, for important political reasons, with the explicit support of Christian Democracy, Nicola Mancino (DC) retained his post as Minister of the Interior. Others who remained in their posts were the Minister of the Treasury, Piero Barucci, and the Minister of Justice, Giovanni Conso, who had replaced Claudio Martelli. Since Giuliano Amato refused the position of Minister of Foreign Affairs, which traditionally has gone to ex-premiers, the portfolio instead went to Beniamino Andreatta (DC), who had failed to gain re-election to the Senate in 1992 and had replaced Franco Reviglio as Minister of the Budget after the latter received a cautionary warrant (*avviso di garanzia*) in March 1993; Andreatta thus overcame the "quarantine" imposed on him for more than a decade by the Vatican and Andreotti for his role in unveiling the scandals involving the Vatican Bank, the IOR. The Budget portfolio was entrusted to Professor Luigi Spaventa, formerly a parliamentarian from the Independent Left. The innovations of Ciampi's government, which to be sure was neither completely detached from the parties nor unresponsive to their requests, were essentially of two interrelated and superimposed kinds: the nomination of personnel without strong political markings; and the recourse to university professors, almost all of whom were not members of parliament. These innovations also provided a way of offering a place in government to the Democratic Party of the Left without forcing the PDS into any direct involvement, while still making a first step toward a future commitment. Professor Augusto Barbera was nominated as Minister for Relations with Parliament, but he punctiliously claimed a share in the formulation of institutional reforms; in turn the ex-President of the Constitutional Affairs Committee of the Senate, Leopoldo Elia, who had not been re-elected in 1992, was named Minister for Institutional Reforms. Senator and Professor Vincenzo Visco was nominated Minister of Finance, while Luigi Berlinguer, Rector of the University of Siena, became Minister of University Education and Scientific Research. Francesco Rutelli of the Green Party headed the Ministry of the Environment. Republican Senator Antonio Maccanico became Undersecretary to the Prime Minister, and Professor Andrea Manzella, also of the PRI, assumed the post of general secretary in the Prime Minister's office. Among the other important nominations, which made the Ciampi government from its inception a "government of professors," was that decided for the Ministry of Public Administration: Sabino Cassese, the leading Italian expert in the field. The choices that Ciampi reached, which were probably settled through close contact with the President of the Republic and were subject to an informal preliminary consideration by the party leaders involved, clearly indicated that the parliamentary base of the government had expanded to include the Republicans, the Greens and the Democratic Party of the Left.

The first challenge to the Ciampi government was issued but a few hours after the swearing-in of its ministers, in the wake of the historic moment when, for the first time after forty-five years, the government ignored the so-called *conventio ad excludendum* (agreement to exclude) that had operated against the PCI/PDS, the largest Communist Party in Western Europe until its renaming in 1991. On the afternoon of April 29, the four-party majority in the Chamber of Deputies — a majority that by this time was solid and compact only when defending its members under investigation or likely to be investigated and that was probably aided by those (in first place, the Lega) who hoped to block the implementation of the referendum mandate by asking for new, immediate elections — rejected all four requests for authorization to proceed against Bettino Craxi that the *Procura* (Public Prosecutor) of Milan had submitted and accepted only the two authorizations proposed by the *Procura* of Rome. Calculated or not, these votes produced as an additional, probably unintentional, and certainly welcomed result the hurried resignations of the three PDS ministers and the minister from the Greens, Rutelli. After four days of waiting in vain for some reconsideration of their decisions, Ciampi substituted the resigning ministers with three other professors and also moved a politician. Valdo Spini of the PSI returned to the Ministry of the Environment and was replaced at the Ministry for the European Community by the ex-President of the Constitutional Court, Professor Livio Paladin. Professors Franco Gallo, Paolo Barile and Umberto Colombo, who were not parliamentarians, went respectively to the Ministries of Finance, Relations with Parliament, and University Education and Scientific Research. Only in the course of the parliamentary debate on the government's program did it become clear how the PDS, the Greens and the League might vote on investiture. Though their previous positions were quite divergent, these parties converged and opted to abstain on the vote of confidence, as did the Republicans. In any case, notwithstanding the withdrawal of their ministerial delegation, the PDS and the Greens turned out to show a benevolent attitude and concrete support toward the Ciampi government.

The Program of the Ciampi Government and Its Implementation

Ciampi completed the formation of the cabinet in record time, overcame with rapidity and understatement the obstacle of the nearly immediate resignation of the ministers from the Left, and gained the confidence of the Parliament. The Ciampi government had next to quickly begin implementing its program. The government's program clearly identified all the unavoidable, difficult questions put on the agenda by the institutional transition and by the pressing economic context, which was complicated by the extraordinary weight of the public deficit inherited from the five-party governments. From the very start, then, the Ciampi government addressed the task of guaranteeing a change in the rules of the game (following above all the indications from the referendum) in a phase in which the national political geography and the balance of power among

Italian parties were being rapidly transformed. The team headed by Ciampi and his staff took into account, in a way that would later be revealed as both careful and shrewd, the time limits put on the government's life. And yet it also dedicated itself to undertaking, and in some cases completing, several important policies intended to reduce the public deficit in conjunction with efforts to contain inflation and regulate wages. The Ciampi government thus sought to meet the targets defined as necessary for convergence with the other European Community economies according to the Maastricht Treaty, as well as to move towards privatization of some state agencies and to effect a profound reform of the public administration.

The fundamental objective that underpinned and linked these programmatic priorities, and that seems to have constantly inspired both the action and style of the cabinet, was the attempt to rebuild, in the brief span of a few months, confidence in Italian state institutions. Such trust — on the part of markets, international political institutions, and Italian citizens themselves (in their role as creditors of the state) — had been rapidly eroded. As an economist and as a high official of the state, Ciampi knew — and reminded others frequently — that trust in public institutions is a fundamental resource, needed to guarantee a stable currency and to stimulate investment and employment, as well as to render effective and efficient any type of initiative that public institutions intend to frame and implement.

From this point of view, "absolute priority" had to be given to the question of electoral reform, as Ciampi declared to the Chamber of Deputies on May 6, when he committed himself to facilitating, with the appropriate regulatory instruments and in agreement with the Presidents of the Chamber and Senate, the approval of an electoral law before the summer recess. He meant for the law to be consistent with the referendum results and the launching of new rules on the financing of political activity. Ciampi was determined not to yield before the open attempts to precipitate early elections under the old electoral laws; it was this determination above all that had maintained the fragile equilibrium upon which Ciampi's government was based, an equilibrium that had been damaged by the vote against the authorization to proceed investigating Craxi. This was the reason why the PDS in the end abstained on the vote of investiture. Indeed, President Scalfaro had written a letter (now made public) in which he indicated three "absolute priorities" for the government: electoral reform, the redefinition of parliamentary immunity, and the defense of the lira. In the same letter Scalfaro confirmed that his fundamental duty was to

respect the will of our voting citizens so clearly manifested by the referendum of April 18; that duty entails following the direct and explicit expression of the popular preference for the definition of new electoral rules, rules that would permit the holding of general political elections under the system that the overwhelming majority of Italians has demonstrated, in voting, that it favors.[7]

This brief passage, which synthesized a concept expressed by Scalfaro on various occasions, identified a clear mandate for the Prime Minister and implicitly, but as anyone could see, it also imposed a time limit on the duration of Ciampi's government.

The government, however, in the persons of Ministers Barile and Elia, was not obliged to intervene with any particular force to allow for the timely approval of the electoral laws. It maintained to the end its declared neutrality with regard to different options: the number of parliamentary seats to be elected under proportional representation (PR) rules and the criterion to be used to allocate PR seats; the possibility of two rounds of voting; and the prospect of some linkage between the election of members of Parliament and the Premier. (On the last two points, though, the warnings of Minister Elia were known.) The government limited itself to putting at the disposal of the Committee on Constitutional Affairs the (most rapid) channel of government-proposed bills (*disegni di legge*) so that the law for constitutional reform that would give the vote to Italian citizens abroad could also be approved by the end of 1993. The government deserved credit as well for establishing in record time the committee of experts that was to redesign electoral districts and for protecting that committee from any unwanted interference.

The electoral laws for the Chamber and the Senate were thus approved on August 4, 1993. In contrast, the politically disastrous and technically dangerous appendix on the vote of Italians abroad elicited vigorous debate and was eventually abandoned. A few days before the expiration of the charge conferred upon it, the government completed the procedure for defining the 707 single-member districts (475 for the Chamber and 232 for the Senate), having assimilated the opinions of the regional governments and the Committee for Constitutional Affairs.

The story of institutional reform under the Ciampi government should also include the presentation and approval of a legislative proposal that, by modifying Article 68 of the Constitution, limited the need to grant an authorization to proceed (in both Chamber and Senate) only to those cases in which the judicial official, for either investigative or precautionary ends, intends to place constraints on the personal liberties of a member of parliament under investigation. A second law, approved in December, was unsatisfactory in its treatment of the important issue of financing for permanent party bureaucracies but addressed electoral campaign budgets and access to the mass communications media.

If the Ciampi government simply forced the pace for those members of parliament who wanted to procrastinate further in the passage of electoral reform, it instead made a decisive difference in working towards a profound reform of the public administration. After a few months under new leadership, the cabinet's staff produced a "Report on the Condition of Public Administration," which in turn paved the way for first a set of guidelines and then a series of legislative and regulatory innovations. As anticipated in the programmatic declarations of the President, the law on public contracts, already under discussion in the Chamber, was approved and "codes of conduct" for personnel in the public bureaucracy were also defined; implementing norms were produced for the law on the so-called transparency of administrative acts (Law 241 of 1990) and greater flexibility in the management of personnel was introduced. Two important innovations in the ministerial apparatus were the transformation of the Post and Telecommunications Administration into an economic agency (the first step towards the subsequent creation of a joint-stock company), and the reorganization of the Ministry of Health with the aim of "regionalizing" health-related public policies. Finally, a new order for the security services was approved; this reform was accelerated as past misconduct in the services' use of powers and financial resources came to light. Apart from the last measure, it is clear that on the whole the new direction taken by Minister Cassese, solicited and supported by the Premier, has served to develop more than just a set of initiatives to deal with immediate circumstances and constitutes a point of departure for a serious medium- to long-run policy package.

Economic policy was the second decisive front in the government's commitments. In its essential terms Ciampi's strategy was fairly clear and linear. The primary budget surplus was already estimated to be lower than the previous forecast by about 25,000 billion lire. This would have undermined efforts to reorder public accounts and would have put at risk the issuing of the second tranche of the international loan scheduled to be granted to Italy from the European Community (which was conditional on the maintenance of policy commitments). This problem led to the first economic package of 12-13,000 billion lire, approved in May, which halved the differential between the previously projected budgetary requirements and that now foreseen by reducing expenditures and increasing fuel prices and several indirect taxes. The government's attempt to curb expenditures and enlarge revenues should have produced a reduction of the deficit and greater confidence on the part of depositors and investors and thus a decline in interest rates and also in the weight of the public debt (at least in the portion made up of interest payments due). On this point, as in its insistence upon containing the inflation rate, the government showed that it acted rightly and shrewdly, "helped along" by the domestic and international recession and above all by the agreement of the cost of labor concluded and signed in the second round of meetings with labor confederations and employers' associations in July. In this accord unions and employers committed themselves to concur with the government in framing budget policies (by negotiating at the various stages of economic and financial planning throughout the year) so as to

(1) reach an inflation rate in line with the average rate in the 'most virtuous' economies of the European Community; and (2) reduce the state debt and deficit and [attain] currency stability.[8]

The tasks, therefore, were to contain inflation in order to maintain the purchasing power of wages and salaries; and, by working to restore confidence in public institutions, to reduce the weight of interest payments in the public debt. By September, at the inauguration of the Levante Fair, Ciampi was able to report rather encouraging progress toward these objectives.[9] These results were confirmed at year's end, due in part to broad parliamentary agreement that protected the approval of the budget from traditional pressures. Inflation stood below four percent and the trade balance showed credits of 24,000 billion lire. The state's current revenues exceeded current expenditures, even though the surplus was not yet large enough to cover the interest on the debt and thus did not entirely eliminate the need for additional borrowing. Nonetheless, these policies and outcomes surely marked an important first step, especially since the revenues already obtained and those foreseeable through the sale of entire companies or of blocks of shares once in public hands would enter separately into public accounts and directly reduce the primary debt. Privatization policies were another feather in the cap of this government's record. The privatization of the Credito Italiano was a success. In only one day, December 5, all available shares were sold, and demand was three times greater than the amount on hand. On the same day that the budget was approved, the privatization of Nuovo Pignone was completed, with 25 percent of total shares sold to General Electric. Naturally these battles that have been won cannot compensate for one of the most difficult periods of recession that the Italian economy has weathered during the last twenty years.

As the government moved towards the Second Republic and sought to restore confidence in state institutions, it pursued a program with largely predictable and inevitable flaws and limitations. The most evident of these concerned policies for employment and a strategy for renewing taxation and fiscal administration. The problem, after twenty years of haphazard financial management, was to make less burdensome — and possibly more equitable — the necessarily bitter policies for dealing with the public debt. It is no accident that the clearest failures and the greatest drops in popularity faced by the Ciampi government appeared at the two points they did: from September to October, when the minimum tax generated polemical debate and was then abandoned by the government; and in December, when the "pharmaceutical manual" was revised[10] and only demographic criteria were used to establish who could be exempt from pharmaceutical co-payments. This stop-gap measure, in the absence of a reliable system for verifying levels of income, worked against equalizing mechanisms in health service policies.

The Organization of the Government's Activity

Ciampi seems to have succeeded in imparting noteworthy coherence to the action of his cabinet, at least on those issues that attracted particular attention from the public or from limited but influential sectors of society. This result was naturally facilitated in a decisive way by the composition of Ciampi's cabinet and by the nature of the mandate that the Premier had received from the President of the Republic and the Parliament, as well as by the criteria adopted in selecting cabinet ministers. In the past, as long as the individual ministers had (or believed they had) a personal legitimation determined by their influence within their parties of origin, and as long as the Premier was (and was perceived by all to be) the exponent of one of the member parties of the coalition, the Premier could either play the role of out-and-out mediator (following the model whose master was Giulio Andreotti) or concentrate his efforts on a few issues and use his authority and visibility to work towards their resolution (as Bettino Craxi did with particular effectiveness, though not always in decisive areas).

It is instead evident that from the start the Ciampi government displayed a style of collegiality and reserve, which was upset only in the dispute (quickly settled) between Minister of the Treasury Barucci and Minister of Industry Savona regarding the strategies to pursue in privatizing state-held firms. Barucci had come out in favor of the formula of the "public company" with numerous shareholders, while Savona argued vigorously for the sale of substantial packets of shares to a single shareholder who would guarantee confidence in the subsequent management of the firms. (Savona cited the risk, which many refuted, that organized crime could hide behind the small shareholders.) Except for this case, it can be said that the criteria Ciampi communicated in a memorandum to his ministers during his first days in office have been basically respected. The key passage of this document required that "the different opinions that emerge in the course of debate and that contribute to the decisions of the government not be rendered public," which underlined that both the delicate and difficult context in which the government operated and the very nature of the government, "different from the coalition governments that have preceded [it], exclude the possibility of any political declarations shaped by partisan considerations."[11]

Again focusing on organizing the collegial activity of the cabinet, the Premier's Office provided a "Plan for the Regulation of the Council of Ministers," in accordance with a specific provision, never implemented until then, of Law 400 of 1988.[12] This set of rules, which was approved in the cabinet meeting of October 28, 1993, and which defined the procedures for meetings, the conservation of documents and the commitment of the ministers in translating government decisions into parliamentary action, made clear an orientation that attributed to the Premier a preeminence within the cabinet that was not merely formal and prescribed a rigorous style of shared responsibility and reserve on the part of individual ministers.[13]

Of course, we have no perfect way of measuring the exact correspondence between these prescriptions and the external image that the executive projected, on the one hand, and the reality of behavior inside the cabinet, on the other. Yet the nature of the Premier's legitimation and the types of relationships that in this cabinet, as opposed to almost all of its predecessors, link the Premier, the other members of the cabinet, and the parties make the notion more than plausible that appearances have corresponded to a real change and a truly collegial style of action.

The Government's Relationships with the Parties, the Media, and Other Institutions

The Premier's style of action both inside and outside the cabinet was not constrained in this case by the obstacles imposed by mutual vetoes of various party secretaries or by conflicts among faction leaders present in the cabinet. That Ciampi wanted, and was able, to do without the traditional practices of mediation is readily shown by the fact that neither of the two institutional devices designed and tested for this purpose in the phase of center-left governments, then again in the first of the five-party governments, then finally codified in 1988 in the law on the Premier's Office, were used in the Ciampi government: the figure of the Vice Premier (who guaranteed the status of the principal partner/antagonist of the party controlling the post of Premier) and the institution of the executive committee within the cabinet (the *consiglio di gabinetto*, made up of the heads of party delegations or the faction leaders of the coalition's parties). Since the parliamentary base of the Ciampi government did not coincide with the parties present within the executive — and given that the leaderships of those parties had almost entirely lost control over the behavior of their respective parliamentary groups — it was even simpler for Ciampi (and in a way he was forced) to distance himself clearly from the traditional practices of interparty consultations outside the cabinet (the so-called "majority summits" of leaders of coalition parties).

In the critical situations that Ciampi confronted — to name a few examples, the rapid passage of the electoral law, demonstrations against firings and *cassa integrazione*, the launching in May of the adjustment of the estimated projected deficit and then the budget package at the end of the year — his principal interlocutors were the President of the Republic, the Presidents of the Chamber and Senate, and the heads of parliamentary groups. In some of these episodes, and especially when presenting to the press the government's plans for public finance, Ciampi declared with a certain pride that he was not heading a "party government" and that he thus was not constrained by any previous extra-institutional consultations. This did not lead Ciampi to establish an overly direct and personalized relationship with the media. He aimed instead at using the mass media to communicate in a very restrained and sober way, largely on "classic" occasions, thus consolidating his image as a *grand commis* (highest-level civil servant) assigned the political leadership of the country; Ciampi lost no opportunity to call upon the mutual trust and support that linked him to the President of the Republic and in a sense he shielded himself behind the rhetorical bent of the President. If the climate of imminent defeat and breakdown that surrounded the parliamentary groups of the ex-four-party coalition guaranteed the Ciampi government notable autonomy, it also threatened to make the government's legislative activity even more uncertain and muddled than was the case in the past.

Ciampi found himself carrying out his institutional mission in a context of decaying party loyalties among parliamentarians of the old four-party governing majority, many of whom were preoccupied by their legal misfortunes and were occupied in attempts to weave new and contradictory alliances or to attain an "optimal" redrawing of their constituency boundaries. In this situation, and given Ciampi's self-imposed deadlines for the realization of his program, the government — predictably — made even greater use of decree-laws than past governments did. For example, over a much longer period (302 days) Amato introduced 76 new decree-laws; the Ciampi government introduced 83 in 250 days. Any mode of calculating percentages and monthly averages of decrees converted into law, expired, or rejected serves to confirm this progressive quantitative increase. For instance, in the course of the Tenth Legislature (June 1987-April 1992), about 16 decrees per month were presented, which already represented a record number; from the start of the Eleventh Legislature to the end of 1993, the monthly average rose to roughly 20. This practice is an indicator of the lack of coordination between the government and Parliament that not even the well-balanced cabinet headed by Carlo Azeglio Ciampi has been able to overcome. Upon taking office Ciampi inherited 103 decrees to submit to Parliament for a first or a repeated attempt at conversion into law, and he had prepared 136 by the start of 1994.[14]

The Government of the Political
and Institutional Transition

We conclude by affirming that the Ciampi government fulfilled the programmatic points it had indicated as top priorities, and that it did so more successfully — with regard to both policy achievements and style of action — than might have initially been imagined.[15] The Ciampi government turned out to be almost exactly what the Prime Minister wanted: "a parliamentary government, a political government, and also a government of institutional guarantees," and a government that made "useful, necessary, honest, and humble" efforts.[16]

Even amid the uncertainties and the difficulties created by the decomposition of the parliamentary groups of the four-party coalition, as long as the minimum and fundamental objectives of the government remained unmet, Ciampi was upheld both by the supporters of an indefinite postponement of parliamentary elections and by those who wanted elections as soon as possible under new rules. But when, with the approval of the new budget, the institutional and political tasks of the Ciampi government could be viewed as completed, the battle to postpone political elections, up to that point fought in the form of parliamentary guerrilla warfare, came out in the open.

Marco Pannella (ex-Radical and head of the Pannella List) collected in a flash the number of signatures needed to introduce a no-confidence motion. Pannella argued that a new, truly political, government was required (headed by Ciampi still, with Mario Segni as Vice Premier and Pannella himself as Minister of Foreign Affairs), but that the new government should not view immediate elections as its sole aim. Debate quickly ensued on the objectives and political consequences of a particularly irregular no-confidence motion. Understandably, those deputies who were destined to be defeated or not renominated hoped to postpone the dissolution of Parliament and thus the date of the next elections.[17] The mere discussion of Pannella's no-confidence motion was designed to give a few more weeks' time to the diverse forces (or rather weaknesses) of the center, to allow them to reorganize and perhaps coalesce in a defensive alignment. The constitutional problem that all of this posed is not new. Indeed, it recurs with virtually every early dissolution of the Parliament.

If we were in Great Britain, the argument runs, then it would be enough for the current head of government to approach the Queen and ask for an early dissolution, even with the most political and the most partisan of motivations: The polls show that the popularity of the current government is very high and that the opposition is in disarray. And Parliament would be dissolved. Notwithstanding the many opinions written on Italian constitutional doctrine in this matter,[18] not all agree that in Italy a similar declaration of the government would suffice. For example, the key move toward the traumatic dissolution of the Ninth Parliament (1983-1987) occurred in late April 1987 when Mino Martinazzoli, the already embittered head of the DC parliamentary group, invited DC deputies to abstain on the vote of investiture of the pre-electoral Fanfani government; the aim was to prevent the formation of a majority including the Socialists, Social Democrats, and Radicals (all of whom voted in favor) and to allow the President of the Republic to dissolve the Parliament.

It should be noted that the dissolution of Parliament after Ciampi's resignation resulted from political and institutional motivations. It was not only justified by the decomposition of the parliamentary majority or prompted by an electoral calculation on the part of the Premier. The dissolution was also designed to allow citizens to use the new electoral system that they had requested through the referendum (as the President of the Republic had urged when he had named Ciampi as premier-designate) and to respond to the need to adjust parliamentary representation to the manifest change in the electorate's preferences. This last argument cannot be easily dismissed. For example, to return to the comparison with Britain, in 1874 the Liberal premier Gladstone advocated general elections (which his party then lost), maintaining that the outcomes of several recent by-elections demonstrated that popular opinion had changed.

Perhaps in the 1993 episode many Christian Democratic parliamentarians wished only to gain a few weeks' time and respite. However it may be resolved, the problem of the procedures to follow for an early dissolution of Parliament does remain open in Italy and it will certainly be on the agenda when decisions are reached on fundamental institutional reforms: What is at issue is how the prime minister with his majority is to be elected and how and when this prime minister can legitimately ask for a dissolution of Parliament and can thus obtain the electorate's verdict on his actions.

Whatever the future holds, it is important to note that 1993 closed with several political paradoxes in Italy. The first is that it will probably turn out to have been easier for Ciampi to enter Palazzo Chigi than to leave it. The second is that the Premier may not in fact be forced to leave Palazzo Chigi immediately, despite the no-confidence motion. The Ciampi government has gained support within the Progressive Alliance; and, as a third paradox, even Massimo D'Alema, often considered the most "party-political" of the leaders of the PDS, is aware that a government headed by Ciampi himself, but with an altered composition and parliamentary base, could continue to be useful — both to the Progressives themselves and to the country at large. Ciampi would be able to guarantee the necessary economic and political continuity that would maintain the confidence of the international economic community as the reform of Italian political institutions proceeded and as Italian citizens absorbed the impact of their first experience of democratic alternation, which might well be on the horizon. With the approach of the parliamentary elections, whose results will of course influence the formation, composition, and leadership of the next government, some might regret both the difficulty of creating a cohesive parliamentary majority and the present impossibility of allowing citizens to vote directly for the government and Prime Minister. Only time will tell whether the Ciampi government should be considered the last government of the First Republic or simply the one, true government of the transition. Already today we may affirm that the Ciampi government must be evaluated positively for having facilitated the institutional transition and political realignment and for having made a notable contribution to what may turn out to be a "constitutional revolution."[19]

Translated by Claire Holman and Carol Mershon

Notes

Although the entire chapter reflects joint work, the first, second and sixth sections were written by Pasquino, the third, fourth and fifth sections by Vassallo.

1. Giuliano Amato, *Una Repubblica da riformare* (Bologna: Il Mulino, 1980).

2. The best analysis of the formation of the Amato government is the work of Stephen Hellman, "Politics Almost as Usual: The Formation of the Amato Government," in Gianfranco Pasquino and Patrick McCarthy, eds., *The End of Post-War Politics in Italy: The Landmark 1992 Elections* (Boulder, Co.: Westview Press, 1993), pp. 143-159.

3. For useful data and a convincing analysis of this subject, see David Hine, *Governing Italy: The Politics of Bargained Pluralism* (Oxford: Clarendon Press, 1992).

4. To quote from Amato's speech in the Senate during the tumultuous session of March 10, 1993: "The conclusion of my experience as Prime Minister, whether it comes in a day, in a month, or further in the future, will be at any rate the conclusion of my political career. I do not pretend, as do others, to be the leading character in too many political seasons, old and new."

5. On the role of the Amato government, its tasks, and its difficulties, see Gianfranco Pasquino, "Il traghetto del governo Amato," *La Rivista dei Libri*, December 1992, pp. 32-36.

6. In order to proceed in investigations of corruption involving sitting members of Parliament, Italy's magistrates have had to request that Parliament vote authorization of the investigation and thus lift the immunity otherwise granted parliamentarians. On changes in these requirements, see section three below. The five-party coalition, which included the Republicans along with the DC, PSI, PSDI, and PLI, governed Italy for most of the 1980s.

7. The complete text of Scalfaro's letter is published in *Vita italiana. Documenti e informazioni*, No. 5, 1993, p. 6.

8. See "Protocollo sulla politica dei redditi e dell'occupazione, sugli assetti contrattuali, sulle politiche del lavoro e sul sostegno al sistema produttivo", July 3, 1993, Attachment 1, *Vita italiana. Documenti e informazioni*, No. 7, 1993, p. 7; and the chapter by Richard Locke in this volume.

9. "Discorso del Presidente del Consiglio dei Ministri Carlo Azeglio Ciampi a Bari - Fiera del Levante (September 11, 1993)," *Vita italiana. Documenti e informazioni*, No. 12, 1993, pp. 109-116.

10. This manual lists the drugs that can be sold at a discount or distributed free to participants in medical insurance plans.

11. "Lettera ai Ministri sulla necessità di una condotta solidale della compagine governativa," Memorandum of May 26, 1993, published in *Vita italiana. Documenti e informazioni*, No. 8, 1993, p. 83.

12. See Pietro Barrera, "The First Institutional Reform: New Discipline in Government Activity," in Raimondo Catanzaro and Raffaella Y. Nanetti, eds., *Italian Politics*, Vol. 4 (London: Pinter, 1990), pp. 6-20.

13. But it should be noted that, with two additional memoranda on November 8, 1993, just after the approval of these regulations, Ciampi saw a need to solicit greater coordination of the efforts of the various ministers in Parliament and to support procedures of oversight and information in accordance with parliamentary rules.

14. Presidenza del Consiglio dei Ministri, Dipartimento per i Rapporti con il Parlamento, "Vicenda parlamentare dei decreti legge nella XI legislatura (situazione al 13 dicembre)," typescript; Presidenza del Consiglio dei Ministri, Dipartimento per i Rapporti con il Parlamento, "Vicenda dei decreti legge del Governo Ciampi alla data del 4 gennaio 1994," typescript. For comparative data from preceding legislatures and an interpretation of the increased use of decree-laws, see Vincent Della Sala, "Government by Decree: The Craxi Government and the Use of Decree Legislation in the Italian Parliament," in Piergiorgio Corbetta, Raffaella Y. Nanetti and Robert Leonardi, eds., *Italian Politics*, Vol. 2 (London: Pinter, 1988), pp. 8-24.

15. Prof. Mario Monti, Rector of the Bocconi University, who was passed over for a ministerial post in the Ciampi government, declared: "If I were forced to make a comparative evaluation, I would say that the Ciampi government is superior to that of Amato in the prestige, independence, and competence of the Premier and the Ministers. But Amato showed greater incisiveness of action: Working in his favor, paradoxically, was the grave state of emergency in which he operated. I believe it is legitimate to expect a great deal from the Ciampi government,

especially in terms of a radical change in the way the country is governed." "La svalutazione ci ha fatto bene," *La Repubblica,* September 12, 1993, p. 47. Today it seems that Prof. Monti has been proven right in his assessment.

16. The first quotation comes from a speech given by Ciampi at the inauguration of the Levante Fair in Bari. "Il mio governo non getterà la spugna," *La Repubblica,* September 12, 1993, p. 7. The second quotation is taken from Ciampi's programmatic declarations made to the Chamber of Deputies on May 4, 1993.

17. About 350 deputies and senators, many of whom were surely signatories of the no-confidence motion, declared their aim more explicitly when they asked Scalfaro to make the parliamentary elections coincide with the European Parliament elections already set for June 12, 1994. These Europeanists disregarded the fact that the EC Council of Ministers had already expressed its opposition to any coupling of this type.

18. See the long commentary, which unfortunately ends in 1983, given by Lorenza Carlassare on Article 88 of the Constitution in "Il Presidente della Repubblica," *Commentario alla Costituzione* (Bologna: Zanichelli, 1983), pp. 1-95. On the crisis of 1987 in particular, see the chapter by Enzo Balboni, "Who Governs? The Crisis of the Craxi Government and the Role of the President of the Republic," in Piergiorgio Corbetta and Robert Leonardi, eds., *Italian Politics,* Vol. 3 (London: Pinter, 1989), pp. 11-24.

19. It is still too early to state with any certainty whether this long, difficult, and conflict-ridden transition should be remembered as a "constitutional revolution." For a positive judgment, see Augusto Barbera's introduction to the useful and effective volume by Carlo Fusaro, *La Rivoluzione Costituzionale* (Soveria Manelli: Rubbettino, 1993).

3

The Referendum on the Electoral Law for the Senate: Another Momentous April

Piergiorgio Corbetta and Arturo M. L. Parisi

The Answer Is "Yes." What Was the Question?

On April 18 and 19, 1993, nearly 29 million Italians answered "yes" to the referendum item that asked whether they were willing to modify the rules for electing the Senate. As was the case for each of the nineteen previous referenda, a series that started with the 1974 divorce referendum, this time, too, the question on the ballot was difficult to read and even more difficult to understand. Certainly the electoral reform was the most complex of the eight referendum items simultaneously submitted to the electorate in April 1993.

To be sure, in the 145 words making up the referendum item, the key point could be identified as the request to suppress a short clause in the law that had until then regulated Senate elections. Article 17, Section 2, of Law No. 29 of February 6, 1948 (reformulated by Law No. 3 of January 23, 1992) stipulated that: "The president of the electoral office in the constituency, in conformity with the results obtained, declares elected the candidate who has won the largest number of valid votes cast in the constituency, *if that number does not represent less than 65 percent of total votes*." The elimination of the words italicized here would have transformed the Senate electoral law from a system that was theoretically "mixed" but actually proportional to one that was "mixed but primarily majoritarian."[1]

To appreciate the simplicity of the referendum item, the voter would have had to know the fact that lay behind the formal provisions for majoritarian competition within the single-member senatorial constituencies. Throughout the forty-five years of the Italian Republic, it was the exception, not the rule, for seats in the Senate to be awarded on a majoritarian basis. It was hardly ever the case that a candidate could reach the 65 percent threshold. And when all candidates missed the threshold, party shares of the vote were tallied region by region and senatorial seats were allocated by a proportional method. In practice, then, the electoral system of the Senate proved to be absolutely proportional. Even more important, however, an adequate understanding of the referendum item presupposed that the voter was able to connect the two systems — the proportional system, whose abrogation was requested, and the predominantly majoritarian system that would result from the abrogation — to broader projects of institutional reform.

Since the campaign for the referendum of June 9, 1991, on the single preference vote, the theme of institutional reform had entered into mass debate. Before that, throughout the 1980s, only a restricted segment of the political class had discussed institutional reforms. In the new context defined by the 1991 referendum, multiple actors spoke on the topic ever more frequently: from the President of the Republic (first Francesco Cossiga, then since 1992 Oscar Luigi Scalfaro), who repeatedly called for urgent institutional reform, to the political parties. Nonetheless, the technical nature and the political implications of the issue at the center of the 1993 referendum suggest that the question that voters answered did not coincide with the phrase written on the ballot.

In an analysis of the 1991 referendum, Patrick McCarthy[2] has emphasized that voters' responses had as their reference point not the literal meaning of the question at hand, but instead the desire for a more general change: Voters were protesting the lack of democracy in the political system and its inefficiency. For the referendum of April 18, 1993, as well, we believe that we should follow the same sort of approach to understand the nature of the question and the numbers of positive answers it elicited. That is, we should start from the fact that in the absence of effective alternatives, the movement for institutional reforms established itself — while advancing through the referendum process — as a response to the Italian political crisis.

The appropriateness of this line of interpretation was already clear in 1991, and it was all the more clearly revealed in the months separating the referendum on the single preference vote and that of 1993. We need not reconstruct here the details of this tumultuous period in Italian history. A brief review of major events suffices to show how a crisis that was already evident two years earlier became even more serious and pressing.

Though the crisis penetrated the entire political order, it was manifested above all in the growing delegitimation and decomposition of the Italian party system, especially the governing parties and their leaders. Two actors in particular held immediate responsibility for the destruction of the overall political equilibrium, even though deeper, more distant causes were certainly also at work. One was the Northern League, a radically new political force that did not in any way fit within the framework of parties and issues that had long characterized Italian politics. The League allowed voters to express and give weight to their increasing intolerance of the traditional political parties. The other actor was the investigating magistrature, which, since the opening of the Chiesa case in Milan in early 1992,[3] has relentlessly brought to light the vast web of political corruption that had developed over time in Italy.

As a result of the combined pressure of these two actors, the old political order had shattered by the time the April 1993 referendum was held. The inexorable crescendo began with the November 1991 municipal elections in Brescia, when for the first time the League snatched first place from the DC in a city that had been one of the DC's long-standing strongholds. Next was the electoral earthquake of the April 1992 parliamentary elections: The League emerged as the only winner and all of the traditional political forces met defeat. The series of local elections held in the latter part of 1992 — from the September provincial elections in Mantova to the December municipal elections in such cities as Varese, Monza, and Isernia — all rendered the same verdict.

Just as the elections have redefined the party system, the actions of the magistrates have delegitimated the leadership of the parties. One by one, those who were once the undisputed leaders of the major parties — Bettino Craxi (PSI), Giulio Andreotti (DC), Arnaldo Forlani (DC), Giorgio La Malfa (PRI), Renato Altissimo (PLI), Carlo Vizzini (PSDI), Claudio Martelli (PSI) — have lost their positions due to judicial initiative. At the end of the process, none of the figures who dominated politics for more than a decade remained at the top.

When the 1993 referendum was held, the old party system was divided, fragmented, and decapitated. Faced with this far-reaching crisis, the electorate looked for some escape: It is in this light that the referendum item should be read. The question put to voters no longer amounted to a choice between two electoral rules: "Do you wish to move from a proportional to a majoritarian system?" It should instead be read as a plea for salvation (even though no savior was in sight):

Do you wish to leave the system we call the First Republic, which has been founded on mediation among parties and among these parties in particular? Do you see proportional electoral rules as one of the major causes of the evils of the past and at the same time as the factor perpetuating the existing parties? Do you think that the majoritarian system will help us to overcome the present crisis?

In this context April 18, 1993, must be viewed as the end of a cycle that opened on another April date: April 18, 1948, when parliamentary elections were first held under the Constitution of the postwar Italian Republic.

From 600,000 Signatures in 1990
to 29,000,000 "Yeses" in 1993:
The March of the Referendum Movement

What we have said about the referendum question explains the reply as well. The overwhelming consensus represented in the "yes" vote has no precedent, as shown below, and is especially surprising in light of the difficulties encountered by the committee organized to collect the signatures required by law.[4] What allowed such a small minority, in such a short span of time, to win over to its side nearly the entire country? Gianfranco Pasquino and Patrick McCarthy[5] have reconstructed the stages of the difficult process that led from the emergence of the initial vanguard of reform promoters to the 1991 referendum. It is worthwhile here to survey the principal events of the next two years.

On October 16, 1991, the drive to gather signatures for the new referendum began. On January 14, 1992, 1,300,000 signatures were deposited in the Court of Cassation. This huge success strongly contrasted with the meager number of signatures mustered for the referendum held in 1991 and eloquently testified to the changed political climate in Italy. (The appendix reports the province-by-province distribution of the signatures gathered.)

The initiative of the Committee for the Referendum on Electoral Laws (COREL) encouraged other referendum proposals, for which different organizing committees were formed. Alongside the three referenda proposed by COREL (two for the Senate electoral laws and one for municipal electoral laws), other proposals were added to form an overall set of thirteen referenda, which was presented to the Court of Cassation in January 1992.

The referenda were then submitted to the Constitutional Court for a judgment on their admissability. On January 16, 1993, the Court admitted ten and rejected three, including one (of the two) proposed by COREL on the electoral law of the Senate. Later both the referendum on electoral laws for city councils and that on the end of special aid to the South would be dropped, since Parliament passed laws that superseded the rule whose abrogation was at stake. In the end, then, eight referenda remained to be submitted to the electorate on April 18, 1993. Table 3.1 summarizes the eight referendum topics and records the official positions assumed by the parties.

The formation of the alignment favoring electoral law revision deserves particular attention. The reform movement this time was able to bring over to its side ever greater numbers of varied political forces. Party leaders who had more or less openly resisted the 1991 referendum had by now been replaced, thus allowing the majority of the party spectrum to endorse

TABLE 3.1 Party Positions on the Eight Referendum Items of 1993

	a	b	c	d	e	f	g	h
DC	yes	no	yes	yes	yes	yes	no	yes
PDS	no	yes	yes	yes	yes	yes	yes	yes
RC	no	yes	yes	-	-	no	-	-
PSI	yes	-	yes	yes	yes	yes	yes	yes
MSI	yes	no	yes	yes	yes	no	no	no
PSDI	yes	no	yes	no	yes	yes	yes	no
PRI	yes	-	yes	yes	no	yes	yes	no
PLI	yes	-	yes	yes	no	yes	yes	no
Pannella List	yes	yes	yes	yes	yes	yes	yes	yes
League	-	-	-	yes	yes	yes	yes	yes
Network	yes	yes	yes	yes	yes	no	yes	yes
Greens	yes	yes	yes	yes	yes	no	yes	yes

Key: Parties
DC   Christian Democracy
PDS   Democratic Party of the Left
RC   Communist Refoundation
PSI   Socialist Party
MSI   Italian Social Movement
PSDI Social Democratic Party
PRI   Republican Party
PLI   Liberal Party

Referendum Items
a. Environmental responsibilities of local health units (USL)
b. Personal use of drugs
c. Public financing of political parties
d. Nominations of directors of savings banks
e. Abolition of the Ministry for State Holdings
f. Electoral laws for the Senate
g. Abolition of the Ministry of Agriculture
h. Abolition of the Ministry of Tourism

the referendum proposals. The PDS, the bulk of whose leadership had since 1990 supported the cause of reform, and the PRI were gradually joined by all the other major forces: from the Christian Democrats, now headed by Mino Martinazzoli, to the PSI of Giorgio Benvenuto, and most importantly to the League. Other actors who had initially backed the reform movement now decided to raise the banner of a "no" vote, arguing that the current Parliament no longer had the legitimacy to issue new rules governing democratic life (although these groups were probably motivated by a preoccupation with defending or reinforcing their position as minority, opposition forces).

We can identify three basic groupings among the traditional political forces, considering the positions they took throughout the two referendum phases, from the gathering of signatures launched in April 1990 to the vote of April 1993. First, some actors gave steadfast support to the cause of the reforms promoted by COREL: the PRI and the majority of the PDS/ PCI. Second, others firmly opposed reform: the PSI (despite Benvenuto's eventual backing of reform) and the majority of the DC (under Forlani as secretary). Third, still other actors shifted their stance: the League switched from a "no" to a "yes;" the MSI, the *Rete* (Network), the Greens, Communist Refoundation and a minority of the PDS/PCI moved from a "yes" to a "no;" and the DC left (identified with Ciriaco De Mita) oscillated between a "yes" and a "no."

Not surprisingly, once a consensus had grown in favor of the reformists' positions, public opinion surveys and general expectations on the eve of the vote uniformly envisioned a sure victory for the "yes."

The Exceptional Success of the "Yes" Front

The day after the vote, the terms chosen most often to describe the referendum results were "avalanche" and "Bulgarian percentages." For once the tendency to hyperbole, typical of an Italian journalism accustomed to seeing earthquakes in any change, seemed to correspond to the dimensions of the phenomenon. Like few other votes in the past, the 1993 referendum was remarkable in light of long-term trends in Italian electoral behavior.

The first exception is paradoxically represented by the close match between survey data before the vote and the results of the vote itself. An examination of the twelve principal opinion surveys conducted in the month preceding the vote[6] demonstrates that the predicted and the actual outcomes were extraordinarily similar.

Even though some variations appeared, the proportion of "yes" preferences never fell below 75% (with one exception) and averaged 81% across all surveys, less than two percentage points under the real result. With the advantage of hindsight we must recognize these signals — which were not taken seriously enough on the eve of the vote — as evidence that voters had clearly defined orientations, even at the start of the referendum campaign. In other words, voters' choices neither depended on the last month's propaganda nor reflected hasty decisions made at the polls. They instead resulted from a process of political mobilization that had progressively spread throughout the country, a "long wave" that had swept Italy since the campaign preceding the 1991 referendum.

The second exceptional feature regards turnout. Even though no political force advocated abstention this time — which instead was the case for the 1991 referendum — the record of past referenda raised some concern, in large part because of the rise in abstentionism. Indeed, the abstention rate had steadily increased ever since the 1976 parliamentary elections. Moreover, nonvoters are typically more numerous in referenda than in parliamentary elections. This phenomenon is known as "added abstentionism," and the major explanation for it centers on the different levels of mobilization in referenda as opposed to parliamentary elections, levels produced by the efforts of party organizations and (for parliamentary races) individual candidates. Not only abstentionism but also, as Table 3.2 shows, "added abstentionism" had grown since the 1974 referendum on divorce. On the eve of the referendum, estimates based on the abstention rate in the April 1992 parliamentary elections and on recent trends in "added abstentionism" indicated that only about 68-70% of the electorate would turn out to vote.

This calculation obviously missed the mark: On April 18-19, 77 of 100 voters went to the polls. If we used this result to estimate turnout at hypothetical concurrent parliamentary elections, we would obtain a participation rate of over 90%, which is extraordinary even within the Italian tradition of voter participation. (Despite recent trends, Italy still exhibits some of the highest turnout levels among democracies.) Our estimation reinforces just how unusual the rate of voter participation was in 1993.

Indeed, the most noteworthy success of the 1993 referendum was attained thanks to this revival of participation: An absolute majority of the electorate was convinced to support the cause of change. Note that the formal rules in Italy would permit a victory in a referendum even on the basis of the assent of a minority of the electorate. According to Article 75

TABLE 3.2 Rates of Participation and "Added Abstentionism" in Eight Referenda

	% voters voting	added abstentionism[1]
1974	87.7	5.1
1978	81.2	12.2
1981	79.4	11.2
1985	77.9	11.0
1987	65.1	23.5
1990	43.1	44.0
1991	62.4	25.0
1993	77.1	10.2

[1] Percent of voters voting in the referendum less percent of voters voting in the most recent elections for the Chamber of Deputies.

of the Constitution, "the proposal submitted to the referendum [vote] is approved if a majority of eligible voters has participated in the vote, and if the proposal receives a majority of valid votes" (that is, excluding blank and spoiled ballots). Thus, it would be possible to register a victory even with less than a quarter of the total electorate in favor of the winning option.

This scenario is not completely removed from reality, as indicated by past referendum results, which are summarized in Table 3.3. Consider a crucial referendum in Italy's history, that of 1946, which pitted the continuation of the monarchy against the introduction of a republic:[7] Only 45.4% of all voters cast a vote in favor of a republic. The figure does not in any way call into question the formal value of the popular verdict (after all, 54.3% of valid votes endorsed the republic); yet since the winning side attracted a minority of all eligible voters, more than a few instances of contestation and accusations of vote rigging ensued. Of all the proposals for abrogating legislation submitted to a referendum vote before 1993, only the one on preference voting in 1991 could claim the backing of more than half of the electorate. The other proposals that were approved, even with high percentages of valid votes, drew the support of a minority of all eligible voters. In some cases, this minority footing explained the difficulties later encountered in Parliament as legislators worked to translate the referendum mandate into new legislation.

Even if prudence had led the proponents of the 1993 referendum not to declare openly that their target was a majority of all eligible voters, they were aware that, due to the proposal's political and institutional importance, the "yes" front could not be satisfied with a victory based on a minority. Belying all timidity and caution, the level of support surpassed every expectation and gave the abrogation of the Senate electoral laws a weight never reached in the past: 60.4% of all eligible voters. This third exceptional aspect of the 1993 referendum constituted an indisputable reference point for the further advance of the reform movement.

A Homogeneous Vote or a Differentiated Vote?

Another significant feature of the referendum outcome was that ratification of the reformists' stance penetrated all of Italy's regions and societal groupings. Data from an exit poll conducted by the Doxa Institute (a prominent Italian polling agency) show that the affirmative vote consistently carried a majority and displayed a very restricted range of variation across social categories. As Table 3.4 reports, the differences between men and women in positive votes cast (as a percentage of valid votes) were minimal; and such differences were small across age groups as

TABLE 3.3   Referendum Results from 1946 to 1993

	% of valid votes		% of all eligible voters	
	Rep	Mon	Rep	Mon
1946 Institutional referendum (Republic vs. Monarchy)	54.3	45.7	45.4	38.3
	Yes	No	Yes	No
Abrogative referenda:				
1974 Divorce	40.7	59.3	35.0	50.8
1978 Aspects of law on public order	23.5	76.5	17.9	58.3
Public financing of parties	43.6	56.4	33.2	43.0
1981 Public order	14.9	85.1	10.7	61.5
Life prison sentences	22.6	77.4	16.5	56.4
Bearing arms	14.1	85.9	10.3	62.6
Abortion (Radical challenge)	11.6	88.4	8.3	63.5
Abortion ("Right to life")	32.0	68.0	23.5	49.8
1985 Cuts in wage escalator	45.7	54.3	34.4	40.9
1987 Liability of judges	80.2	19.8	45.3	11.2
Parliamentary Committee of Inquiry	85.0	15.0	48.2	8.5
Siting nuclear reactors	80.6	19.4	45.8	11.0
Local funding nuclear energy	79.7	20.3	45.0	11.4
Foreign nuclear energy	71.9	28.1	41.0	16.1
1990 Hunting regulations	92.2	7.8	37.7	2.3
Hunting on private property	92.3	7.7	37.9	3.2
Regulation of pesticides	93.5	6.5	38.7	2.7
1991 Single preference vote	95.6	4.4	57.1	2.7
1993 Senate electoral laws	82.7	17.3	60.4	12.6

Sources: ISTAT, *45 anni di elezioni in Italia*, Roma, 1990; Ministero dell'Interno, *18-19 Aprile 1993 Referendum popolari*, Vols.1 and 2, Roma, 1993.

well. Table 3.5 documents the slight distinctions separating provincial capitals and other municipalities, where "yes" votes overall stood at 79.5% and 84.1%, respectively. The differences across geopolitical zones are more substantial: positive responses to the referendum represented 83.3% of valid votes in the industrial Northwest; 93.1% in the "white zone," the traditionally Christian Democratic Northeast; 87.6% in the "red zone" in central Italy, long the stronghold of the PCI/PDS; and 77.1% in the South. Following we further discuss the South's divergence from the national trend.

TABLE 3.4   "Yes" Votes as a Percentage of Valid Votes in the Referendum on the Senate Electoral Law by Sex and Age Group (N = 7820)

Age group	Men	Women	Both sexes
18-35	79.9	83.3	81.6
36-54	80.5	84.0	82.3
55 and above	85.8	83.5	84.6
Total	81.8	83.6	82.7

Source: Cattaneo Institute calculations from Doxa data.

TABLE 3.5   "Yes" Votes as a Percentage of Valid Votes in the Referendum on the Senate Electoral Law by Geopolitical Area and Capitals/Other Municipalities (N = 7820)

Area	Provincial Capitals	Other Municipalities	Total
Industrial	80.2	84.8	83.3
White	93.4	93.0	93.1
Red	87.2	87.7	87.6
South	75.9	78.0	77.1
Italy	79.5	84.1	82.7

Key:
Industrial zone: Piemonte, Valle d'Aosta, Lombardy, Liguria.
White zone: Veneto, Trentino Alto Adige, Friuli Venezia Giulia.
Red zone: Emilia Romagna, Tuscany, Marche, Umbria.
South: Lazio, Abruzzo, Molise, Campania, Puglia, Basilicata, Calabria, Sicily, Sardinia.

Source: Cattaneo Institute calculations from Doxa data.

One uncertainty about the outcome, both at the start of the campaign and even more so on the eve of the vote, was prompted by the new position taken by some parties and movements that had sided in favor of a "yes" on the 1991 referendum on the single preference vote. Even though the DC and PSI leaderships, which had been hostile to reform in 1991, now declared their support in 1993, more than a few reformists feared that the new adherents would not be numerous enough to offset the withdrawals from their camp. Indeed, the shifts to the "no" front announced by the leaderships of organizations that had at first favored a "yes" (the MSI, the *Rete*, and Communist Refoundation) appeared to pose a serious threat, for their electorates were judged to be highly loyal and disciplined. The promise of new recruits to the reformists' cause, who would follow the conversion of party leaderships that in the past had been arrayed against reform, did not seem to be equally firm and well founded: The electorates of the parties that had most recently joined the "yes" front, the DC and the PSI, had in large part subscribed to reform since 1991; and it was reasonable to doubt that those segments remaining in favor of proportional electoral laws could be moved by party leaders' formal statements of position alone, without strong organizational commitment and political determination.

Again belying all fears, and as emphasized in the press on the basis of the first exit polls, the vote to alter the Senate electoral laws proved instead to represent the majority of the electorates of all parties, with the exception of the MSI. As depicted in Table 3.6, the ranking of "loyalty" in the referendum was headed by the League (92% of its electorate cast a positive vote), followed by the DC and the PRI (89%), the PDS and the PLI (86%), and the PSI (84%). Hence even the electorates of parties that manifested strong resistance to the reform (the case of the DC) or housed an explicit, organized, and militant minority in the "no" camp (the case of the "Ingrao component" in the PDS) were largely persuaded by the arguments in favor of electoral law reform. Even more noteworthy was the behavior of the electorates of parties openly advocating a negative vote: 56% of those who voted for Communist Refoundation in the 1992 parliamentary elections opted for a "yes" in 1993, as did 59.5% of those voting for the *Rete* and 78% of those voting for the Greens, thus disregarding the advice of their parties. Even the MSI leadership could not boast great satisfaction, since 44% of that party's electorate ignored its instructions.

Closer scrutiny of Italy's two principal geopolitical divisions does not undermine this portrayal of broad support for electoral law reform. The MSI had a homogeneous electorate (displaying rather similar percentages of "yes" votes in the Center-North and South), as did virtually all other parties. The *Rete* marked the most salient exception in this regard, as Table 3.6 discloses, for almost half of its electorate in the South rejected the referendum proposal, whereas fully two thirds of its electorate in the Center-North embraced reform.

Thus, many voters did not comply with the directives of party leaders who had abandoned the referendum movement, and this accounted for another record that no one had imagined as realizable on election eve: The number of affirmative votes was greater in 1993 than in the referendum of June 9, 1991. A comparison of the absolute number of voters in 1991 and 1993 (which makes sense given the substantial stability in the size of the electorate across the two referenda) reveals that nationwide two million voters in 1993 added their weight to the twenty-seven million "yeses" of

1991, as Table 3.7 details. Of course, these aggregate data hide any compensating flows in opposite directions. And yet these figures demonstrate beyond doubt that the vast majority of what has been called "the people of June 9" remained loyal to the cause of reform in 1993.

TABLE 3.6 "Yes" Votes as a Percentage of Valid Votes in the Referendum on the Senate Electoral Law by Area and by Party Vote in 1992 (N = basis for calculating percentages)

Party	Center/North	South	Italy		(N)	
DC	94.3	84.1	89.1	(765)	(846)	(1611)
PDS	87.6	84.0	86.2	(756)	(366)	(1123)
RC	50.3	63.3	56.0	(210)	(160)	(370)
PSI	88.1	79.0	84.3	(386)	(323)	(708)
MSI	49.6	43.0	44.0	(140)	(158)	(297)
PRI	93.1	83.2	89.2	(116)	(75)	(191)
PSDI	82.5	78.8	80.2	(42)	(56)	(98)
PLI	88.8	81.1	86.2	(120)	(51)	(171)
Greens	84.1	67.0	77.8	(558)	(86)	(243)
Pannella	84.8	83.2	83.7	(74)	(55)	(129)
League	92.4	89.8	92.2	(660)	(21)	(681)
Network	67.8	48.7	59.5	(60)	(82)	(142)

Key:
Center-North: the first three zones indicated in Table 3.5
South: as in Table 3.5

Source: Cattaneo Institute calculations from Doxa data.

TABLE 3.7 Comparison of "Yes" Votes in the 1991 Referendum on the Single Preference Vote and in the 1993 Referendum on the Senate Electoral Law

Area	1991	1993	Difference (1993 - 1991)	Index (1991 = 100)
Industrial	7,576,358	8,942,226	1,365,868	118
White	3,552,382	3,983,940	431,558	112
Red	5,158,141	5,765,869	607,728	112
South	10,645,241	10,245,340	- 399,901	96
Italy	26,932,122	28,937,375	2,005,253	107

Sources: See Table 3.3

This statement does not hold for all areas of the country, however. Table 3.7 reports the substantial and largely uniform increase in positive votes in the North and Center from 1991 to 1993. In the South the trend was negative, with the "yes" camp losing roughly 400,000 voters from one referendum to the next. The territorial differences in electoral behavior noted above are thus reconfirmed.

A Triumph for the "Yes" Front, but not Utter Failure for the "No"

The overwhelming endorsement of a "yes" seems to lend plausibility and foundation to another frequent description of the referendum results: "plebiscite." This definition aptly expressed the object and implications of the referendum pronouncement. It was generally agreed that, even though the referendum formally addressed an aspect of the electoral laws for the Senate, it called into question the constitutional form of the State.

The same cannot be said for the subject that the term "plebiscite" often evokes. In some commentaries, an emphasis on the magnitude of the reformists' achievement accompanied the insinuation that the subject of the referendum pronouncement was not "the people" as understood in a democracy but "the common people," the *plebs*, to whom neo-patricians had left no choice other than to respond affirmatively or to remain silent. Not by chance, some exponents of the "no" stance more or less explicitly formulated this thesis in order to justify to themselves (more than to others) the dimensions of their defeat. To some "no" advocates, this focus on the near-unanimity behind the "yes" seemed to be the only way to belittle their opponents' victory and to reconstrue their own debacle as some sort of conspiracy, if not fraud.

This interpretation was not simply self-serving, for the emphasis on the defeat of the "no" was a dominant feature of all commentaries, regardless of the political position voiced. And when we compare the outcome with the hopes of the "no" camp and the fears of the "yes" side evident on the eve of the referendum, it is difficult not to agree with *Il Manifesto*, a newspaper identified with the extreme left, which saw in the "ferocity" and "cruelty" of the returns "the defeat of the No and especially the `left No.'"[8] Indeed, even though no one ever dared to forecast a "no" victory, the expectation on the eve of the vote was that support for efforts to preserve the proportional system might expand. This expectation was fostered by the activism and discipline in the ranks of the "no" alignment. Moreover, it found corroboration in surveys of voters' attitudes in recent months, which all showed that the "no" forces were gaining strength.

Whereas no analysis can discredit the "yes" victory, a correct reading of the data discloses that not only did the "no" option not retreat, but it advanced. To provide evidence for this assertion we must refer to the votes cast in the 1992 parliamentary elections for those parties that in 1993 championed the "no" position. Despite the revival of participation in 1993, "added abstentionism" appeared this time as well, so that we must subtract from the 1992 electorates the estimated portion of those voters who abstained in the referendum, assuming that abstentionism was equally distributed across parties. With these adjustments computed, the performance of the "no" at the national level is clearly positive. As Table 3.8 documents, the "no" camp started with a potential base of 5,500,00 votes and obtained over 6,000,000.

This result is the product of two contradictory trends. In the North and Center potential "no" voters swung to the "yes" side, yielding a total outflow of about 400,000 votes, as Table 3.8 illustrates. In the South, however, negative votes exceeded not only the expected number (listed in column B of the table) but also the number of votes won by the "no" parties in the 1992 parliamentary elections (column A). Hence in the South the "no" front not only succeeded in eliminating the normal rate of "added abstentionism" within its own electorate but also marshaled support from some of those who in 1992 voted for parties that now officially endorsed the "yes" position. Such conversions were especially striking in Molise, Campania, Calabria and Sicily, where negative votes surpassed by 70% the estimate based on the 1992 results.

TABLE 3.8   Comparison of "No" Votes in the 1993 Referendum on the Senate Electoral Law and Votes Won by the "No" Camp in the 1992 Chamber Elections

Area	A 1992	B 1992	C 1993	D Difference corrected (C - B)	E Indexed (B =100)
Industrial	1,622,592	1,525,236	1,340,526	-184,710	88
White	656,226	623,415	535,318	-88,097	86
Red	1,202,194	1,130,062	1,008,691	-121,371	89
South	2,715,060	2,226,349	3,154,374	928,025	142
Italy	6,196,072	5,505,062	6,038,909	533,847	110

Key:
A: Votes for the "No" Camp in 1992 (Communist Refoundation, MSI, *Rete*, Greens)
B: Votes for the "No" Camp in 1992 excluding added abstentionism
C: Negative votes in 1993
D: Difference C - B
E: Negative votes in 1993 setting B at 100.

Sources: See Table 3.3

The origins of these shifts are difficult to establish from the available data. Nonetheless, conversions to the "no" camp were particularly numerous in heavily Christian Democratic provinces (in rank order: Benevento, Avellino, Agrigento, Messina, Isernia, and so forth.). To judge from this evidence, the analysis conducted on the "no" side, which attributed the growth in part to a "semi-clandestine or open campaign of segments of the DC,"[9] would seem to hold. Yet data from exit polls on the party preferences of "no" voters — which unfortunately given the limited numbers of cases can be analyzed only in the aggregate, for the entire South — do not support that hypothesis. Turning again to Table 3.6, which distinguishes percentages of positive votes by party preference (and indirectly, of course, complementary percentages of negative votes) in the Center-North and the South, the exit polls indicate that the percentage of negative votes in the South was not greater for the DC than for other parties (the share of "no" votes ranged from roughly 15% to 20% of the electorates of all parties formally backing the "yes"). In light of these data, we conclude that the "no" front does not seem to have exercised any greater appeal for the DC electorate than for other parties' electorates in the South.

Conclusion:
On the Persistence of the Southern Difference

In sum, geographic distinctions stand as the only real difference that can be identified in the extent of agreement on a change in the Senate electoral laws. To be sure, as we have emphasized, the consensus on the "yes" was spread throughout the country. Even so, the vote reflected one of the most salient cleavages defining the Italian political system: the cleavage between the Center-North and the South.

Throughout our analysis, every time the territorial variable entered into play it served to confirm the contrast made so familiar to us by studies of political and electoral sociology. Whether we examine the success of the "yes" camp or the tenacity of the "no," we can discern the boundary separating two Italies: the Italy to the north of Rome and the Italy to the south. At the same time, each of these two Italies is homogeneous across its constituent regions — a feature found above all in referenda, since in parliamentary elections the imprint of the different territorial rooting of the parties is visible.

To drive home the importance of the geographic divide, we consider the map of support for the Republic in the institutional referendum of June 2, 1946. Figure 3.1 compares the 1946 and 1993 referenda and reveals that the two results show the same pattern. Almost five decades ago, as in 1993, all of the regions of the South displayed percentages of pro-Republic (now, pro-reform) votes that lay below the national average. In 1993, the nation-wide average of "yes" votes (out of all eligible voters) was about 60%; whereas the vote favoring electoral law reform in the regions of the Center-North hovered around 70%, with limited variations, the "yes" vote in all regions of the South was under the national average and, most often, was even under 50%. (For detailed region-by-region results, see the documentary appendix to this volume.)

☐ "yes" votes (as % of eligible voters) above the national average
▨ "yes" votes (as % of eligible voters) below the national average

FIGURE 3.1 Percentage of votes in favor of the Republic in the referendum of June 2, 1946, and percentage of "yes" votes in the referendum on electoral reform of the Senate of April 18, 1993, by regions

The two referenda are of fundamental institutional significance, and in both cases the South contributed its weight to the cause of preserving the pre-existing institutional regime. Whereas in 1946 monarchist and fascist forces were aligned to defend "the old," in 1993 the survival of the proportional system depended on an unusual convergence between the extreme right and the extreme left: This is clearly not a trivial distinction. And yet the different way in which the two Italies have confronted "the new" has ancient roots. Even though the cycle that opened in the April 1948 parliamentary elections has now closed, the long-standing divide between North and South endures and will shape Italian politics after 1993.

Translated by Claire Holman and Carol Mershon

APPENDIX

Number of signatures gathered in public squares and at notaries' offices for the referendum on the electoral laws, by region and province[a]

Aosta	317	Bologna	19,557	Napoli	27,430
Valle d'Aosta	317	Ferrara	2,816	Avellino	1,469
		Forlì	8,340	Benevento	1,569
Torino	29,273	Modena	27,082	Caserta	755
Alessandria	2,208	Parma	17,292	Salerno	12,531
Asti	719	Piacenza	5,221	*Campania*	*43,754*
Novara	2,767	Ravenna	6,805		
Vercelli	5,295	Reggio Emilia	8,261	Bari	18,771
Cuneo	2,915	*Emilia Romagna*	*95,374*	Brindisi	2,926
Piemonte	*43,177*			Foggia	3,873
		Firenze	6,429	Lecce	5,060
Genova	25,567	Arezzo	1,550	Taranto	8,552
Imperia	3,107	Grosseto	1,093	*Puglia*	*39,182*
La Spezia	913	Livorno	5,389		
Savona	3,024	Lucca	3,664	Potenza	561
Liguria	32,611	Massa Carrara	4,289	Matera	1,454
Milano	84,358	Pisa	1,518	*Basilicata*	*2,015*
Bergamo	6,383	Pistoia	2,400		
Brescia	7,154	Siena	895	Reggio Calabria	2,308
Como	7,432	*Toscana*	*27,227*	Catanzaro	2,874
Cremona	6,506			Cosenza	10,848
Mantova	3,475	Ancona	3,722	*Calabria*	*16030*
Pavia	4,523	Ascoli Piceno	1,450		
Sondrio	374	Macerata	956	Palermo	6,841
Varese	6,118	Pesaro	126	Agrigento	404
Lombardia	*126,323*	*Marche*	*6,254*	Caltanissetta	3,635
		Perugia	2,665	Catania	12,108
Trento	1,620	Terni	1,018	Enna	1,144
Bolzano	2,351	*Umbria*	*3,683*	Messina	1,660
Trentino Alto Adige	*3,971*	Roma	94,146	Ragusa	314
		Frosinone	3,061	Siracusa	907
Trieste	6,154	Latina	1,395	Trapani	1,783
Gorizia	1,410	Rieti	404	*Sicilia*	*28,796*
Pordenone	1,526	Viterbo	496		
Udine	2,001	*Lazio*	*99,502*	Cagliari	32,057
Friuli Venezia Giulia	*11,091*			Nuoro	1,700
		L'Aquila	666	Oristano	1,800
Venezia	3,428	Chieti	3,334	Sassari	16,000
Belluno	3,828	Pescara	153	*Sardegna*	*51,557*
Padova	15,641	Teramo	588		
Rovigo	3,163	*Abruzzo*	*6,741*	Totale	684237
Treviso	9,398				
Verona	2,186	Campobasso	1,143		
Vicenza	7,835	Isernia	-		
Veneto	*45,489*	*Molise*	*1,143*		

[a]Signatures affixed in municipalities and gathered by the ACLI (Association of Italian Christian Workers) are excluded. Total signatures: about 1,300,000.

Source: Comitato referendum leggi elettorali.

Notes

1. See A. Ciancarella, "Basterà la maggioranza relativa per essere eletti nei 238 collegi," in *Guida ai referendum*, Supplement to *Il Sole 24 Ore*, April 4, 1993, p. 31; and the chapter by Richard Katz in this volume. The Constitution provides only for abrogative referenda, that is, popular votes that decide whether or not current legislation (or a portion of a law) will be abolished.

2. P. McCarthy, "The referendum of June 9," in S. Hellman and G. Pasquino, eds., *Italian Politics*, Vol. 7 (London: Pinter, 1992), p. 11.

3. Mario Chiesa, a nursing home president in Milan, was arrested for corruption in February 1992. This marked the start of the still-continuing chain of arrests for political corruption in Italy. See D. Della Porta, "Milan: immoral capital," in S. Hellman and G. Pasquino, eds., *Italian Politics*, Vol. 8 (London: Pinter, 1993), pp. 98-115; and the chapter by Della Porta and Vannucci in this volume.

4. See G. Pasquino, "The electoral reform referendums," in F. Anderlini and R. Leonardi, eds., *Italian Politics*, Vol. 6 (London: Pinter, 1992), pp. 9-24.

5. McCarthy, "The referendum of June 9;" Pasquino, "The electoral reform referendums."

6. *Panorama*, April 25, 1993; *La Repubblica*, April 18, 1993.

7. The 1946 referendum pre-dated the Constitutional provision for abrogative referenda and indeed was held simultaneously with elections to the Constituent Assembly. For details of the controversy surrounding the result, see Denis Mack Smith, *Italy and Its Monarchy* (New Haven and London: Yale University Press), pp. 338-341.

8. *Il Manifesto*, April 21, 1993.

9. See *Ibid.*

4

The 1993
Parliamentary Electoral Reform

Richard S. Katz

When Italian voters overwhelmingly approved the referendum of April 18-19, 1993 abrogating several sections of the Senate electoral law [Law February 6, 1948, No. 29 as amended], they sent a clear message that they wanted institutional reform. They also left the country with a fundamentally unworkable electoral system. The message was amplified by the fact that it was accompanied by several other referenda implicitly criticizing the way the parties had managed both their own affairs and the affairs of state and as well by the fact that it followed similar messages sent by previous referenda.

This referendum, however, additionally left a situation that required the parliament to make further, and more profound, reforms for practical as well as for moral reasons. In particular, because the Council of Ministers (the cabinet) remained equally responsible to each chamber of the parliament, it was untenable to allow the electoral systems in use for the two chambers, and consequently the likely balance of forces among the parties within the two chambers, to be radically different.

Once the results of the referenda were announced, the reform effort moved quickly, with the final version of the law for the Chamber of Deputies approved in the Senate on August 3, 1993 and the final version of the law for the Senate approved in the Chamber of Deputies the next day. This rapid progress was spurred first by the fact that premature elections had been made extremely likely by the repudiation of the governing parties implicit in the overwhelming acceptance of the April referenda, their more explicit repudiation in the municipal elections of June 6 along with the spectacular rise of new formations such as the Lega Nord, La Rete, and the Democratic Alliance, and the ever-growing ripples of the *Mani pulite* investigations into corruption and the resulting decapitation of the existing political class. Second, many of the preliminary debates required for such a major reform had already been held; although the bicameral commission for institutional reform had not been able to produce a proposal of its own in time to head off the referendum, the issue had been extensively considered, both in Parliament and in the popular and academic press.[1]

Perhaps most significant in both speeding and shaping the eventual reform, however, was the fact that the referendum itself did not leave a void (as would have been the case had the Senate electoral law been abrogated completely), but rather left a new system that, unworkable though it might have been in that form, could be said to have received overwhelming popular endorsement. As a result, the range of options to be seriously considered by the parliament was seriously restricted.

Objectives of Reform

The referendum drive and the parliamentary attempts at electoral reform that both preceded and followed it were motivated by several complaints about the old system and objectives for the new. In much of the debate, the key word was "governability," but there was little consensus as to what specifically this term meant, or how it could be achieved.

The most general desire was for governments with more secure parliamentary majorities, and hence greater stability. Among the alternatives proposed at one time or another were bonus seats for a coalition winning a majority of the popular votes; a "constructive vote of no confidence" patterned on the German system; direct election of the Prime Minister; and revision of the electoral law so as to weaken or eliminate small parties. Implicit in these proposals was the assumption that the result would be the introduction of alternation in government: not just alternation of individual ministers, but alternation of governing coalitions. A concomitant goal of all the reform proposals was "aggregation," i.e., encouraging small lists to merge into larger, but fewer, parties. As Mario Segni, the leader of the Electoral Reform Movement and prime mover of the referendum, argued during the debate on the new law, "governability cannot be assured by any technique of constitutional engineering, unless there is also 'a simplification and homogenization of the political scene.'"[2] At the same time, however, there was also a desire to maintain the possibility for minority views and groups to find voice in parliament.

A second widely cited, but somewhat less clear, objective was to increase the direct accountability of the elected to the electors. On the one hand, this reflected a desire that the people, either directly or through the transparent operation of the electoral system, choose the party or coalition of parties or indeed the particular individuals to form the cabinet. On the other hand, it reflected a desire to free the choice of individual representatives from the confines of party and ideology, and encourage voters to decide on the basis of the personal character and qualifications of the candidates. That personalized choice of representative and stability of parliamentary majorities are likely to prove incompatible appeared not to dawn on many people, who sometimes advocated the same reform as productive of both.

A third objective of some was the weakening of the grip of party barons, and indeed of party organizations altogether. Additionally, many hoped for a massive renewal of the political class, the pensioning off of those who had governed Italy (badly, in their view) and the injection of new blood into parliament. In the words of Radical leader Marco Pannella, it was essential to strike at the heart of the parties, to "close down the parties."[3]

One problem was that even when there was agreement about objectives, there often was not agreement about the likely consequences of particular institutional reforms in the particular circumstances of Italy in the 1990s. Often, these disagreements were found within as well as between the parties. Additionally, these objectives were not mutually compatible; most obviously, in a parliamentary system, strong government is unlikely to coexist with weak parties. Even more important, however, many of these objectives, even if widely perceived to be in the public interest, were seen to be incompatible with the personal and organizational interests of the parties and leaders who would have to write the new laws. In proverbial terms, many found themselves "between a rock and a hard place." Especially after the municipal elections in June 1993 (using a new, two-ballot run-off, electoral system adopted earlier in the year and showing a collapse of support for the governing parties of "earthquake" proportions)[4] failure to pass reforms was seen to be not only morally indefensible but politically suicidal as well. Yet, the leaders of the major parties in the parliament were precisely those slated to be pensioned off, and if the result was to be a two-party system, then nearly half the seats in parliament were held by parties that would be putting themselves out of business.

The Pre-Reform Electoral System

In order to understand the reforms adopted and to assess their potential impact on the Italian political system, it is necessary first briefly to summarize both the old electoral system and the system that would have been in place had the results of the referendum simply been allowed to stand.

Electoral Laws Before April 1993

Under the old system, the electoral laws for the Senate and Chamber of Deputies looked quite different, but in operation worked very similarly, with the important exception of the use of intraparty preference voting for the Chamber but not for the Senate.[5] For the Chamber, the electoral system was simply list proportional representation in 31 districts using the Imperiali quota and a national distribution of remainders (plus one single-member constituency for the Valle d'Aosta). For the Senate, the Constitution dictated that the twenty regions formed the principal constituencies (*circoscrizioni*). Each region was then divided into a number of single-member districts (*collegi*). The relationship between the number of *collegi* and the number of seats assigned to each region varied, but overall the number of *collegi* (238) was roughly equal to 3/4 of the total number of senators to be elected. The voters within the territory of each *collegio* voted for a single candidate. If one candidate received at least 65% of the vote, he or she was immediately declared elected, but this generally occurred in only one or two *collegi* (e.g., the candidate of the South Tyrolean People's Party in the *collegio* of Bressanone in Trentino-Alto Adige). The votes received by all the candidates in the region in those *collegi* in which no candidate achieved the 65% threshold were then totalled by party group (*contrassegno*), with the remaining seats (usually all of them) allocated among lists using the d'Hondt highest average method of proportional representation (and allocated within lists among individual candidates in order of the percentages of the vote received by the individual candidates within their own *collegi*). In essence, with regard to the division of seats among the parties, the system was, like that for the Chamber of Deputies, simply one of proportional representation.

Compared to those used in other European countries, both electoral systems were hyperproportional and extremely favorable to the representation of small parties. Thus, in the 1992 election, 16 separate lists won representation in the Chamber (6 of them with less than 2% of the national vote), while 18 groups (8 with less than 1% of the national vote) won representation in the Senate. Further, the seats were so divided among the parties that if one assumed the impossibility of a coalition including the Lega Lombarda and either the DC or the PSI, and assumed the continued exclusion of the ex-PCI (now the PDS and RC) and the MSI-DN, then no majority government except a coalition of the DC, PSI, and at least one other party was even mathematically, let alone politically, possible. The result of apparently permanent government by the DC, or more recently by the DC and PSI in coalition, was not stability, although it may have been immobilism. Instead, at the time of the referendum Italy had its 51st postwar government. It is against this background that the referendum on the Senate electoral system took place.

The Impact of the April 1993 Referendum

Because the Italian rules on referenda allow only the abrogation of existing laws, the range of changes that potentially could be introduced by that device was quite limited. There was no way, for example, in which the French two-ballot system could be introduced through the mechanism of an abrogative referendum. What was done, through the clever deletion of just eleven words (plus a few other words whose removal was desirable to clean up the remaining language) was, first, to abrogate the 65% threshold for direct election of a candidate in his or her *collegio*, so that 3/4 of the 315 elected senators would be chosen by the Anglo-American single-member plurality (SMP, or first-past-the-post) system; and, second, to modify the method of calculating the group totals on the basis of which the remaining seats (now reduced to 1/4 of the total) would be assigned by proportional representation, so that only the votes of directly elected candidates, rather than all votes cast in any *collegio* in which a candidate was directly elected, would be excluded. The result was to make the Senate electoral system substantially different from that of the Chamber of Deputies in fact as well as in form.

One way to assess the impact of these changes is to ask what the distribution of seats would have looked like if the law as amended by the referendum had been applied to the 1992 distribution of votes. The results of this exercise are shown in Table 4.1, which shows as well the distributions of votes and seats for both chambers of the parliament actually resulting from the 1992 election.[6] Several things are immediately clear. First, in marked contrast to the actual results, which gave the DC roughly one third of the seats in each of the parliamentary chambers, the post-referendum Senate system would have given the DC an absolute majority (58.7%) of the seats. Second, the number of groups with representation in the Senate would have been reduced from eighteen to twelve. Third, it was not simply the smallest parties that would have been hurt; indeed, two of the six parties that would have been eliminated had substantially more votes than four of the parties that would have survived. Rather, both size and geographic distribution of support would have been important to the outcome. While four groups with less than 1% of the national vote would have won representation, in only one region would a group with under 5% of the regional vote have won any seats (Lombardy, 3.1%), and in a majority of the regions, no group with under 10% of the regional vote would have done so. Fourth, in raw numbers of seats changing hands, the DC's greatest gains would have come at the expense of its erstwhile coalition partners: PSI (24 seats lost); PRI (7 seats); PLI (4 seats); PSDI (3 seats). The other big loser would have been RC. If one conceives of two big blocs, the "government" and the "opposition of the left", then in each case the principal losers would have been the junior partners in the respective bloc.

To say that Table 4.1 shows the results of applying the post-referendum law to the 1992 vote distribution is not the same as saying that it shows the likely result had the 1992 election been held under that law. Precisely because results like those displayed in Table 4.1 are what would have been expected if neither parties nor voters altered their behavior in the light of a new electoral system, they indicate why changes in behavior would be anticipated. In particular, both common sense and inference from the experience of other countries suggest that voters would desert small parties, and similarly that parties able to find congenial allies would form electoral alliances or even merge, while others would simply disappear. Both the speculative nature of the exercise, and the urgency of those speculations, were confirmed by the local elections in June.

TABLE 4.1   1992 Election Results and Hypothetical Outcome Under New Electoral Laws

	Actual 1992 Election Results				Senate Results Applying Post-Referendum Law to 1992 Votes
	Chamber of Deputies		Senate		
	Vote	Seats	Vote	Seats	
DC	29.7	206	27.3	107	185
PDS	16.1	107	17.1	64	62
RC	5.6	35	6.5	20	7
PSI	13.6	92	13.6	49	25
MSI-DN	5.4	34	6.5	16	7
PRI	4.4	27	4.7	10	3
PLI	2.9	17	2.8	4	
PSDI	2.7	16	2.6	3	
Fed. dei Verdi	2.8	16	3.1	4	1
Lega Lombarda	8.6	55	8.2	25	19
Lega Aut. Veneta	0.4	1	0.4	1	
Lega Alpina Lumbarda			0.4	1	
La Rete-Mov. Dem.	1.9	12	0.7	3	1
PPST	0.5	3	0.5	3	3
L. Valle d'Aosta	0.1	1	0.1	1	1
Lista per il Molise			0.1	1	
Per la Calabria			0.4	2	
Federalismo-Pen.Uv.	0.4	1	0.5	1	1
Lista Pannella	1.2	7			

The New Electoral Law

Although the question of electoral reform had been on the political agenda for many years, the referendum led to a widespread agreement on two points: that new parliamentary elections were necessary; and that before those elections could be held, it was imperative that a new electoral law be adopted.[7] In early May, Prime Minister Ciampi confirmed that electoral reform would be a high priority for his government, making it clear that if the parliament did not act, he would.

> What is clear is that there are only two paths: one parliamentary and the other governmental. If there is sweeping agreement in Parliament on the new electoral law, my government will endorse it. If instead there is not, I might even propose for the Chamber of Deputies the system decided by the referendum and now in force for the Senate.[8]

Threats that the matter would be taken out of Parliament's hands proved effective in spurring action again in July, when President of the Chamber of Deputies Giorgio Napolitano, exasperated by a seemingly endless stream of dilatory amendments and the consequent shuttling of the reform legislation back and forth between the two chambers, defined the completion of the new law by August 5 to be a "solemn commitment," and threatened an immediate dissolution of the parliament if this deadline were not met.[9]

The most important changes wrought by the new electoral laws for the Senate and Chamber of Deputies, and those which naturally received the greatest attention by the media and informed observers, are those concerning the allocation of parliamentary seats among party lists and individual candidates. These are not the only significant changes made, however, nor were they the only ones considered. Moreover, the positions of some important actors changed over the course of the debate. This section seeks to explain and assess the reforms adopted, and comments more briefly on those rejected or postponed.

Allocation of Seats Among Parties

The referendum revealed the voters' clear rejection of proportional representation, but in the views of many, it left open three questions regarding PR's replacement. First, while all major actors accepted that single-member constituencies would predominate in the new system, it was not clear whether the English SMP system endorsed by default in the referendum, or some variant of the French two-ballot majority system, should be chosen. At least initially, the DC, fearing a politics of everyone-against-the-DC, favored SMP, pointing particularly to its endorsement by the referendum (e.g., Nicola Mancino's statement that "such an overwhelming yes cannot but bind the Parliament to a mixed system, English single-member constituency for 75 percent of the seats and proportional for the remaining 25").[10] In this the DC was supported by Marco Pannella, the PRI, and the Northern League. Mario Segni, who during the referendum campaign had carefully avoided taking sides between those favoring single-round and those favoring two-round systems, came out in favor of the so-called photocopy solution, "the transposition for the Chamber of Deputies of that already approved for the Senate, because that is a formula that has already had popular investiture and therefore legitimization."[11] The PDS, PSI, PSDI, PLI, and Greens all supported some version of the French system, while some observers speculated that if the second round were limited to only two candidates the PRI, the Northern League, and even Mario Segni, the leader of the Popular Reform Movement and prime mover behind the referendum, might support a two-ballot system. Indeed, by the end of May Segni had switched sides to support such a system.

Beyond the argument that the referendum bound the parliament to maintain the SMP system, debate revolved around the question of the relative capacities of the two single-member systems to produce a bipolar, national result in the absence of true bipolarity in the voters' preferences and in patterns of party competition. Some commentators, apparently making a simple-minded application of "Duverger's Law," asserted that SMP would naturally produce a two-party result. Others claimed it would produce regionalized party systems, with the Lega dominating in the North, the PDS in the Center, and the DC in the South. Opponents of the French system claimed it would produce a crazy-quilt of alternative alliances in varying districts, thus destroying any clarity of the result, and any chance for the voters to decide directly who would govern, while its advocates pointed to the French case itself as evidence that this system would lead to competition between two broad blocs, even if the particular parties representing the blocs in the second round of voting varied among districts. This question was resolved in mid-June, when the Chamber of Deputies rejected a series of amendments to the proposal of Sergio Mattarella (DC), and the SMP principle was supported by the DC, MSI, PSDI, RC, and Lista Pannella, with the PDS, PLI, PRI, and Greens opposed. A majority of PSI deputies, as well as a few Republicans, also supported the SMP system.[12]

The second question was whether the single-member seats would be the only route to Parliament, or whether there would also be some system of proportional compensation seats. The natural, and expected, consequence of single-member election districts is that only large parties have any hope of winning seats (although "large" must be defined locally). To assure some, albeit reduced, representation for minorities, there was a general consensus that there should be some seats awarded by PR to "compensate" the small parties for the disadvantage that single-member districts imposed on them. Thus, the effective question was what the relative balance between single-member and PR seats ought to be. Although Mancino suggested a 75/25 split in the interview just cited, in early May, the official proposal of the DC (that of Mattarella) was for a 40% proportional adjustment, in late May reduced to 30%, and ultimately (mid-June) to 25%. Segni, on the other hand, called for the proportional adjustment to be reduced to only 10%.[13]

In the end, the electoral systems finally adopted for the Chamber of Deputies and for the Senate are broadly similar, and follow the general outline of the system left in place after the referendum. In each case, the country is divided into a number of multimember *circoscrizioni*, to which seats are in the first instance assigned, primarily on the basis of population. (The allocation of seats is shown in Table 4.2) For the Senate, the regions continue to serve as *circoscrizioni*, while for the Chamber some of the larger regions are subdivided to form 26 *circoscrizioni* (in place of the 31 *circoscrizioni* of the old system).[14] Each *circoscrizione* is to be divided into a number of single-member *collegi* corresponding to 3/4 of the seats assigned to it. Each of these *collegi* will elect one member by the first-past-the-post system. The other 1/4 of the seats are to be apportioned by PR, but at this point the two electoral systems diverge, both in the way in which the PR seats are to be apportioned among parties (the third question concerning allocation of seats) and in the way in which the particular candidates who will fill those seats are to be chosen (the subject of the next section).

Senate. For the Senate, the d'Hondt highest average method left in place by the referendum will continue to be used to assign the proportional compensation seats. Each elector will continue to have one vote, to be given to a single candidate in the *collegio* where the elector votes. After the winners in the *collegi* have been determined, the d'Hondt formula will be applied at the regional level to the regional vote totals of candidates affiliated with each of the groups, with the votes received by the candidates already elected in the *collegi* subtracted. (This adjustment was labelled *scorporo*).

Chamber of Deputies. The system enacted for the Chamber of Deputies is quite different. Each elector will have two ballots, one for the choice of a single candidate in his or her *collegio*, and one for the choice of a party list in the *circoscrizione*. These votes need not be given to the same party. Unlike the Senate system, which allows for independent candidacies, every candidate in the *collegi* must be affiliated with one or more of the party lists for the PR seats; where a candidate is affiliated with more than one list, every candidate in the same *circoscrizione* who is affiliated with one of those

TABLE 4.2   Geographic Distribution of Seats Under the New Electoral Laws

	Chamber of Deputies		Senate	
	Single Member Seats	PR Seats	Single Member Seats	PR Seats
Valle d'Aosta	1	0	1	0
Piemonte			17	6
Torino	19	6		
Vercelli, Novara, Cuneo, Asti, Alessandria, Biella, Verbano-Cusio-Ossola	17	6		
Lombardia			35	12
Milano	31	10		
Varese, Como, Sondrio, Lecco, Bergamo, Brescia	32	10		
Pavia, Cremona, Mantova, Lodi	11	4		
Trentino-Alto Adige	8	2	6	1
Veneto			17	6
Verona, Vicenza, Padova, Rovigo	22	7		
Venezia, Treviso, Belluno	15	5		
Friuli-Venezia Giulia	10	3	5	2
Liguria	14	5	6	3
Emilia Romagna	32	11	15	6
Toscana	29	10	14	5
Umbria	7	2	5	2
Marche	12	4	6	2
Lazio			21	7
Roma	32	10		
Viterbo, Rieti, Latina, Frosinone	11	4		
Abruzzi	11	3	5	2
Molise	3	1	2	0
Campania			22	8
Napoli	25	8		
Caserta, Benevento, Avellino, Salerno	22	7		
Puglia	34	11	16	6
Basilicata	5	2	5	2
Calabria	17	6	8	3
Sicilia			20	7
Palermo, Trapani, Agrigento, Caltanissetta	20	7		
Messina, Catania, Ragusa, Siracusa, Enna	21	7		
Sardegna	14	4	6	3

lists must be affiliated with the others. (E.g., if one candidate in the *circoscrizione* of Emilia Romagna were to be affiliated with the PDS, RC, and Verdi, then every candidate in Emilia Romagna who was affiliated with any one of the three lists would have to be affiliated with the other two as well.)

The effective vote for each list in the *circoscrizione* (the *cifra elettorale circoscrizionale*) is computed by taking the total number of votes cast for the list itself, and is then reduced on the basis of the votes received by candidates in the single-member contests. The reduction or adjustment (*scorporo*) made to the list votes of the party or parties with which each winning candidate is affiliated is equal to the number of votes actually required for his or her victory - that is, one more than the number of votes received by the candidate who places second in the same *collegio*. This rule, however, is subject to the additional limitation that the deduction cannot be less than 25% of the valid vote cast in the *collegio*, except that the number of votes that the winning candidate actually obtains serves as the upper limit for the subtraction.[15] If the winning candidate is affiliated with more than one list, the deduction is divided among the relevant lists in proportion to their raw list vote totals. Once the list totals at the level of the *circoscrizioni* have been computed, they are to be forwarded to the National Central Electoral Office, which allocates the PR seats first among the parties, and then to individual *circoscrizioni*, using the Hare quota largest remainder method. Only parties that received at least 4% of the total valid vote at the national level take part in the distribution of the PR seats.National Central Electoral Office, which allocates the PR seats first among the parties, and then to individual *circoscrizioni*, using the Hare quota largest remainder method. Only parties that received at least 4% of the total valid vote at the national level take part in the distribution of the PR seats.

Two differences between the Senate and Chamber systems need to be assessed. The first is with respect to their treatment of small parties. Initially, the system for the Chamber is clearly more favorable to small parties, both because the Hare quota method is more favorable and because national allocation of seats means that the effective district magnitude is much larger.[16] On the other hand, the Chamber system involves a statutory threshold, whereas the Senate system does not. In the parliamentary debates, it was claimed that the regional allocation of proportional compensation seats for the Senate would imply a threshold of at least 10%, but this conclusion must be read with caution. Since the allocation of PR seats is made only after the operation of the *scorporo*, the thresholds of representation (minimum vote needed to win a seat) and exclusion (maximum vote possible without winning a seat) must be computed on the basis of this reduced total. Thus, for example, if one assumes that the average plurality winner in Sicilian *collegi* will have 30% of the vote (in 1992 the figure was over 31%) and that there are 7 parties with candidates (in 1992 there were 13), then a party would need only 8.8% of the vote to be assured of at least one of Sicily's 7 PR compensation seats, and might win one with as little as 5.4% of the vote.[17] For the largest *circoscrizione* (Lombardia), the corresponding figures would be 5.4% and 3.9%. In addition, and even more significantly, these figures are computed regionally, whereas the threshold for the Chamber is computed nationally. But party strength is not uniform throughout the country. Thus, although La Rete had less than 1% of the national Senate vote in 1992, it had nearly 10% of the vote in Sicily, more than enough to guarantee at least one seat. This explains, for example, why the SVP has challenged the 4% threshold for the Chamber, but not the Senate system.

The second difference is between the single and double ballot methods of voting. The justification for having a separate list ballot for the Chamber was to prevent minor party candidates standing in the *collegi* from destroying the hoped-for two candidate clarity of the single-member result; it was hoped that small parties would participate in broader coalitions in the *collegi* instead of presenting their own candidates simply to increase their claim on the PR seats, since these would be based on a separate vote in which the small parties would have their own candidates.[18] This presumably will continue to be a problem in the Senate. On the other hand, the separation of the ballots creates an important conflict of interest within each party. That is, because of the *scorporo*, each party's list candidates are more likely to win seats if its *collegio* candidates lose. Indeed, in the limiting case, each party that hopes to win at least one *collegio* rationally ought to nominate two complete sets of *collegio* and list candidates under two separate *contrassegni*. For example, imagine the DC expecting to win many *collegio* seats. If it (1) ran those candidates under the label DC-SMP, attached to a phantom PR list, and (2) added a list of PR candidates under the label DC-PR as a formally separate party, attached to phantom *collegio* candidates, and (3) instructed all of its voters to vote for the DC-SMP candidates in the *collegi*, but the DC-PR list with their list votes, it could then avoid any deduction from its list total based on the victories of its (or technically "their") *collegio* candidates. Even though such a blatant attempt to circumvent the intention of the law is unlikely to materialize in practice, this possibility highlights the potential for intraparty conflicts of interest that is entailed in the new law.

Allocation of PR Seats Among Candidates

In determining which individual candidates will fill each party's share of the PR seats, the new Senate system again retains the decision of the referendum. Once each party's share of the PR seats is determined, the corresponding number of its candidates who did not head the poll in their *collegi* are elected, in order of their personal vote percentages. Thus, many *collegi* will have two senators, although every *collegio* will have at least one. Other novelties are that each candidate may stand in only one *collegio* and may not be a candidate for both the Senate and the Chamber of Deputies, and that the candidacy of individuals who are not affiliated with a party group, and will not take part in the distribution of the PR seats, is allowed.

For the Chamber of Deputies, the PR seats allocated to each party in each *circoscrizione* are assigned to individuals on the party list, in the order submitted by the party. If the party list does not include enough candidates, the additional seats go to otherwise defeated candidates from the *collegi* in the same way as used for the Senate.[19]

Choice of Individuals

Several provisions of the new laws bear on the question of which individuals will be elected. First, although it was briefly the subject of a back-bench revolt, the individual preference vote *(voto di preferenza)*, as just suggested, has been abolished in favor of blocked lists. Thus at no point will voters have a choice of candidates *within* a party. While this runs against the anti-party current, it is probably necessary if there is to be any hope that the result of SMP will be strong and cohesive parties as in Britain rather than the independence of every representative as in the United States.

A second important provision with respect to the choice of individuals is the prohibition of multiple candidacies. Under the old system, an individual could stand in several districts, and if elected in more than one could choose which seat to take. In making that choice, the candidate would also decide which other seat(s) would become vacant, and therefore in effect determine which otherwise defeated candidate(s) would be lifted into Parliament. Under the new system, a candidate may stand in only one *collegio*, the only exception to the prohibition on multiple candidacies being the possibility of appearing on the lists of one's party in up to three Chamber of Deputies *circoscrizioni*, as well as standing in a single Chamber of Deputies *collegio*.

Both electoral laws make explicit reference to the representation of women. For the Senate, there is simply the exhortation that elections should favor a balance of representation between women and men, while for the Chamber, lists that include more than one name are required to alternate male and female candidates. Neither is likely to make much difference. For the Senate, representation of women depends entirely on the choice of the parties to nominate women in winnable *collegi*; for the Chamber, this is tempered by the requirement that at least the second individual on a multimember party list be a woman, but: (1) parties need not have more than one name on their lists; (2) assuming the lists are constructed man-woman-man-woman rather than the reverse, a woman will be elected only once the party wins its second PR seat; and (3) even if every individual on a party list were elected, the number of women thereby elected might represent as little as 1/24 of the total.[20] If the experience of other countries, that parties are least likely to nominate women to winnable seats when the electoral system is first-past-the-post, generalizes to Italy, then the reforms taken as a whole may well reduce the representation of women.

In the past, when a seat became vacant, it was filled by the candidate who would have been elected at the last general election had his or her party been assigned one more seat in the relevant district. Under the new system, this will be the case only for vacancies occurring in the PR compensation seats. For the single-member *collegi*, there will instead be a special election.

Districting

Because both chambers of parliament effectively were elected by proportional representation from large districts, under the old law the boundaries of constituencies made little difference. Although, for example, the largest Senate *collegio* in Lombardy had more than seven times the number of votes cast in 1992 as the smallest, it would make no difference to the eventual distribution of seats among the parties, because that was based on the regional totals. Under the new laws, however, the drawing of *collegio* boundaries may be absolutely crucial to determining the outcome in both chambers.

Districting problems can be described under two headings apportionment (referring to the equality of population of the individual *collegi*) and gerrymandering (referring to the drawing of boundaries, even within the strictures of population equality, for partisan advantage). The problem of apportionment is addressed directly by the injunction in the law that the population of each *collegio* not deviate by more than 10% in either direction from the average population of *collegi* within the same *circoscrizione;* where the representation of linguistic minorities is at stake, the allowable deviation is increased to 15%. While not as strict as the limits in the United States (virtually no deviation from equality allowed) or New Zealand (5%), this is more stringent than the requirements imposed in Britain (25%) or France (20%).

Potentially more important is the possibility that boundaries would be drawn on a partisan basis. Here the general principle is that if there were perfect foreknowledge and no restrictions on the placement of boundaries, then it would always be possible to draw districts so that a party with 25% of the votes would win 50% of the SMP seats. The new laws address the possibility of this type of manipulation in two ways. The first is to give the drawing of district boundaries over to a commission of experts (the president of the National Statistical Institute and ten university teachers or other experts in relevant fields). The other is to put restrictions on the commission's freedom of action. *Collegio* boundaries are to guarantee socio-economic and historic and cultural homogeneity. More particularly, *collegi* are to be contiguous (unless they include islands) and should not include communes from more than one province nor divide a commune unless the commune itself will be more than one whole *collegio*.[21]

Unfortunately, it is not always possible to respect communal and provincial boundaries and still draw *collegi* that are within the allowable range of population disparities. For example, the allowable range of population for *collegi* in Toscana is roughly 109,000 to 134,000. The commune of Livorno, with roughly 171,000 people, is too large to be only one *collegio*, but too small to be two.[22] Similarly, the province of Matera is too large to be one *collegio* but too small to be two; Agrigento is too big to be two *collegi* but too small to be three; the only way to divide Molise into three constituencies while respecting provincial boundaries is to give one *collegio* to Isernia (population about 95,000) and two to Campobasso (average population about 121,000 each). If these boundaries were respected, there would be quite significant population disparities. The commission drew tentative boundaries that violated the norm against dividing communes in a few justifiable cases. They have been approved with minimal modifications. There have been no cases denounced as manipulations for partisan advantage.

Votes for Non-resident Italians

Although in the past Italians living abroad had their travel home to vote subsidized, those who could not return to the communes in which they were registered were effectively disenfranchised. At the initiative of the MSI-DN, the new electoral laws envision that Italians resident abroad will elect a number of representatives from constituencies defined by the continents. Since this provision was recognized to be blatantly contrary to the Constitution (which specifically allocates all deputies and senators to constituencies within the national territory[23]), the procedures to amend the Constitution and provide for the election of twenty deputies and 10 senators by Italians living abroad were initiated at the same time the new electoral laws were securing final passage. In a stormy meeting of the Senate held November 10, the bill was finally rejected, defeated not only by the negative votes of the PDS and the Lega, but also by the many absences in the ranks of the governing majority.

Ballot Access

Under the old law, parties that had formed parliamentary groups or won at least one seat in either chamber were not required to submit nominating petitions in order to appear on the ballot at the next election. The new laws remove this privilege, and every *collegio* candidate will require the signatures of at least 500 electors of the *collegio* on his or her declaration of candidacy. This means that a party presenting candidates in every *collegio* will need a total of over 235,000 signatures.[24] While this figure is less than 1% of the number of votes cast in the 1992 election, it is also substantially more than the total membership of most Italian parties.

Rejected Proposals

There was general agreement among all parties that reforms roughly like those actually adopted were unavoidable. Given overwhelming popular support for the referendum, the likely costs of not enacting reforms were perceived to be unacceptable, even if the reforms themselves might prove costly to the parties then in power. Some members of Parliament, however, proposed substantially more far-reaching reforms during the course of the debate. Many of these were even more threatening to the parties in power and their leaders, and in the absence of the specific imperative imposed by the referendum, they were not adopted.

Term Limits

One manifestation of discontent with the current political class was the adoption of a term limitation amendment by the Senate at the beginning of July. Introduced by PDS Senator Concetto Scivoletto and supported by the Lega, the "piazza pulita" amendment would have disqualified from candidacy anyone who had served in the Chamber of Deputies or the Senate in three legislatures (whether or not consecutive), or for more than fifteen years. The leaders of all the established parties, virtually all of whom would have seen their parliamentary careers brought to an end, opposed the amendment as contrary to the Constitution. The amendment was defeated in the Chamber of Deputies later in the month.[25]

Direct Election of the Prime Minister

After several weeks of complaining that the end result of the reforms proposed would still be governments formed by the party secretaries, on July 22 Mario Segni of Alleanza Democratica announced a proposal for direct election of the prime minister. Under this proposal, the premier would be elected by the French two-ballot majority system; unlike the French or American presidents, however, the premier's term would coincide with that of the parliament, so that either a vote of no confidence or the dissolution of parliament would result in new elections of both parliament and prime minister. To force turnover in office, an individual could only be elected premier in two consecutive elections, after which he or she would have to stand down for at least one term.

The proposal, which could only be implemented by constitutional amendment, drew both support and opposition from a broad area of the political spectrum. Giorgio La Malfa (former secretary of the Republican Party) and Augusto Barbera (PDS, but near to Alleanza Democratica) indicated support, but Franco Bassanini (also PDS) criticized its plebiscitarian and authoritarian tendencies.

Final Passage, Immediate Aftermath, and Future Prospects

The reforms received final approval in the Senate on August 3, with 128 votes in favor, 29 opposed, and 59 abstentions. Final approval in the Chamber of Deputies came the next day on a vote of 278 votes to 78, with 153 abstentions. Core support for the legislation came from the DC, PSI, PSDI, and the Lega, with opposition primarily coming from the MSI, the Rete, and the PLI. PRI and PDS members abstained in both chambers. Members of Rifondazione comunista abstained in the Senate, but voted against the reforms in the Chamber of Deputies, while the Greens voted "no" in the Senate and abstained in the Chamber of Deputies. Mario Segni, whose referendum drive had spurred the whole process, in the end abstained.

Even before the reforms were finally approved, two challenges beyond that implicit in Segni's call for direct election of the Prime Minister had already been announced. On one side, as already mentioned, the South Tyrolean People's Party challenged the constitutionality of the 4% threshold for PR seats in the Chamber of Deputies, and indeed appealed to Austria for assistance.[26] On the other, Marco Pannella threatened to organize referenda against both the very existence of PR compensation seats and the requirement that all candidates for the Chamber of Deputies be tied to party lists.

Prime Minister Carlo Azeglio Ciampi welcomed the reforms as a clear sign of the "vitality and solidarity of republican institutions."[27] Others were less favorable. Political scientist Gianfranco Pasquino, one of the early proponents of electoral reform for Italy, found the new system excessively complicated. "Worse than the Irish and the Greek laws, and I

have mentioned the two most complicated laws that I am familiar with,"
he commented, while DC Deputy Giovanni Alterio referred to "That ugly
mess from Piazza Montecitorio."[28] And beyond the complexity of the
parliamentary electoral laws themselves, these reforms left Italians with
the prospect of going to the polls three times in 1994 over just a few months,
each time with a different electoral system — two-ballot majority for
mayors, two versions of SMP with proportional compensation seats for the
Chamber of Deputies and the Senate, and straight list PR for the European
Parliament.

Although it is certain that the new electoral laws, in conjunction with
the "meltdown" of the previous party system, will radically alter the
Italian political landscape, it is impossible to predict what the outcome will
be. At the very least, the result will be greatly affected by the pattern of alliances that forms. For example, one analysis of the likely result in the
single-member seats for the Chamber of Deputies contrasted a scenario in
which the PDS and Alleanza Democratica allied with another in which the
PDS instead allied with Rifondazione Comunista and the Rete; the projec-
tion for the first case was 251 seats for PDS/AD, 90 seats for the Lega, and
77 seats for the DC; for the second it was 143 seats for PDS/RC/Rete, 139
seats for the Lega, and 162 seats for the DC. A different analysis projected
that a center-left alliance of PDS and part of AD, the *laici*, socialists, and
Greens would win 196 seats overall against 216 for an alliance of DC,
Popolari, and the rest of the *laici* and socialists, and 165 for the Lega
(without allies), or alternatively that a left alliance (PDS, Rifondazione,
Rete, Greens, and some socialists) would win 196 seats against a center-left
alliance of DC, Popolari and most of the laici and socialists (228 seats) and
the Lega (175 seats).[29] Clearly all this depends on assumptions about what
alliances the other parties will or will not form and about how the voters
will react. Even more fundamentally, it depends on precisely how the
district boundaries are drawn. And finally, given the fluidity of the Italian
situation, the outcome is likely to depend as well on when the elections are
held. Although speculation in the autumn clearly pointed to elections in
the spring of 1994, in late August DC secretary Mino Martinazzoli was still
talking about the possibility that the 11th Republican Legislature might
last its full constitutional term — until 1997.[30]

Notes

1. For example, Gianfranco Pasquino, "That Obscure Object of Desire: A New
Electoral Law for Italy," *West European Politics* 12, April 1989, pp. 280-94.
2. *Il Sole 24 Ore*, July 16, 1993, p. 2.
3. *La Repubblica*, May 20, 1993, p. 4.

4. For example, in the North the DC fell from 22.7% of the popular vote to 10.4% while the PSI collapsed from 17.2% to only about 1%.

5. Richard S. Katz and Luciano Bardi, "Preference Voting and Turnover in Italian Parliamentary Elections," *American Journal of Political Science*, February 1980.

6. The calculation of the hypothetical outcome of the 1992 Senate election under the post-referendum law is based on the votes for individual candidates as reported in *I deputati e senatori del undicesimo parlamento repubblicano* (Roma: Navicella, Editoriale Italiana, 1992). Except for the votes of candidates actually elected, these figures are not definitive.

7. E.g., interview with Minister of the Interior Nicola Mancino reported in *Il Giornale*, April 21, 1993, p. 5; comments by PDS secretary Achille Occhetto on RAI, April 30, 1993; comments by President Scalfaro on RAI, May 1, 1993.

8. *La Repubblica*, May 4, 1993, p. 2

9. *La Repubblica*, June 23, 1993, p. 11.

10. *Il Giornale*, April 21, 1993, p. 5.

11. *Il Sole 24 Ore*, July 6, 1993, referring to remarks made April 24.

12. *La Repubblica*, June 17, 1993, pp. 2-3; *Il Giornale*, June 17, 1993, p. 3.

13. *Il Sole 24 Ore*, June 16, 1993, p. 2.

14. In addition, the Valle d'Aosta remains a single-member *circoscrizione*.

15. All this can be illustrated by again applying the new rules to the votes cast in the 1992 election. For example, in Collegio 6 of Lombardy, the DC candidate received 46,622 votes and would have been elected under the new system. The second-place candidate (Lega Lombarda) received 28,123 votes. Thus, the reduction to the DC list total for Lombardy would have been 28,124, except that this was only 21.4% of the total vote cast in the collegio. As a result, the actual reduction would have been 32,885 votes, which is 25% of the total. In Collegio 13, however, where the DC candidate was in first place with 31,637 votes (23%), the reduction would only have been those 31,637 votes, since the full 25% would have been more votes than the winning candidate actually received.

16. Michael Gallagher, "Comparing Proportional Representation Electoral Systems: Quotas, Thresholds, Paradoxes and Majorities," *British Journal of Political Science* 22, 1993, pp. 469-96; Rein Taagepera and Matthew Shugart, *Seats and Votes* (New Haven: Yale University Press, 1989).

17. The formula for the threshold of representation is $1/(s+1)$ and that for the threshold of exclusion is $1/(s+p-1)$, where s is the number of seats to be assigned (in the case of PR compensation seats for the Senate in Sicily, this is 7), and p is the number of parties. In each case, the results would be multiplied by 0.70, to reflect the fact that 30% of the votes have already been deducted by the operation of the *scorporo*.

18. See, for example, the interview with Massimo D'Alema, PDS floor leader in the Chamber of Deputies, reported in *La Repubblica*, June 15, 1993, p. 10.

19. The number of PR seats won by a party might exceed its number of candidates for three reasons: the maximum number of individuals allowed on each list is only 1/3 (rounded up) of the number of PR seats for that *circoscrizione*; although each individual may be a candidate in only one *collegio*, a *collegio* candidate may also be part of the list for one of the parties with which he or she is

affiliated in that *circoscrizione;* and an individual may appear on party lists in up to three *circoscrizioni.*

20. This figure is 1/2 (the required proportion of women on the list) of 1/3 (the maximum number of names on the list relative to the number of PR compensation seats) of 1/4 (the proportion of the total number of seats allocated by PR). This theoretical minimum for women's representation would be "achieved" only if a single party won all of the PR compensation seats in a *circoscrizione* and nominated no women in the *collegi.*

21. Legge 4 agosto 1993, n. 277, Art. 7.

22. Other examples simply among provincial capitals would be the communes of Piacenza, Modena, Ferrara, Ravenna, Perugia, Salerno, and Reggio di Calabria.

23. Art. 56 and 57.

24. Party lists for the Chamber of Deputies also require nominating petitions, but since these may be signed by the same individuals who sign the declarations of candidacy for *collegio* candidates this does not impose any substantial additional burden.

25. *La Repubblica,* July 2, 1993, p. 10; July 22, 1993, p. 7.

26. *Die Presse,* September 9, 1993, p. 4.

27. AFP broadcast in English, August 4, 1993.

28. *Panorama,* August 15, 1993, p. 9.

29. The first two projections were made by the ufficio elettorale of the PDS, while the second two are by "Forum elettorale per la riforma." *La Repubblica,* October 8, 1993, p. 7.

30. *Il Giornale,* August 24, 1993, p. 4.

5

Reinventing the Left:
The Origins
of Italy's Progressive Alliance

Martin Rhodes

Nineteen ninety-three will be seen as a landmark year on the Italian Left. True enough, the dramatic changes that have revolutionized the Italian political system in the early 1990s make it difficult to state with any certainty just which events were pivotal or precisely when the point of no return was reached. Moreover, some observers have argued that Italy's "quiet revolution" may turn out to have been no more than a cosmetic melodrama, and that when the dust eventually settles, the key character- istics of the old order will re-emerge. Yet at the beginning of 1993, it would have been difficult to imagine that the fragmented and querulous forces of Italy's Left, ranging from the politically, morally and financially bankrupt Socialist Party (PSI) on its right, through to the grab-bag of far-left and new-left groups in *Rifondazione comunista*, would, in less than a year, be on the verge of forging a progressive left alliance with the former communist Democratic Party of the Left (PDS), the Greens, the centrist Democratic Alliance (*Alleanza democratica*), the anti-Mafia *Rete* ("Network"), Socialist- Christians and the Independent Left. Although the events preceding the creation of this alliance were certainly melodramatic, their consequences will be far from cosmetic. What we have been witnessing in Italy is nothing less than a long overdue reinvention of the Left.

The inauguration of the Progressive Alliance *(Alleanza progressista)* on February 2, 1994, was only the first step — albeit a giant one — towards a reconstitution of the Italian Left, and there were plenty of pitfalls in its path, not least its ideological diversity. But its creation confirmed that a number of critical developments had almost run their course: The Socialist Party had disappeared as a credible, independent political force;

a significant section of the old, secular center had come to accept that its future lay not with a reconstructed, Catholic center-right, but with a progressive center-left; and, perhaps most significantly, the former Communists in the PDS now acknowledged the imperative not of a united Left led by themselves but of the need to abandon the cult, symbolism and hegemonic pretensions of the old party and engage in a broad, social democratic alliance. The transition made by all the partners of the new coalition during 1993 had been a difficult one and their apprehensions and qualms were still evident in the weeks following its constitution. However, by early 1994 their own political trajectories and the rapidly changing context — including the introduction of a new electoral system and the rise of a potent alliance of populist forces on the right — had left them with no other viable alternative.

This chapter explains the emergence of Italy's new left-wing alliance by following the trajectories of its component parts during 1993. Of course, it is rather artificial to analyze each alliance partner separately in this way: They clearly evolve as part of a complex, shifting relationship that finally gels in a common program for government and an agreement to contest elections under a single symbol. There is also a danger that history can be falsified by assuming the inevitable convergence of diverse political developments. Nevertheless, I argue that there is a certain inevitability or logic in the evolution of the Italian Left during 1993. As the year wore on, a number of options were closed and the opportunities for renewal were narrowed. By year's end only three real choices remained for forces spanning the progressive center and the Left: alliance, merger or oblivion.

The Remarkable Death of the Socialist Party

By far the most spectacular series of events on the Italian Left during 1993 concerned the Socialist Party. Consequently, its path towards the new Progressive Alliance was the most tortuous. As recently as late 1991, an observer of Italian politics could assume that the PSI would be able to dictate the future of the Left, arguing that, following the 20th Congress of the Communist Party (PCI) — which became the 1st Congress of the PDS — "the PDS faced the same challenges that had plagued the PCI: its credibility as a party of government, and its isolation from the Socialists, with whom an alternative government must be eventually constructed."[1] Even a year later — following the crisis of Craxi's leadership of the party and the emergence of a significant challenge from his former heir apparent (delfino), Claudio Martelli — it seemed possible for the party to rescue itself by engineering a rapid and far-reaching renewal.[2] But 1993 has seen, if not the death of the Italian liberal-socialist tradition, then certainly the death of the party that Craxi had attempted to use as the vehicle for his *mitterrandist* project of unifying the Left. The revelations of extensive Socialist Party corruption and the contradictions created by Craxi's own "presidential" style of leadership simply tore the party apart.

Discontent within the PSI was triggered by the first revelations of the Milan scandal in February 1992 and by the poor performance of the party in the April 1992 general elections and in regional polls in June and September the same year. The mounting tensions split the previously unified Socialists into three factions that became quasi-official at the PSI National Assembly in late November 1992: the faithful *craxiani* (supporters of Craxi), with 63 percent of the assembly vote; the Martelli-led Socialist Renewal group, with 32.5 percent; and a tiny third group (with 4 percent of delegates) led by Valdo Spini, who wanted a reform of the party but not civil war. Craxi's preferred heir — and, indeed, the natural leader of the liberal-socialist area after Craxi's departure — was Giuliano Amato, his faithful lieutenant since the late 1970s and at this point Prime Minister. In late 1992 — having been accused by magistrates in Milan of violating the law on party financing on forty occasions since 1985 — it seemed just a matter of time before Craxi would step down, to be replaced by either Martelli or Amato, although the latter had shown little enthusiasm for the task. But the calamitous events of February 1993 changed everything. Not only was Craxi's *coup de grâce* finally delivered that month, when new allegations made his already difficult position untenable, but the charges also claimed another major casualty in his erstwhile challenger, Claudio Martelli. Indeed, Martelli was the first to go when he resigned both from his Justice portfolio and the Socialist Party on February 10, after having received a cautionary warrant from magistrates investigating the fraudulent bankruptcy of the Banco Ambrosiano in 1982. A day later Bettino Craxi resigned from his post as party secretary.

Their fates had been sealed by testimony from Silvano Larini, the Milan city architect and *éminence grise* of the Milanese PSI who had been arrested in December after eight months on the run. Originally accused of collecting bribes for work on the Milan Metro system, Larini's name was now linked to a *Union de Banque Suisse* (UBS) bank account in Lugano that was allegedly used for payments from the Banco Ambrosiano in the early 1980s before its collapse and the suspicious death of its chairman, Roberto Calvi. Astonishingly, both Craxi and Martelli now faced charges of fraudulent bankruptcy in connection with the Ambrosiano affair and both were accused of arranging illegal funding for the PSI through Calvi and Licio Gelli (grandmaster of the P2 masonic lodge). Although these allegations sent a shock wave through the Italian political system, the *Tangentopoli* ("Bribe City") scandals had already claimed a number of illustrious victims in the party, including the reprobate former Socialist Foreign

Minister, Gianni De Michelis. And as 1993 wore on, the PSI was to be plagued by a seemingly endless series of revelations, exposing a complex web of corruption linking mainly Socialist and Christian Democrat politicians to government officials and both public and private-sector industrialists.[3]

The departures of Craxi and Martelli also heralded a procession of illustrious resignations, accompanied by the desertion of the party by hundreds of activists throughout the country and a complete collapse of its support at the polls: In the 1990 local elections, the Socialists scored more than 17 percent of the vote (benefitting from their traditional networks of local patronage) but in the partial municipal, provincial and regional polls held in June 1993 four months after Craxi's departure, they were all but annihilated, attracting just 2 percent of the vote. To make matters worse for Craxi's successors, it soon became clear that the party's moral and political bankruptcy also extended to its finances. Thus, when on February 12, 1993, Craxi was replaced by Giorgio Benvenuto (the former general secretary of the Socialist-Social Democratic labor confederation, the *Unione Italiana del Lavoro*), Benvenuto inherited a dwindling membership, a once efficient but now irreparable electoral machine, as well as debts estimated to be more than L200 billion by the end of the year. And as it soon turned out, given Craxi's domination of the party — and the absence of even a residual identity independent of him at its lower levels — Benvenuto could be leader of the party in name only. Not only was he constantly impeded by the *craxiani* still congregating and conspiring in the corridors of PSI headquarters in Via del Corso in Rome (the *craxiani* had only supported Benvenuto in order to manipulate him) but he would also prove to be the victim of interference by Craxi himself.

Benvenuto used the occasion of the PSI's mid-March National Assembly in Rome to attempt a burial of *craxismo*. The Belsito conference center — shortly to be sold to help pay off the party's debts — was thronged with unknown faces, and Benvenuto addressed them with a speech that dissociated the party from its recent inglorious past and from Craxi's intemperate denunciations of the *"Mani pulite"* ("Clean Hands") investigations. During a visit to London that month, Prime Minister Amato said that Craxi had no political future. But the burial was premature. Though by no means vital and healthy, *craxismo* was a lingering presence that still exerted a malignant influence over the party. It was this knowledge that led Norberto Bobbio — the philosopher and long-time intellectual and moral pillar of the party — to refuse to endorse the new leadership, regardless of Benvenuto's ostensible break with his predecessor.[4]

The continued influence of *craxismo* was revealed when the party's new power structure was installed towards the end of March. The appointment of Gino Giugni — an academic and a symbol of rectitude in the party — as the PSI's new president was designed to help renovate the leadership. But it turned out to be the only significant innovation. For when Benvenuto put together his executive committee, the *inquisiti* (those under investigation) were there in force, including De Michelis (with five cautionary warrants), Paris Dell'Unto (two), Giusy La Ganga (two), Raffaele Rotiroti (two), Giulio Di Donato (two), Rino Formica (one) and Biagio Marzo (one). Ugo Intini had said that while Benvenuto could choose the members of the secretariat "we [the *craxiani*] will choose the names for the executive." Benvenuto was also outmaneuvered on the secretariat, which was downgraded to the status of "secretariat office." To cite the *craxiano* Di Donato, "the real leadership is now exercised by the executive, while the secretariat office will be a technical body, composed of the secretary's staff, his collaborators, the head of the press office."[5]

In these circumstances, it was hardly surprising that Benvenuto's "leadership" was to prove short-lived: After 100 days as secretary he resigned on May 20 along with six members of the party's executive and Gino Giugni, now Labor Minister in the new Ciampi government. Unable to establish and wield real control over the party, Benvenuto also had to cope with divisions on policy and further corruption allegations against major party figures. First, the PSI split on the electoral reform referendum, with the *craxiani*, led by Ugo Intini, Gennaro Acquaviva, Margherita Boniver and Pierluigi Romita, joining Craxi in the "No" camp, while others in the party not only backed the "Yes" campaign but supported the PDS in its call for a two-ballot, French-style system against the single-ballot option that was eventually chosen. Second, throughout Benvenuto's period in office, the party became tarnished with further corruption revelations and was battered by public outrage at the refusal of Parliament at the end of April to lift Craxi's immunity on the most important charges laid against him.[6] The decision provoked the resignation of the three PDS ministers appointed in the new Ciampi government,[7] but more importantly for the PSI it also provoked the resignation of three of its most senior politicians: former minister Giorgio Ruffolo; the former leader of the FIOM-CGIL, the metalworkers' union, Roberto Cassola; and Giacomo Mancini, a key figure in the internal party opposition to Craxi.

In an attempt to improve the party's image, Benvenuto agreed that members under investigation — especially those in Parliament and the main party apparatus — should be suspended, producing a major clash between the *inquisiti* and the new leadership in the first week of May. In the end, the *inquisiti* agreed to leave their posts if they were replaced by members from the same faction, which would maintain the internal party balance. From then on, the knives were out for Benvenuto and he abandoned the leadership ten days later. The *craxiani* had won. But his greatest enemy had been the power still exerted by their leader within the party.

When Benvenuto finally resigned from the PSI on July 14, he commented that "Craxi was not there physically but it was as if he were present: The party felt like his orphan. Craxi was not there but he was everywhere." When asked whether "it would seem that rather than leaving the PSI you have left Craxi or, more precisely, his ghost," Benvenuto grinned and replied, "Thank you, that's exactly it."[8]

Defending the PSI's image had in any case become a fairly hopeless task by this stage. In March, the Socialist senator Franco Reviglio was forced to resign from the Finance portfolio after becoming the fifth minister in the Amato government to be caught up in the corruption investigations. The charges alleged the receipt of illegal funds while Reviglio had served as chairman of the Socialist public-sector fiefdom ENI (the National Hydrocarbons Agency) from 1983 to 1989. In the same month, his Craxi-appointed successor at ENI, Gabriele Cagliari, admitted to paying L4 billion to a representative of the PSI to win a contract on a power station being built by ENEL, the state electricity authority.[9] In April, Claudio Martelli received a second cautionary warrant (accusing him of receiving stolen property and belonging to an international fraud ring that used stolen bank securities as collateral to secure credit and loans) while two cautionary warrants were issued against Gianni De Michelis for illegal party financing. A third linked De Michelis, three of his former ministry staff and his personal secretary to the embezzlement and misdirection of funds designated for aid to developing countries. In May, Salvo Andò, the Socialist Defense Minister in the Amato government, was placed under investigation for alleged vote rigging involving the Mafia in his native Catania and Martelli received his third warrant for corruption, relating to an alleged kickback of L400 million on a power station contract at Brindisi for which his secretary, Sergio Restilli, was arrested. On the same day, Bettino Craxi was questioned by a Belgian magistrate investigating alleged irregularities in the sale of Augusta helicopters to the Belgian armed forces. In sum, the party's image was by now beyond redemption.

Benvenuto's successor, Ottaviano Del Turco, was elected with 82 percent of the party's vote on May 28, just prior to the PSI's heavy losses in the municipal and provincial polls in June. Formerly adjunct secretary general of the Socialist-Communist CGIL labor confederation (under Bruno Trentin of the PDS), Del Turco set out to salvage what remained of the party. He failed: He was to remain secretary for seven months, but the party simply slipped out from under him. Del Turco attempted to circumvent the *craxiani* and to pursue Benvenuto's project of removing the *inquisiti* from positions of influence in the PSI, while also attempting to create a future for the party by striking new tactical alliances. However, this strategy was to prove impossible to implement. As Fausto Vigevani, the general secretary of the FIOM (the metalworkers' union in the CGIL), commented when resigning from the party in the first week of June, "Del Turco will fail just as Benvenuto did. The PSI cannot be reformed or renewed. The external political, social and cultural — not to mention the internal — conditions simply do not exist."[10] Moreover, Del Turco had few resources to employ. Already in May, the day-to-day functioning of the party had ground to a halt when, due to L1 billion in unpaid bills, SIP and ENEL cut off the PSI's phones and electricity. For a party that is estimated to have pocketed L50 billion in kickbacks and bribes, this was an extraordinary state of affairs. But it was paralleled in the Social Democratic Party (PSDI), where the resignation of its secretary Carlo Vizzini in March was provoked by the bankruptcy of the organization and by the ignominy of criminal investigations into the activities of some of its leading members, including former secretary Antonio Cariglia.[11]

Meanwhile, the PSI's influence in the country at large had all but disappeared: Not only had its popular support evaporated, but it now had only three members in the government and only one significant portfolio (Defense, held by Fabio Fabbri).[12] During the summer months, the extent of the PSI's demoralization and decrepitude became abundantly clear. When on July 4, the party abandoned its former headquarters in Via del Corso in Rome, an important material and symbolic defeat had been conceded. The desertion of the party by its senior ranks also began to accelerate. Enzo Mattina left the party on June 30, stating that "it is impossible to renew the credibility of socialism in Italian society while remaining in the PSI"; and he was followed in the second week of July by former secretary Giorgio Benvenuto, who began an uncertain journey towards the Democratic Alliance and the PDS. Only two major figures in Benvenuto's *Rinascita socialista* faction, Mauro Del Bue and Enrico Manca, remained in the party. Internationally, Del Turco and the PSI had become an embarrassment. In the first week of July, both Del Turco and the PDS secretary, Achille Occhetto, attended the congress of the French Socialist Party in Lyons. But Del Turco was ignored and Occhetto chosen to speak as the voice of Italian socialism, a role that in former times had always been played by Craxi who, although still vice-president of the Socialist International, had been left off the congress invitation list.

However, Del Turco had at least been thinking strategically. By midsummer he appeared to be set on taking the party into the centrist Democratic Alliance while resisting invitations from Occhetto to ally with the PDS. In early July, Mario Segni and his Catholic *Popolari per la riforma* had joined the Democratic Alliance, suggesting for many in the PSI — including Del Turco — that their future now lay with the liberal-democratic center. For Del Turco, this represented something of a U-turn: In January, he had advised the Republican secretary, Giorgio La Malfa, to "abandon the illusion of bringing a piece of the Catholic world into the liberal-democratic camp" since Segni was a leader of "a reformist Right that must be countered by a reformist Left."[13] But as became clear at the PSI Convention in Rome in the third week of July (designed to relaunch the party with a new name and symbol), Del Turco's reassessment of the Democratic Alliance was not shared by all PSI leaders. A large section of the party now saw an alliance with the PDS as the only alternative. When Enrico Manca suggested this to Del Turco in late June, the latter commented that "the last time I heard something like this was from Lelio Basso at the congress in '63,"[14] suggesting a parallel between Basso's split from the PSI of Pietro Nenni in 1964 (in protest against the party's participation in a center-left government led by the reformist Christian Democrat, Aldo Moro) and the present situation. Basso created the PSIUP (Socialist Party of Proletarian Unity), which subsequently split into several factions, some of which joined the PCI, while others linked up with such new-left groups as the PdUP (Party of Proletarian Unity) or DP (Proletarian Democracy).

However, if Del Turco saw himself as a contemporary Nenni, he was assuming that the bulk of the party would follow him into a broad center alliance and that such an alliance would have the potential to form a government. He was wrong on both counts. First, as had already become clear, the party was not behind him. The *craxiani* continued to follow their own path, which would lead them ultimately towards the new right-wing alliance formed under Silvio Berlusconi in early 1994, while many of those who might have backed Del Turco had either already left or now had only one foot in the PSI and the other in another camp; and of these, only some (as in the case of Giugni and Spini) shared Del Turco's predilection for the Democratic Alliance and even they were more favorably disposed than Del Turco towards the PDS. Second, as the year wore on and Segni parted company with the Democratic Alliance (returning, with his *Popolari per la riforma*, to the Catholic center-right), it became clear to those already in the Democratic Alliance that they did not have governing potential and that the logic of a single-ballot, first-past-the-post system required *them* to forge an alliance with Occhetto's PDS. Indeed, many had been made uncomfortable by the presence of Segni in the organization, and would find the company of the secular Left much more amenable. In turn, Segni's departure allowed the PDS leadership of Occhetto and Massimo D'Alema to reconsider their reluctance to forge an alliance with the political center and narrowed Del Turco's strategic choices to one — alliance with the PDS within a larger center-left electoral confederation.

Meanwhile, the PSI continued to be buffeted by further revelations of corruption involving Craxi and Martelli, and in November and December, both admitted for the first time to receiving illicit funds.[15] By year's end, after a clumsy attempt by the *craxiani* to undermine Del Turco, a fundamental split in the party had become inevitable. In the first week of

November 1993, Benvenuto guided the "Socialist diaspora" towards the PDS when one thousand Socialists met to constitute the *Unione dei socialisti verso l'unità dei progressisti* (Union of Socialists towards the Unity of Progressives). And by mid-December, Del Turco had no alternative but to follow them, accompanied by his supporters and the old *martelliani* (Del Bue, Mario Rafaelli, Mauro Sanguineti and Francesco Tempestini), a handful of former *craxiani* (Formica, Dell'Unto, Nicola Capria and Silvano Labriola), and the *Circolo Rosselli* group led by Valdo Spini and Gino Giugni. With Bettino Craxi went Intini, Andò, Boniver, Paolo Pillitteri and Franco Piro, plus Di Donato, De Michelis, Marzo, Claudio Signorile and Felice Borgoglio. Henceforth, there were two "PSI's", two parliamentary groups and two leaders of Socialist deputies: Franco Piro headed the largest group (which was still faithful to Craxi) while Nicola Capria led the smaller one backing Del Turco. The constituent assembly of Del Turco's new "party" in mid-January received the imprimatur of Pierre Mauroy, the president of the Socialist International, and 74 percent of the delegates opposed the renewal of Craxi's membership. Some of the *craxiani* now began to gravitate towards Segni's new *Patto per l'Italia* while others began to move further right, towards Berlusconi's *Forza Italia* and Umberto Bossi's *Lega Nord*. This, the fourth schism since 1947, was to terminate the history of the party. The liberal-socialist tradition would henceforth survive only as one current alongside others in the Progressive Alliance.

From Unity of the Left to Progressive Alliance:
Occhetto and the Communist Metamorphosis

Occhetto's strategy of steering the PCI towards a new era in the form of the social-democratic PDS has been variously described as opportunistic, as a class betrayal or as a qualified success given circumstances beyond his control. For Tobias Abse, articulating the position of the left-wing breakaway party, *Rifondazione comunista*, Occhetto aspired not to an overtly reformist moderate party of labor, firmly linked to the trade unions, but rather to a "nebulous leader-centered inter-class coalition." In this view, the PDS/PCI betrayal of the Left was revealed in its decision to back the austerity policies of the Amato and Ciampi governments and in its joining with center-right Catholics such as Mario Segni in the "Yes" camp in the referendum campaign for electoral reform.[16] For Stephen Hellman, however, Occhetto's greatest sin was a lack of vision, a tendency to stride forth boldly into the future with no clear sense of direction: "With no broad social movements to feed a new political force, the transformation Occhetto hoped to carry out merely euthanised the old party and then revealed that the leadership of the new party really did not have a very clear idea of what it wanted."[17] But for Michele Salvati, Occhetto's "strategy" was dictated by contextual developments and by his own party's entrenched position in the consociational structures of the First Republic. Thus the PCI/PDS could neither make the critical break with the status quo nor champion the "moral revolution." Instead it was the *Lega Nord* that became the driving force for change and the PDS that had to respond, however clumsily, to the cataclysmic events of the early 1990s. Given the pace of change and the immobilism and division within the PCI/PDS, Salvati concludes that it was a minor miracle that the schism produced by the *svolta* created a mainstream social-democratic force with some 16 percent of the vote and a party the size of the French Communists on the left (in the form of *Rifondazione*).[18] In this interpretation, Occhetto can be seen as a relatively skillful steward of an ineluctable transition.

Moreover, given the disappearance of Craxi and the PSI as a credible force for left-wing renewal, by early 1993 Occhetto had the opportunity to push forward the transformation of his own party within a broader project for the Left as a whole. Not only did he now have the political space in which to do this (the PDS had become the only pole of attraction for other left-wing forces after years of vying with the Socialists) but by early 1993 his was the only establishment party in Italy with its national organization still intact. This was to prove invaluable in forging new, experimental alliances during the year as a testing ground for the future Progressive Alliance. Indeed, I would argue that Occhetto proved to be a much more acute tactician during this critical year than he is usually believed to be.

The year began with Occhetto facing two major problems: how to govern the party and how to respond to the new imperative of alliance formation. By 1993, democratic centralism was dead and the previously monolithic PCI was by now irremediably divided into factions that were able to go their different ways and engage in independent tactics of alliance (indeed, some twenty PDS deputies had already joined the centrist Democratic Alliance).[19] To those on the left of the PDS, such as Pietro Ingrao, Occhetto's talk of "party pluralism" and a "third way" was close to heresy. Already in mid-1992, Occhetto had launched the second phase of the PDS *svolta*, promising an end to the traditional cadre system and a thorough-going response to the recent revelations concerning PDS corruption.[20] And as Occhetto declared to the PDS National Assembly in Rome in the last week of March 1993,[21] "I believe neither in a leader-centered party nor in an oligarchic party but rather in a third way between democratic central-ism and factionalism." As yet, it was unclear just what this form of organization would look like, but Occhetto did describe "a brain trust for developing projects and programs" and outlined the search for what he termed a "decentralised centralism" (in a dreadful disclosure of his desperation to bridge old and new); this "decentralized centralism" would involve the regional secretaries in "a political and cultural collegial unit that would reconsider the very notion of the center and would genuinely include a multiplicity of forces in the center of the party." Mauro Zani, the Emilian leader in charge of party organization, stated clearly that the PDS now rejected its traditional, Leninist form of organization: "We are well aware of the fact that the era of the so-called party-apparatus is over. In fact we intend to work from the premise, with courage and the necessary radicalism, that the entire tradition of organization practiced during the postwar period has largely exhausted its utility." He was careful to add, however, that while the party must engage in far-reaching reform, this must not push the party to the point of disarray: A degree of internal party discipline was still required, as suggested by Occhetto himself.[22]

This was an important qualification, for it betrayed the extent to which "party form" was becoming a critical element in the strategic debate that, by spring 1993, was dominated by discussions of alliance. At this stage, the PDS leadership had still to appreciate the extent to which a successful alliance would require it to abandon the old notion of "left-wing unity" (led by itself) in favor of an alliance of forces with no single, predominant member and would require it to replace outdated hierarchical structures with a confederal form of organization. To date, the party's alliance strategy had not exacted such sacrifices. Thus, the alliance with Segni and his electoral reform movement against the old order of the CAF (Craxi-Andreotti-Forlani) coalition[23] had not only been tactically successful (it had allowed the PDS to attack the institutions of the First Republic despite its extensive participation in them through parliamentary committees and local coalitions); but it had also left the internal structures of the PDS undisturbed. In early 1993, Occhetto hoped to continue on this path, and the best way of doing so was through the adoption of an electoral system like that used in France, where two rounds of voting allow parties to engage in alliances without surrendering their autonomy. As Occhetto declared at the March National Assembly, "The real problem is to create a greater distinction between the level of the party and that of democratic alliances and progress in representation. The parties with greater strategic responsibilities and wider electoral alliances [may serve] as the meeting point of different ideas."[24] It was clear that in Occhetto's vision, the party and the alliance would come together after the first ballot and before the second run-off ballot.

Even though Occhetto worked hard in favor of the adoption of a two-round, first-past-the-post system, by early May the PDS was virtually the only major force left supporting it. And when it came to the vote in mid-June, the two-round option was heavily outvoted in the Chamber of Deputies by 383 to 134. The PDS had struck an agreement with most Republicans, the Greens, the Liberals and some Socialists, while ranged

against the two-round camp were the DC, the *Lega Nord*, almost all of the
PSI (the *craxiani* outnumbered the supporters of Benvenuto — who had
backed the PDS — in the Chamber of Deputies), *Rifondazione comunista*, the
neo-Fascist MSI and the Social Democrats. The June vote in the Chamber
was an important defeat for Occhetto and others seeking a thoroughgoing
overhaul of the political system that would also make the country more
governable. Not only did it mean that Occhetto had now to revise his
conception of the relationship between parties and alliances (for pre-
electoral pacts would now be essential, making party distinctions more
difficult to defend). But, in addition, as Michele Salvati points out, the new
rules approved in August[25] were likely to "magnify the localistic tendencies that are splitting the country: it is a gift for the *Lega* which will obtain
most of the 75 percent, first-past-the-post MPs in the North, and a gift for
the local 'barons' in the South, who will run under any banner, DC, PSI or
whatever (local) list suits them best."[26]

The spring and early summer had been a difficult time for Occhetto.
Opinion polls indicated that the PDS was losing support to *Rifondazione
comunista* on its left. *Rifondazione* had managed to bolster its support in the
labor movement by branding the PDS leader of the CGIL, Bruno Trentin,
an enemy of the working class after he backed the abolition of what
remained of the Italian system of wage indexation (the *scala mobile*) in
1992;[27] and also by attacking the PDS's endorsement of the austerity
policies pursued by both the Amato and Ciampi governments. *Rifondazione* banners dominated the demonstrations in the early part of 1993 that
challenged the authority of the main union confederations and attracted
support from the *Rete* and left-wing Greens.[28] Then in May, the PDS was
split over participation in the new Ciampi goverment (Occhetto was in
favor but his deputy, Massimo D'Alema, was against). The division was
only resolved when its ministers — Vincenzo Visco at Finance, Augusto
Barbera at Parliamentary Relations and Luigi Berlinguer (the cousin of
Enrico Berlinguer) at University Education and Scientific Research —
were withdrawn after just ten hours, ostensibly in protest at Parliament's
defense of Craxi's political immunity from prosecution.[29] But worse was to
come in the form of potentially highly damaging corruption allegations in
the second week of May[30] and the simultaneous departure of Pietro Ingrao,
the leader of the party's left wing, who declared that the party was a
"political mutation" of its former self and was no longer his political home.
An exodus of his faction (around a third of the party's base) was expected
at first; but while thirty trade unionists in the Democratic Communist
faction exited with Ingrao, most of his supporters have stayed with the
PDS.

Occhetto's battered leadership was given a reprieve with the party's
success in the partial municipal elections held on June 6 and 20. Indeed, this

triumph may well have prevented the anticipated hemorrhage of left-wing membership. Held under the new rules approved in March — which introduced a popular vote for mayor in towns of more than 15,000 people — these elections stipulated a second-round run-off between the two leading candidates in the mayoral race (if no candidate received a majority in the first round) and provided the PDS with a useful testing ground for its alliance strategy. Involving a roughly representative sample of the electorate (covering some 11 million voters in 1092 towns, six provinces and the entire region of Friuli-Venezia Giulia), the elections confirmed the growing strength of the *Lega Nord* (it became by far the largest party north of the Po). The municipal elections also demonstrated the tenacity of the PDS, which, despite the recent corruption revelations, managed to act as a rallying point in the Center and South, forging alliances with a variety of local partners including the Republicans, the Greens, the *Rete* and Segni's referendum movement. The PDS, with its partners, took 73 of the 145 mayoralties contested. These results proved beyond any doubt not just the utility of alliance formation but, given the advances made by the *Lega*, its absolute necessity.

But alliances with whom and on what basis? Regardless of the success of electoral partnerships in June, the formation of broader coalitions was still fraught with problems through much of the second half of the year. The greatest problems for the PDS derived from its relationship with the Democratic Alliance and Segni's reform movement on its right and with *Rifondazione* on its left. Relations with the PSI, the *Rete* and the Greens were by no means unproblematic, but ultimately they proved simpler to resolve. In essence, these problems stemmed from two issues of dispute: the full abandonment by the PDS of any hegemonic pretensions on the Left, allowing for an alliance of "equals"; and a dampening of ideological distinctions sufficient to develop a program for government, as now required by the new single-round, first-past-the-post electoral system in place for three fourths of the parliamentary seats.

To turn first to the forces to the right of the PDS, at the start of the year, relations between Occhetto and the Democratic Alliance were close, as were those between Occhetto and Mario Segni. But during the second half of the year, the situation became more complex. In May, Segni announced the creation of his new *Popolari per la riforma* party — having abandoned the DC earlier in the year — and after the June elections Segni held talks with the Democratic Alliance, which led to their merger in mid-July. Already in June, a rift had opened up between Occhetto and Segni: Once the cement of common membership in the "Yes" camp on electoral reform had disappeared, the incompatibilities of their respective projects became clear. Occhetto now saw Segni as a competitor seeking to build and lead a new aggregation of forces, linking his reformist Catholics to former members of the old secular center and the liberal Left. Indeed, when Segni invited the PDS to dissolve itself in a large center-left, reformist alliance, Occhetto was dismissive and curt, arguing that this was "a little like Craxi when he said 'we represent socialist unity.' This is a completely erroneous way of thinking. And we won't accept it."[31]

The rift between Segni and Occhetto was extremely disappointing for those PDS leaders who were already playing a prominent role in the Democratic Alliance (AD) alongside former Socialists and Republicans. It was especially so for Augusto Barbera, the principal PDS figure in the referendum movement and a close collaborator of Segni. Tensions between the latter and Occhetto meant that an embittered Barbera was unable to take his place in the AD's new coordinating committee in July. Fearing for the future of the center-left coalition, he declared that "Segni and Occhetto have not yet understood the opportunity they have to sustain the unity that made the referendum movement so successful. They thus end up encouraging those in the AD who want to create a modest "fourth pole" and those in the PDS who still dream of an impossible unity of the old Left."[32]

Barbera had touched on the most sensitive issue as far as the PDS was concerned: its inclination to think in terms of a unity of the Left formed and led by itself, a project that the demise of the PSI had made much more realistic. But Barbera was also guilty of wishful thinking. Given the confessional character of Segni's *Popolari*, they made unlikely bedfellows for either the PDS or the liberal-socialists in the AD camp. As Giuliano Amato remarked in late May, Segni's natural home lay with the other reformist forces emerging from the carcass of the DC: "He should now stay with Martinazzoli. Segni's political trajectory came to an end with the electoral law. He cannot present himself as the exponent of Catholic culture, nor can he be the expression of neo-Marxism."[33] Amato's prescience was proven in the autumn when Segni opened a dialogue with Mino Martinazzoli (then the DC secretary and in January founder of the DC's successor, the *Partito Popolare*), which led to his departure in early October and the subsequent formation of the *Patto per l'Italia.*

Segni's split from the Democratic Alliance was lamented by Augusto Barbera, who mourned the failure of "virtuous partnership" on the center-left, suggesting that Segni had succumbed to "strong pressures from the Church hierarchy."[34] But as it turned out, Segni's departure was to facilitate a potentially more durable "virtuous partnership" between the AD, the PDS and other forces on the Left. The fact that a dialogue between these forces had continued regardless of the mutual distrust between Occhetto and Segni had clearly contributed to the latter's decision to leave. Many in the AD believed that the future of the movement would be brief without PDS involvement, although they were concerned about a simultaneous improvement of relations between Occhetto and *Rifondazione*. Segni's departure also encouraged former Socialists whose membership in the AD had been conditional on a *rapprochement* with the PDS. One indicator of the gradual coalescence of forces around the PDS emerged from the *Festa dell'Unità* in late August and the first fortnight of September. Del Turco signalled his movement towards the PDS by making the important symbolic step of becoming the first Socialist secretary ever to attend a PCI/PDS *Festa*, although he made clear his concern that there should be no alliance with *Rifondazione*. In mid-September, Occhetto delivered a speech that declared "Yes to Alliance but not in the center" and that produced a positive reaction from most of the leading figures in the AD and outright enthusiasm from the left-wing Greens. Simultaneously, Occhetto was holding talks with representatives of *Rifondazione* (principally Armando Cossutta and Lucio Magri) on an accord; important differences persisted, however, including the fact that the PDS and *Rifondazione* were competitors in the forthcoming Rome election, the former backing the leading Green politician, Francesco Rutelli, and the latter Renato Nicolini.

Nothing could be achieved while Segni remained inside the Democratic Alliance. Once he had left, Occhetto moved quickly to dispel any lingering anxieties among his potential allies. Del Turco's Socialists were still pulled in two directions and initially applauded Segni's departure from AD because there was now the possibility of an alliance among his *Popolari per la riforma*, the PSI, the lay parties, Marco Pannella and the ecologists in a sort of "third force" that would "find a place in the clearly progressive area between the PDS and the DC."[35] However, this scenario was unlikely given the collapse not just of the PSI but also of the other parties of the lay center. Both the Republicans and the Liberals — or, rather, what remained of them — were already split between pro-Segni and pro-PDS camps, and the fears of the latter concerning Occhetto's intentions were alleviated in mid-October when he made clear his commitment to an alliance of progressive forces extending from the center to the left and declared his willingness to abandon the PDS symbol when contesting elections. Leoluca Orlando — who had stated in the summer that "the dream of the *Rete* is to disappear into a progressive pole that will be a greater *Rete*" — was also reassured.

The one remaining doubt of the centrists and Socialists concerned the relationship between the PDS and *Rifondazione*. By contrast, Orlando's *Rete* and the Greens would refuse to join any broad alliance that did not include *Rifondazione*. Early in 1993 some observers speculated that a further schism could divide the former Communists due to tensions within *Rifondazione* between Lucio Magri and the former PdUP/Ingrao left on the one hand and hard-line traditionalists such as Armando Cossutta and Lucio Libertini on the other. Under different circumstances these tensions might have produced a new party to the left of the PDS spanning the Ingrao current in the PDS, the Magri current in *Rifondazione*, and possibly the left-wing Greens (originally in Proletarian Democracy) and part of the *Rete*. However, the new imperatives of alliance formation under the new electoral laws made this outcome much less likely, regardless of increased tensions within *Rifondazione* arising from Cossutta's ejection of Sergio Garavini from the party leadership in mid-1993 and his virtual imposition of Fausto Bertinotti (leader of the CGIL current *Essere sindacato*) as his successor. These events provoked considerable discontent among members of the party who had once been part of the *Manifesto* group, led by Luciana Castellina and Lucio Magri; and Garavini's replacement by Bertinotti seemed to indicate an increasing antipathy in the party towards the PDS. Indeed, discussing their support for Ciampi's new austerity package in mid-September, Bertinotti referred to Occhetto and D'Alema as "the new nephews of Craxi."[36] However, by late December the leadership line in *Rifondazione* had switched to one of full approval for alliance with the PDS, a strategic U-turn that Cossutta described as "an historical obligation."[37] Given the new facts of life created by a strongly majoritarian electoral system, the phrase "historical necessity" might have been more appropriate.

Two developments accounted for *Rifondazione's* change of heart and for the PSI's and AD's acceptance of *Rifondazione* as a member of the Progressive Alliance: the results of the local elections in December and the emergence of *Forza Italia*, the new populist force on the right led by media magnate Silvio Berlusconi. The election results confirmed the role of the PDS as the one organized force able to rally the Left and provide it with national organizational support — a fact that *Rifondazione* was now also forced to acknowledge. The PDS and its electoral allies made a clean sweep of the six major cities where polling occurred (Genoa, Naples, Rome, Trieste, Venice and Palermo) and in the 129 towns with over 15,000 inhabitants, they captured 53 administrations. The PDS had firmly staked its claim to be the central force in a broad leftist alliance that would fight the next general elections. That claim had already been advanced by Occhetto in November in a speech that signalled a number of important strategic revisions: the acceptance of the need for a broad alliance rather than a unity of the Left in which other groups would be merely satellites of the PDS; the confirmation that such a broad alliance should confer equal respect on both small and large forces; the end of the PDS's previous suspicion of moderates in the center; the acceptance of a common symbol (a point already conceded in September); and the abandonment of attempts at control by a narrow party apparatus.[38] The PDS claim was now bolstered by the launching of Berlusconi's *Forza Italia* and the prospect that *Forza Italia* might form an alliance for government with the two other

populist forces on the right, the neo-Fascist MSI (which had also performed well in the December elections) and Umberto Bossi's *Lega Nord*.

Conclusions

Occhetto's success in wooing into electoral wedlock his former opponents on both left and right was in large part the product of fortunate
circumstances, not inspired strategy. After all, the PDS was still clearly
responding to history rather than making it. But Occhetto had also proved
to be insightful and astute in appraising a rapidly evolving situation and
in assessing how best to bend to his advantage developments that eluded
his full control. In retrospect, Occhetto's expression of antipathy toward
Segni after the latter forged his pact with the Democratic Alliance in July
turned out to have been an intelligent maneuver, although at the time it
was seen by many — including a number of key figures in the PDS itself —
as a potentially costly tactical error. Squeezed uncomfortably between
the new right-wing alliance and the Progressive Alliance on the left, it
appeared in early 1994 that it was instead Mario Segni who had miscal-
culated.

Even though the Progressive Alliance and the PDS rose rapidly in the
opinion polls after forming the new pact in late January, this support was
quickly eroded in subsequent weeks by the sudden surge in popularity for
Berlusconi's new movement. But such fluctuations represented conjunc-
tural difficulties. Of longer term significance are the structural problems
of the Progressive Alliance. The reinvention of the Left is still far
from completion. Indeed, in early 1994 the Alliance resembled a hastily
prepared prototype betraying the rather awkward compromises struck
by those involved in its assembly. The main compromise concerns
ideology, although practical matters such as the allocation of candidates
have created the immediate grounds for contention among the partners.
The Alliance's "declaration of intent" presented in the first week
of February 1994 managed skillfully to paper over divisions on policy
by accommodating the preferences of all of its partners. Its six main
points were: a democratic pact based on a "closer relationship between
rights and needs"; a redistribution and decentralization of power to
produce a new balance between national unity and local autonomy; the
promotion of growth while restoring the health of public finances; efforts
to create employment and safeguard the cultural and environmental
heritage; a commitment to make the economy more dynamic, combatting
the abuse of the welfare state and modifying public intervention, if
necessary through privatization; an attempt to moderate the impact of
austerity policies by spreading sacrifices widely and by protecting the

poorest in society; and the building of a society cleansed of corruption in which the public role of education, training, health and social services is strengthened, and economic growth balanced with ecological protection.[39]

Apart from the obvious contradictions (tackling Italy's massive public sector debt would be difficult if one simultaneously were to strengthen social services and education), the vagueness of the charter reveals not only the obstacles to overcoming the ideological divisions within the progressive camp, but also the more general difficulties facing the Left everywhere in Europe as it attempts to preserve social democracy in a hostile climate. The task of the opponents of the Progressive Alliance — united by both their populism and their common cause of economic liberalism and rigor — is far simpler. Although they too may fall out over disputes of territory and list allocations, their ideological distinctions are easier to reconcile and their policy prescriptions will conform with, rather than resist, the pressures coming from the international economic environment. In sum, they may prove to be the "natural party of government" in hard times.

The key tensions in the progressive camp will appear between the PDS and its allies to the right and the *Rifondazione* and Greens on its left. It is unclear how long the new left and far left can accommodate themselves to a program for the economy that, in essence, differs little from that of the Amato and Ciampi governments. Indeed, the PDS now prides itself on its early commitment to privatization and will seek to bolster its reputation further as a party able to calm the jitters of the money markets. After the December elections, Occhetto launched a "charm offensive" to convince the national and international business communities of his party's "capital-friendly" character, making a commitment to help Prime Minister Ciampi secure the passage of the 1994 budget and arguing that the economy could be revitalised without increasing debt levels by selling off state assets worth some L30,000 billion. If they come to power, however, the PDS and its partners in the Alliance will be faced with some highly unpopular choices and may well have to implement further cuts in welfare state spending and witness an increase in unemployment. In that event they will also have to respond to increasing social unrest. We have seen this scenario before: This is precisely what occurred in France after Mitterrand's U-turn in economic policy in 1984, which provoked the departure of Communist Party ministers from the cabinet. In similar circumstances in Italy, it is hard to imagine how *Rifondazione* — and perhaps also the *Rete* and the Greens — could do otherwise.

The knowledge that the Alliance may prove fragile once in power — and the exploitation of this issue by Berlusconi's media circus — will certainly contribute to its electoral problems. But there are other difficulties, chief among them being the return of the PCI's `consociational' past to haunt Occhetto and his comrades. By the end of 1993, 112 *pidiessini* had fallen afoul of the corruption investigations. In October 1993, Bettino Craxi began to collaborate with the *"Mani pulite"* magistrates in order to ensure that his own allegations against the PDS were fully publicized and investigated.[40] Craxi's allegations ranged from claims that the PDS had drawn illicit financing from public works and transport contracts in Milan, through to accusations that the PDS had received extensive funding from Moscow until the late 1980s and had established a counter-intelligence network in Italy linked to the KGB. Given Craxi's grudge against the PDS leadership, many of these allegations could prove to be groundless. Nonetheless, as more testimony from a variety of sources is becoming available, especially regarding the financing of the party from the cooperative movement and from other business sources (as part of deals involving the other establishment parties) the involvement of sections of the PCI/PDS in the spoils system of "partycracy" appears irrefutable. These revelations will complicate, burden and perhaps delay the process of renewal and unification that the PDS and its partners have initiated. Before it can reinvent the Left, the PDS may have to go considerably further in reinventing itself.

Notes

1. S. Hellman, "The Difficult Birth of the Democratic Party of the Left," in S. Hellman and G. Pasquino, (eds.), *Italian Politics: A Review, Volume 7* (London: Pinter, 1992), p. 68.

2. See M. Rhodes, "The 'Long Wave' Subsides: The PSI and the Demise of *Craxismo*," in S. Hellman and G. Pasquino (eds.), *Italian Politics: A Review, Volume 8* (London: Pinter, 1993) pp. 66-82.

3. On the corruption scandals see Donatella della Porta's chapter in this volume and her "Milan: Immoral Capital," in S. Hellman and G. Pasquino (eds.), *Italian Politics: A Review, Volume 8* (London: Pinter, 1993), pp. 98-113.

4. See G. Baget Bozzo, "Il rifiuto di Bobbio," *La Repubblica*, March 31, 1993. As Baget Bozzo points out, the *craxiani* were still trying to advance their own malevolent agenda: "This group wished that the judges be disarmed, that the immunity of politicians be sustained and that the extent of wrongdoing should provide the moral and legal basis of this immunity."

5. *La Repubblica*, March 19, 1993.

6. The Chamber of Deputies authorized the lifting of immunity on only two of the six requests, those concerning corruption in Rome and violation of the laws on party financing. The Milan magistrates believed that the Parliament exceeded its rights in rejecting the other requests, including corruption and receiving illicit funds in Craxi's political base of Milan. Led by Francesco Saverio Borelli, Milan's chief public prosecutor, the magistrates decided to fight the Parliament's decision not to lift the immunity of Craxi.

7. See below for the implications for the PDS.

8. *La Repubblica*, July 15, 1993.

9. The ENI affair is a complex one, involving multiple deals and covert kickback arrangements that have been linked to other public sector companies such as ENEL. Before committing suicide in the third week of July (after 133 days in prison) Cagliari admitted to knowing about at least L50 billion worth of illicit funding channelled through ENI and its subsidiaries to the Socialist and Christian Democratic parties. Former ENI finance director, Florio Fiorini, informed Italian magistrates that ENI had channelled L1.2 billion per annum to the DC, PSI, Liberals and Social Democrats throughout the 1970s and L40 million a month to the DC and PSI in the 1980s. ENEL was also linked to illicit Socialist Party funding by the testimony of Valerio Bitetto, who says he was placed by Craxi on the ENEL board to procure bribes. The ENEL connection also brought down Franco Nobili, who was forced to resign as the chairman of IRI, the state holding company, after his arrest in mid-May for allegedly helping arrange a L600 million payment to the Socialists arising from an ENEL contract.

10. *La Repubblica*, June 5, 1993.

11. Having always aspired to the PSDI leadership, Vizzini was forced to resign after ten months in post. (His father had been a close collaborator of Giuseppe Saragat, the founder of the PSDI after splitting with Nenni's Socialists in the late 1940s.) Vizzini found that the rent for the PSDI's headquarters had not been paid for years and that, with debts amounting to L20 billion, public funding for the party had been going straight to the PDSI's largest creditor, the Banco di Napoli. On May 1 he was succeeded by Marco Ferri, who became secretary of an ex-party.

12. The others were Valdo Spini at Environment and Gino Giugni at Labour.

13. Cited in *La Repubblica*, July 20, 1993.

14. *La Repubblica*, June 24, 1993.

15. In June, magistrates informed Craxi and Franco Castiglione, a Socialist senator, that they were under investigation for allegedly receiving L360 million passed on via intermediaries from Craxi's long-standing adversary Olivetti, for the supply of information equipment to the Justice Ministry in the early 1990s. But the most damning indictments have emerged from the Montedison/Enimont affair. In July, testimony from Giuseppe Garofano, a former chairman of Montedison, and from two other former executives of the Ferruzzi group, Carlo Sama and Giuseppe Berlini, revealed that kickbacks worth L130 billion were handed over to leading politicians at the time of the Enimont breakup. Craxi allegedly received L75 billion and Arnaldo Forlani (then secretary of the Christian Democrats) L35 billion. L20 billion was said to have been divided between Paolo Cirino Pomicino (also of the DC), Claudio Martelli and others including Vincenzo Palladino, a vice-president of the Banca Commerciale Italiana and a Socialist appointee. Palladino held shares in Montedison while Raul Gardini, the Montedison chairman, and the politicians negotiated ENI's purchase of Montedison's 40 percent stake in Enimont at an inflated price, from which Gardini is alleged to have paid at least L120 billion in bribes, mainly to the Socialists and Christian Democrats.

In mid-December 1993, while giving evidence in the trial of Sergio Cusani, the consultant close to the PSI (who is accused of bribery and corruption and helping to falsify the Montedison group's accounts), Martelli admitted to illicitly receiving

L500 million from Carlo Sama (formerly managing director of Ferruzzi-Montedison). Sama admitted giving money to Martelli and surprised the court by saying that he had also given between L5 billion and L7 billion to Bettino Craxi for the party's 1992 parliamentary election campaign. In the same week, Milan magistrates asked that Craxi be sent for trial along with twelve others on corruption charges relating to a L17 billion insurance deal, involving a carve-up of the lucrative insurance business covering the 130,000 employees of ENI in favour of SAI, an insurance company controlled by Salvatore Ligresti, the Milanese construction magnate. Craxi was described as one of the main instigators of the deal. A week earlier, Craxi had admitted while giving testimony in the Cusani trial that he had been fully aware of the illicit financing of political parties but denied taking money himself or receiving money from businessmen on behalf of the PSI.

16. See T. Abse, "The Triumph of the Leopard," *New Left Review*, 199, 1993, pp. 3-28.

17. S. Hellman, "The Left and the Decomposition of the Party System in Italy," in R. Milliband and L. Panitch (eds.), *Real Problems, False Solutions: Socialist Register 1993* (London: The Merlin Press, 1993), p. 207.

18. M. Salvati, "The Travail of Italian Communism," *New Left Review*, 202, 1993, 117-124.

19. Led by the PDS deputy from Trieste Willer Bordon, Augusto Barbera, the director of *L'Unità* Walter Veltroni, Claudio Petruccioli and senator Carlo Rognoni, this was a sufficient number to form a separate parliamentary group. Some members of this group wanted to go much further than Occhetto in reforming the PDS. Indeed, Willer Bordon wanted parties in the center and on the Left to dissolve and make the Democratic Alliance the Italian equivalent of the U.S. Democratic Party, thereby ending what he and his colleagues saw as an outdated cult of party and personalized leadership.

20. Occhetto announced the second phase of the *svolta* in an emotional speech made in the People's Hall in the working-class Bolognina district of Bologna on May 29, 1992. The speech was partly a response to news that a warrant had been issued for the arrest of his shadow defense minister, Gianni Cervetti.

21. Like the other establishment parties, the party's finances were in a parlous state. The 1993 National Assembly was the most spartan for many years, costing only L50 million due to PDS debts of around L44 billion.

22. *La Repubblica*, March 28-29, 1993.

23. The so-called CAF alliance of Bettino Craxi, Giulio Andreotti and Arnaldo Forlani originated in spring 1989 and was reaffirmed in summer 1992, before the inauguration of a new government led by Andreotti. The allies had two major objectives: to bolster the power of the Christian Democratic center and right against that of the DC left led by Ciriaco De Mita (the former DC secretary and prime minister who is a long-standing opponent of both Andreotti and Forlani); and to allow Craxi (also an old enemy of De Mita) to extend the influence of the PSI in public-sector management and the state machine while securing his own claim to succeed Andreotti as premier (see Rhodes, *op. cit.*, p. 68).

24. *La Repubblica*, March 28-29, 1993.

25. For details, see the chapter by Richard Katz in this volume.

26. See Salvati, *op.cit.*, p. 119.

27. On the end of the *scala mobile* see the chapter by Richard Locke in this volume.

28. See Abse, *op.cit.*, p. 23.

29. Although the PDS abstained on Ciampi's vote of investiture and once the government was installed the PDS continued to provide Ciampi with its abstentionist support, its absence from the cabinet has probably helped the party to distance itself from the `old regime'.

30. By the summer of 1993, some seventy PDS officials had been accused of corruption, including the former administrative manager of the Turinese PCI, Primo Greganti, who was arrested in February; the secretary of the Neapolitan PDS, Benito Vasca; the party's former administrative director, Renato Pollini; and the head of the PDS-controlled construction cooperatives, Fausto Bartolini. Greganti confessed to raising illicit funds for the PCI when he was a party official in Milan. Pollini and Bartolini were arrested in May in connection with inquiries into alleged kickbacks from the state railways, which were claimed to have gone to the Christian Democrats, Socialists and the PDS. The leader of the PDS in Lombardy, Gianstefano Buzzo, had also been detained and accused of receiving kickbacks linked to thermal energy plant contracts. Testimony from a former ENEL executive, Valerio Bitetto, had implicated the PDS deputy leader, Massimo D'Alema, in the arrangement of kickbacks linked to ENEL contracts in the early 1980s.

31. *La Repubblica*, July 14, 1993.

32. *La Repubblica*, July 16, 1993.

33. *La Repubblica*, May 27, 1993.

34. *La Repubblica*, September 11, 1993.

35. *La Repubblica*, October 3-4, 1993.

36. *La Repubblica*, September 18, 1993.

37. *La Repubblica*, December 23, 1993.

38. See F. Adornato, "E Occhetto approdò alla Seconda Repubblica," in *La Repubblica*, November 7-8, 1993.

39. See *La Repubblica*, February 1, 1994.

40. In October Craxi accused Ugo Pecchioli, the chairman of the Chamber's oversight committee on the secret services, of having run a branch of the KGB in Italy staffed by PCI members. The ensuing "*Gladio rosso*" ("*Red Gladio*") affair has clearly damaged the party. Craxi subsequently made further allegations that a number of PDS officials and politicians had benefitted from the Milanese system of kickbacks, reaped largely from public works and transport contracts. In late January 1994, Angelo Tromboni, the former PCI secretary of the Ivrea federation, was arrested on corruption charges (he was then a manager of companies linked to the *Lega delle cooperative*, the large Italian cooperative organization). Craxi was attempting to prove that the former Communists had received substantial funds from Moscow and illicit financial support through an extensive set of deals involving the party-controlled cooperatives. On February 16, 1994, the Progressive Alliance suffered a heavy blow when Massimo D'Alema was placed officially under investigation by judges in Rome on allegations of illicit party funding through the cooperative network.

6

The Last Year of the Christian Democratic Party

Douglas Wertman

The Christian Democratic Party (DC) billed 1993 as the year that would see the transition from the old to the new DC following Mino Martinazzoli's election as DC secretary in October 1992. Did Martinazzoli's election bring an end to the indecision and conflict that marked intraparty politics after the DC's major defeat in the April 1992 parliamentary elections? Martinazzoli, a long-time member of Parliament and one of the northern leaders of the traditional left faction, was chosen as secretary expressly because of his reputation as an honest politician with "clean hands." While some DC leaders may have supported his election because they believed that cosmetic change would once again be enough, many others turned to Martinazzoli because they believed that real reform was necessary and hoped that Martinazzoli would have the legitimacy to push through reform. The results of his first fourteen months as secretary, however, fell far short of the hopes of those wanting real change; by late 1993, the transition had produced few concrete results.

The difficulties that had faced the DC at the beginning of 1993 — reforming the party, shedding the many DC leaders and officials implicated in the widespread corruption scandals and replacing an old political class with a new one, defining the party's new mission, and developing alliances with other political forces — remained unresolved at the end of 1993. Divisions within the party over the speed and nature of reform and over electoral and governmental alliances, resistance by traditional elites unwilling to relinquish power and to support Martinazzoli's reform efforts, and the hesitant leadership of Martinazzoli all contributed to this lack of progress in shaping a new DC. In late July 1993, in the wake of the poor DC showing in the June local elections, the DC held a much-heralded four-day Constituent Assembly with the goal of propelling the party toward real change. But the follow-up was minimal in the second half of 1993; and the National Congress, which it was hoped would actually bring about and codify real reform of the DC, was postponed from fall 1993 to early 1994. As the postscript to this essay explains, the DC Congress was indeed held in mid-January 1994, and the DC went out of existence. It was replaced by a new Catholic party, the Italian Popular Party (PPI), also headed by Martinazzoli, while a conservative minority of the DC split off to form the new Christian Democratic Center (CCD). It is too early at the time of writing to say how different from the DC or how successful the Popular Party will be.

Martinazzoli, though very thoughtful and well-intentioned, displayed caution, gradualism, and indecision during 1993 in trying to steer a course between the traditional elites who wanted limited change and the most radical reformers who wanted much greater change that would have represented a clean break with the past and removed all the traditional factional leaders from power. Martinazzoli worked to avoid splitting the DC and defined his strategy as one of "reforming without renouncing" the DC's past and of emphasizing the DC's Christian roots and identity. During 1993, Martinazzoli was also required to perform a balancing act within the DC over the equally divisive question of which parties should be the object of DC efforts at alliance in the 1993 local elections, in subsequent parliamentary elections, and in the formation of any future government coalition. As a result primarily of these internal divisions but also because of the standoffish attitude of some other political forces, the DC was largely unsuccessful in forming alliances in the June and November 1993 local elections.

Another important factor in the DC's failure to "reinvent" itself has been its inability to define a new mission and concrete program for the party. The DC's original mission — to be a barrier against communism, to protect and maintain democracy in Italy, and to anchor Italy firmly in Europe and the Atlantic Alliance — is no longer relevant in the post-Cold War world, and the DC has become largely a machine for holding on to power. As Gianni Baget Bozzo has argued, the DC has become a "void" in terms of ideas and programs.[1] In fact, the debate within the DC in 1993 produced few concrete policy proposals. It focused largely on pure politics and abstract discussions of the party's nature rather than on substantive policies or real change.

Of course, Italy's political corruption is also a key consideration. The old political system is in disrepute as one revelation after another since February 1992 has uncovered widespread, systematic political corruption. About 500 Christian Democrats — ranging from top leaders to lower-level officials and including managers from state and private corporations and fully one-quarter of the DC's members of Parliament — have been arrested or notified they are under investigation in the many ongoing judicial inquiries on the kickback, or "Bribe City" (*Tangentopoli*), scandals and on the complicity of political figures with organized crime, in particular the Mafia in Sicily and the Camorra in Naples. Many individuals from the other four parties that have governed Italy for much of the postwar period — the Socialists, Republicans, Liberals, and Social Democrats — have also been implicated, and all four of these parties face the threat of extinction. Nevertheless, more of those arrested or under investigation come from the DC than from any other single party. As by far the largest government party and the "linchpin" of the political system for the entire postwar period, the DC is viewed as having much of the responsibility for this network of bribery and payoffs as well as for the serious economic and social problems of the country and the poor performance of Italy's public services. As a result both of this baggage and the party's failure in 1993 to make real progress in reforming or re-defining itself, the DC saw its electoral support go into free fall in the June and November-December 1993 local elections.

Trends in Christian Democratic Electoral Support

The DC suffered a series of disastrous electoral defeats in the 1992-93 period that took it from one new historic low to another. The suddenness and magnitude of these losses underline the difficulty the party (as the PPI) will have in winning back many of these votes in the absence of substantial intraparty reform and, at this point, possibly even with such reform. Compared to the 34.3% it won in the 1987 parliamentary elections, the DC dropped to 29.7% in the April 1992 parliamentary elections, then to about 20% in the June 1993 local elections, and even further just five months later to only 11% in the November-December 1993 local elections. By late 1993 the DC's electoral strength was less than a third of its support in the 1950s, 1960s, and 1970s and less than half of what it had been as recently as the then historic low reached in the April 1992 elections. The DC's uncontrolled fall in the 1992-93 period offers a stark contrast to most of its electoral history. Between 1963 and 1979, in fact, the DC had the most stable nationwide vote support of any major party in Western Europe, remaining between 38.3% and 39.1%. In 1983, the DC fell to 32.9%, a new postwar low at that time, but from 1983 through 1990 it stabilized in the range of 33%-35%.

In the June and November 1993 local elections, electors voted both for a mayoral candidate (in two rounds) and for a party list for seats in the municipal council (in the first round only).[2] In June 1993, the DC won 18.8% of the vote in the 122 communities with populations of 15,000 or more where elections were held, and its candidates for mayor made the second round runoff between the top two finishers in about half of the races (in 66 communities). However, DC candidates failed to reach the second round in the three largest cities holding elections — Milan, Turin, and Catania — and won the mayoral position in only nine of the 66 communities in which they made the second round; none of these nine were among the largest communities in which the DC had second-round candidates. In the November 1993 local elections — held in 428 communities throughout the country that together have about one-quarter of Italy's electorate — the DC did even more poorly. It won only about 11%, and, of the six largest cities where mayoral elections occurred — Rome, Naples, Palermo, Genoa, Venice, and Trieste — a DC-backed candidate took one of the top two first-round places only in Trieste (and in Trieste the candidate was also supported by the Democratic Party of the Left). The DC, as it prepared for the November elections, proved unable to learn or adapt from its failings in the June elections; in most cases, the DC did not form alliances, it delayed in picking mayoral candidates, and, in the end, it often settled on candidates who were not competitive or even well known in the local community.

What is the import of these trends? In April 1992, despite its losses, the DC remained Italy's largest party by a sizable margin. In June 1993, the DC was still Italy's largest party — though by a much smaller margin than a year earlier. In late 1993, the DC was no longer the single largest party; at best, it appeared to be just one of the four largest parties in Italy. While the June and November local elections were held in only a portion of the country and used an electoral system that differs significantly from the system adopted for the next parliamentary elections, the overall trajectory and the depth of voter rebellion against the DC and the other government parties suggest that these results were much more than just a transitory protest against the DC.

One consequence of these trends was already seen in mid-1993. The DC took the experience of the June local elections very much into account in pushing for the electoral system approved for the Chamber of Deputies in August 1993 and, in particular, in resisting both the two-round system preferred by the Democratic Party of the Left (PDS) and any direct election of the prime minister. In fact, the combination of two rounds and direct election of the mayor — which made for a much more personalized campaign and in many cases left DC supporters with no DC candidate on the second round — had proved disastrous to the DC in the mayoral races because of its inability to ally itself with other parties. When it was approved in August, the one-round system (with 75% of the seats allocated by plurality, single-member district competition and 25% by proportional representation) appeared likely to allow the DC to garner a higher proportion of the seats than in the local elections even if it failed to achieve electoral alliances with other parties. However, the further drop in the November elections — and the January 1994 split into the PPI and CCD — may throw off many of these calculations made by the DC in the summer of 1993.

The results of the November elections have also raised serious questions about the DC's strength in southern Italy, which, before November, was presumed to be the DC's last bastion and the source of a substantial number of DC seats in the 1994 parliamentary elections. Over the past two decades, in fact, the most striking trend in the composition of the DC's electoral support has been its "southernization." This has occurred in most, though not all, elections since 1972, but it took place to a much greater extent in the April 1992 parliamentary elections than in any previous ones.[3] In other words, after those elections — and even after the June 1993 local elections — a much greater share of the DC vote nationwide came from the South than was once true. Prior to the November elections, it appeared that the DC faced no strong alternative for centrist/moderate votes or Catholic votes or even center-right/conservative votes in the South; in contrast, a strong regional party, the Northern League, has taken a large number of votes from the DC and other long-established parties in the last three years to become by far the largest political force in northern Italy.

Therefore, the most important and stunning development of the November 1993 local elections was the degree to which the Italian Social Movement (MSI) — which won the largest share of the votes in both Rome and Naples — undercut the DC vote in the South. In the Rome city council elections, the MSI received 30.9%, compared to only 12.0% for the DC. In Naples, the MSI won 31.2% and the DC only 9.9%. While the MSI has had a pariah status in Italy throughout the postwar era, this is less true in the South than the North, and the absence of a better alternative apparently led a substantial number of those who had previously voted for the DC and the other centrist parties to support the MSI. This balance of forces and the MSI's success in drawing votes away from the DC are unprecedented. In the previous high point of protest votes, the 1972 parliamentary elections, the MSI reached almost 15% in the Rome area and over 18% in the Naples area, but in those elections the DC won about twice as many votes as the MSI in Rome and Naples and maintained roughly the same level of votes it had won in the 1968 parliamentary elections.[4]

Even with this enormous success of the MSI, the DC (now PPI) still appears to be somewhat stronger in the South (or at least parts of it) than in the rest of the country. In fact, the best DC results in the November 1993 local elections were in small and medium-sized towns in the southern regions of Calabria and Campania. Any parliamentary elections held in

1994 will likely yield a further southernization of a much reduced DC (PPI) parliamentary delegation, though this southernization will probably be less pronounced than had been expected prior to the November local elections.[5]

The weight of the South is likely to continue to grow in the DC's (PPI's) parliamentary delegation at a time when DC/PPI leaders in the North — especially those of the reformist wing — are pushing for a greater role in the party in order to bring about change. While there are advocates and opponents of reform in both the North and the South, the most eager, vocal reformers in the party, led by the DC secretary in the Veneto, Rosy Bindi, come predominantly from the North. Some of this pressure has created resentment among a number of DC leaders from the South, and the North-South tensions in the DC/PPI are likely to increase as the reformers in the North see the southern DC/PPI as a drag on its ability to win seats in the North. Whether the dramatic results in the South in the November local elections and this major new threat from the MSI to the southern DC/PPI — most of whose leaders had been relatively complacent about the 1994 parliamentary elections even after the June 1993 local results — will in any way further stimulate reform efforts in the South remains to be seen.

Intraparty Reform

Reform of the DC has been on the party's agenda for almost twenty years. The DC's losses in the 1975 local and regional elections first fixed attention on the question of intraparty reform. Since then, this issue has at times risen in importance and at times receded, but it has never disappeared. Electoral defeats have repeatedly stimulated discussion about reform, but subsequent electoral recoveries, coupled with the continued dominance of the DC by the top factional leaders, have put a damper on real change.[6] In other words, the issue of reform has persisted in the DC since the mid-1970s largely because reform itself has progressed so little. Attempts to reform the DC in the run-up to the April 1992 elections, including the Assembly held in December 1991 to develop a new reform agenda for the DC, yielded few concrete results.[7] Even the drop of 5% in the 1992 elections to a then new postwar low did not catalyze the party to undertake urgent change, but resulted in six months of indecision and internal conflict leading up to the naming of Martinazzoli as party secretary. Moreover, even after the DC elected Martinazzoli, many within the party continued to resist serious reform; in fact, Martinazzoli's initial efforts in November 1992 to reform party institutions were blocked by traditional party leaders.

An effort early in 1993 to work toward basic reform of the party was the new membership drive officially launched on January 23 by Martinazzoli and Franco Marini, the ex-leader of the CISL trade union confederation and ex-minister of Labor chosen by Martinazzoli as the head of the party's organizational department.[8] This was seen as a prerequisite to any fundamental change in the party because of the nature of DC rank-and-file membership, which many believe has long been artificially inflated (not primarily by non-existent "phantoms," but by inactive members who join the party at the behest of a party boss). The incentive for this inflation — and, therefore, the reason for trying to attack this problem — is that the distribution of memberships among different groups or factions determines the selection of delegates to the provincial, regional, and national party congresses that elect the DC leadership at each level. Martinazzoli and Marini, in other words, undertook a complete revision of the membership in order to undercut party bosses who control packets of memberships through patronage. All existing memberships were nullified as of January 1, 1993, and each individual wanting to join the new membership lists of the DC was required to go personally to the local party section (not previously required), sign the party's programmatic statement, and pay the modest membership fee at that time. A list of the members was then to be made public to assure that no one was made a member without his or her knowing it. After the roughly two-month membership drive, DC membership was approximately cut in half, for about 600,000 did not renew their membership. However, this membership drive appears to have been largely ineffective as an instrument of reform. Many of those who refused to re-join the party were apparently the more reform-oriented who quit out of dissatisfaction. In fact, while it is widely believed that the artificial inflation was much greater in the South and a number of studies have shown that fewer southern members are active participants in party life, the exodus was much greater in the North and Center than in the South. In most provinces of the North and Center, at least 60% did not renew their membership, while in the South the non-renewal rate was less than 20%. In a number of areas of the South, the new membership drive never even occurred.

The single most important effort to propel reform of the DC was the Constituent Assembly held from July 23 to 26 in the wake of the very poor DC showing in the June local elections.[9] This meeting was attended by eighty DC members of Parliament, 125 representatives of the provincial and regional party organizations, the twenty DC party group leaders in the twenty regional legislative assemblies, and the members of the DC's National Executive Committee; an equal number (about 225-250) of *esterni* (people from outside the party), most of them from organizations of the Catholic subculture, also participated as voting delegates at the meeting.

This Assembly was preceded by one a few weeks earlier in the Veneto called by the new DC secretary there, Rosy Bindi, a 42-year-old university professor and highly religious Catholic; the Veneto DC proposed profound change, including the removal of not only those under investigation but also all "old faction leaders" (however that was to be defined). Bindi's proposals generated a great deal of opposition and criticism. For example, Gerardo Bianco, the DC group leader in the Chamber of Deputies, said that Bindi's way of refounding the DC is its "destruction."[10] Clemente Mastella, a DC deputy since 1976 and one of the most outspoken southern critics of the northern radical reformers, said, "We are confronted with an unacceptable diktat, a coup d'état inside the DC."[11] The debate at the national Constituent Assembly addressed the reform of the DC, the alliances the party should undertake, and the general concern over the party's survivability. Martinazzoli managed to avoid a split in the party at the national Constituent Assembly; the final resolution he proposed, which represented a compromise between the views of the radical reformers and those of the traditionalists on party reform, avoided a commitment on future alliances with other parties and was approved with only three dissenting votes.

At this Constituent Assembly, Martinazzoli announced that the DC would, following ratification by the Party Congress, change its name to the Italian Popular Party, though he said the party should keep its symbol (a red cross on white with the word *libertas*, or liberty, on it) and its links to its Christian roots. This name change was meant to signal a new DC, but in itself is of limited consequence.[12] The DC has long referred to itself as a popular party, meaning one with mass support drawn from all social classes. Its predecessor party was the Popular Party, which existed from 1919 to 1926. This name change, in other words, is a cosmetic exercise and not the kind of dramatic event that it was for the Italian Communist Party (PCI) when it became the Democratic Party of the Left (PDS); this latter change was coupled with a debate over the party's heritage and program and resulted in the splitting out of the left-wing faction to form a new party named Communist Refoundation, a party that won 5.6% of the vote in the April 1992 elections. Comparing the DC's name change to that decided by the Communists, Martinazzoli said, "they had to renounce their origins, we want to return to ours."[13]

To stress that Martinazzoli's efforts had little effect is not to argue that no change occurred in the DC in 1993. First, many long-time DC leaders are now out of power because they are under investigation by the magistrates for corruption or for complicity with organized crime, and, as a result, many of the old factions are weakened or broken up. Even the factions of some top leaders not now under investigation have been greatly weakened by the corruption investigations of lesser factional leaders. Among the many DC figures under investigation are such important figures as Giulio

Andreotti, Antonio Gava, Paolo Cirino Pomicino, Giovanni Goria, Vincenzo Scotti, Carlo Bernini, Vittorio Sbardella, and Giovanni Prandini. These and many other former DC leaders under investigation were not allowed to attend the DC's Constituent Assembly in July 1993. Most prominent of these is Andreotti, who had come to symbolize the DC's permanence in power and who is now under investigation for collusion with the Mafia. He has been a top figure in Italian governments since the late 1940s, has been prime minister seven times, and led a faction that held fully 18% of the votes at the party congress in 1989. Any analysis of the DC in 1993 cannot fail to note that Giulio Andreotti, whether or not he is guilty of conspiring with the Mafia (a charge he strongly denies), is finished politically and that his faction, losing him and a number of his key lieutenants, is no longer a major force in the DC.

In addition, some new leaders emerged within the DC in 1993. The most well known of these is Rosy Bindi, who became the DC secretary in the Veneto, one of the former strongholds of the DC, after the removal of Carlo Bernini, who is under investigation. Following the departure from the DC in spring 1993 of Mario Segni, a long-time DC deputy from Sardegna who led the reformist referendum movement in Italy, she became the most outspoken and prominent figure within the DC's more radical reform group.

Moreover, the DC — like the other four parties that have governed Italy in the postwar period — has been forced to change the way it operates, to restructure its finances, and to downsize its facilities and permanent bureaucracy. These parties have seen the major source of their funding cut off as a result of the investigations that have ended the widespread use of bribery and kickbacks; this source provided much greater resources than the DC or the other parties could hope to get through regular contributions and the public financing given parties. According to Emilio Rubbi, named DC administrative secretary in mid-1993 as a replacement for Severino Citaristi (the person who has the record so far for the largest number of notices of investigation from the magistrates — more than forty), the DC has rented out the local party headquarters buildings it owns throughout the country and moved into smaller offices, is selling or leasing a large office building on the outskirts of Rome owned by the party, is closing other offices, has sold the party's part ownership of the Naples daily newspaper *Il Mattino*, has cut the number of telephones and cars, and is firing a sizable number of its paid permanent functionaries at the national, regional, and provincial levels.[14]

In sum, change did occur within the DC in 1993: A number of long-time leaders who are now under investigation have been forced out of power, many of the traditional factions have been greatly weakened, and a limited number of Catholics from outside the party have been given leadership positions in the DC. In addition, in response to the corruption scandals, Martinazzoli has put a number of local party organizations under administration by a special commissioner pending the holding of local party congresses and the election of new leadership groups in these local organizations. Nevertheless, as a result of divisions within the party, resistance from party barons, and hesitation by Martinazzoli, fundamental reform of the party has not taken place. The Constituent Assembly did not provide the boost, or jump start, to reform that many had hoped it would. As of late 1993, Martinazzoli had only very sparingly used the special powers to reform the DC that he had been granted at the time of the Constituent Assembly. The downsizing and modification of the DC's National Executive Committee (*Direzione*) in mid-1993 did not eliminate the influence of long-standing party leaders since it continued to allow all ex-party secretaries and all DC ex-prime ministers to be members along with the fifteen new members.

An egregious example of the very slow, halting pace of reform is the fact that the DC national party congress was again postponed from fall 1993 until early 1994, probably in an effort to put off further any showdown over the nature and degree of reform. Under the DC Party Statutes a national party congress, which would determine and formalize major changes in the DC's rules, in its name, and in its leadership group, should be held every two years, but the last one before January 1994 took place in February 1989, which in the current climate of Italian politics seems many light years ago. Thus, at a time when renewal is essential, the DC was by late 1993 nearly three years beyond its own statutory limit for calling a new national congress.

The DC's Alliance Options
in a Redefined Party System

From the late 1940s until the late 1980s, the Italian party system was a very stable one. Voters were offered roughly the same choices from one election to the next, as few new parties (and then only small ones) emerged, and few old parties were eliminated. Furthermore, in most cases, the change in the strength of individual parties was small from one election to the next. In the 1990s, by contrast, the party system is undergoing sweeping change. These changes have forced new choices on the DC.

Apart from the turmoil in the center, the new party system that is now emerging in Italy is marked by three larger parties — the Democratic Party of the Left (PDS) on the left, the Northern League on the right, and the Italian Social Movement (MSI) on the right/far right — and several smaller ones, including the Network on the left and Communist Refoundation, the left-wing splinter from the PDS, on the far left. The PDS has in recent years halted or even reversed the decline it (then the Italian Communist Party) had undergone since the late 1970s. The PDS did well in the June and November 1993 local elections, though its success was to a great extent based on its ability to coalesce with other groups. In fact, the PDS was particularly successful in winning mayoral races (where it formed part of coalitions) but less successful in municipal council races (where it ran alone and actually lost about 3% compared to the 1992 parliamentary elections). The Northern League, which arrived on the political scene only in the mid-1980s and won just 0.5% of the vote in the 1987 parliamentary elections, has come from obscurity in the last five years to be by far the largest party in northern Italy today and, despite its virtual non-existence south of Rome, possibly the largest in the country as a whole. The neo-fascist MSI has seen a major resurgence, especially in the South, in the November 1993 elections; the MSI won a higher proportion of the vote in these elections than in any previous postwar national or major local elections.

By contrast, the center of the Italian political spectrum, which has furnished Italy's ruling parties for the entire postwar period, is in a state of near collapse in late 1993. A variety of old center/center-left/center-right political forces, including the DC, are now fighting for their survival and a number of new forces are trying with very limited success to establish themselves. Four of the traditional government parties — the Socialists (PSI), the Republicans (PRI), the Social Democrats (PSDI), and the Liberals (PLI) — face the threat of elimination in parliamentary elections in 1994 after having won only a handful of votes in the November 1993 local elections. The fifth and largest, the Christian Democratic Party, while not in late 1993 on the edge of extinction, is — at 11% of the vote — much, much weaker than at any time before 1993.

The new centrist forces — Democratic Alliance and Mario Segni's Popular Movement for Reform (*Popolari per la Riforma*) — each won only a small share of votes in the November 1993 elections and show no signs of taking off by themselves as larger political forces. The Democratic Alliance (AD) was created by individuals who come primarily from a number of the center/center-left parties; its adherents include the current party secretary of the Republicans, Giorgio Bogi, some from Catholic associations, several Greens, some dissident Socialists, and even a number of PDS members. Thus far this disparate group, though part of some coalitions (often including the PDS) that have elected mayors, has not been able to get more than a small proportion of the votes for its individual candidates for the municipal councils.

Over the past few years, the top leader of the referendum movement that gave birth to AD was Mario Segni. Segni, a DC deputy since 1976, formed his own group called Popular Movement for Reform in October 1992 and left the DC in April 1993. Since then, Segni has changed his political strategy a number of times. In July, he was one of the founding leaders of AD, in August he opposed an AD alliance with the PDS after flirting with the idea, in early fall he had a seeming reconciliation with Martinazzoli and left AD, and later in the fall he drew back from being too close to the DC. In the November local elections Segni supported common mayoral candidates with AD and the PDS in Rome, Venice, Genoa, and several other places and with AD but not the PDS in Naples. In late 1993, Segni and a number of centrist businessmen and intellectuals launched another political project, called the Pact for Italy (*Patto per l'Italia*), with the hope of getting one million signatures on petitions supporting this movement. Though he is one of the most respected and popular political leaders in Italy today, his personal popularity has not translated into electoral support for his movement, which has so far won only a very small share of the vote. At the same time, in late 1993, Segni is being touted by many as the figure who has the best chance of bringing together a centrist electoral alliance of both old and new political forces, including the DC. The DC, which itself contained a variety of political viewpoints running from center-left through center-right, long chose to locate itself in the center. In mid-1993 Martinazzoli described the DC as a "forward-looking party of the center."[15] Many others, especially on the left, have called the DC a conservative party, but its long-time placement between the Communists on the left and the MSI on the right has helped build the image of the DC as a centrist party. Furthermore, the DC in past elections has always received the votes of a substantial majority of the Italians who view themselves as centrist.[16] This has been very beneficial for the DC because the largest number of Italian voters place themselves in the center of the political spectrum. For example, in a fall 1993 survey, 17.2% of Italians defined themselves as centrist, 16.2% center-left, 11.2% center-right with 15.4% leftist, 6% rightist, and 3% on the extreme left or right; 31% did not answer.[17] While an abstract term such as centrist is not directly translated by the average voter into a voting choice, it is generally indicative of favoring a moderate, non-extremist position. It is clear, moreover, that many Italian voters want a choice other than the PDS, the League, and the MSI. In fact, while this is not to deny that these three parties each have many strong supporters, all three undoubtedly also drew many protest votes that were more a rejection of the DC and the other long-governing centrist parties rather than a convinced, positive choice. Many of these centrist voters have deserted the DC or other centrist parties in 1993 out of dissatisfaction with the corruption in, and poor functioning of, the political system. Whether the DC can regain any of these centrist voters from the PDS, League, or MSI will depend both on how these parties are able to define themselves to the electorate in the future and on whether the DC is able to reform itself and become once again an acceptable choice. It will also depend on the ability of the DC and other centrist forces to form an alliance prior to the next parliamentary elections. A centrist electorate exists as a potential reservoir of support, but the centrist parties remain largely in disarray in late 1993. Other new movements or figures continue to enter the scene, including media magnate Silvio Berlusconi, who, in response to his fears of a leftist victory in the upcoming parliamentary elections, is pursuing the idea of an alliance of the various centrist and even right-wing forces. Given the upheaval in the party system, the question of alliances is ever more pressing for the DC and other centrist political forces. In late 1993, however, the DC to a large extent still found itself politically isolated. Martinazzoli, in looking toward the November elections, got ahead of reality when he declared on October 9 that the DC's "isolation is finished" and on October 16 that "we won't go to the vote alone as we did in the previous local elections."[18] In fact, one of the key factors in the DC's inability in both the June and November elections to win the mayoral positions in Italy's largest cities or even in most of its medium-sized towns was its failure to form electoral alliances with other parties. Though the centrist forces have so far shown no great ability to ally with each other and the current electoral strength of all the centrist forces would still not add up to a great deal, three potential solutions for the center exist: the DC/PPI will form an electoral alliance with some of the other centrist forces (though an alliance that looks like a warmed-over version of the old government coalition would probably be of little benefit, a key reason for having someone like Segni at its head); the non-DC/non-PPI centrist forces will form a bloc separate from and in competition with the DC (a solution preferred by a number of the leaders of Democratic Alliance); or, worst of all for the center, it will remain fragmented.

The other major question about alliances facing the DC and other centrist forces is whether to ally themselves with either the PDS or the League in the next parliamentary elections or in the government formed after those elections — assuming that either of those parties would be interested in such an alliance. Some DC leaders, especially some of the most eager reformers from the North who directly confront the threat from the League, would like to see the DC form an electoral alliance with the PDS in the North to cut into the number of seats won by the League in the plurality, single-member district competition. Through early 1994 Martinazzoli has tried to avoid making a choice, to a great extent because of differences within the DC between the reform wing, which has preferred to ally with the PDS, and the more conservative wing (the bulk of which now constitutes the CCD), which does not want to be forced into an agreement with the PDS. Interestingly, in a September 1993 national survey, DC voters preferred a coalition with the PDS over one with the Northern League by a two-to-one margin.[19]

Conclusion and Postscript

Nineteen ninety-three was a dramatic year for the Christian Democratic Party as it suffered a tremendous fall in its electoral support. And 1993 turned out to be the last year of the DC, Italy's permanent governing party for the past fifty years. The November election results and the impending parliamentary elections put the DC under enormous pressure. In mid-January 1994, the long-postponed DC National Congress was finally held and officially changed the name of the party to Italian Popular Party.

The new Popular Party is a renamed, somewhat purged DC. In fact, many of the top leaders who dominated the DC until recently, including such key figures as Giulio Andreotti and Arnaldo Forlani, were not permitted to attend this congress or to be part of the birth of the new party. Furthermore, a portion of the old DC split away. The conservative wing of the DC, containing roughly 15% of the party leadership, refused to be part of the Popular Party and broke off to form the Christian Democratic Center (CCD). Most important, the CCD, in contrast to the Popular Party, is oriented toward the center-right and possibly even an alliance with some of the forces on the right. This split is understandable — and even predictable — given the intraparty disagreements in 1993 over alliances and reform and given the electoral disasters that befell the party in 1993.

The Popular Party has inherited some advantages from the DC. Foremost among these is that it still has multi-faceted subcultural roots in the Catholic world that provide a core of electoral support and can serve as the source from which a new political class can emerge. The Catholic subculture is clearly a minority force in Italy, and support for the DC from the Church and the Catholic subculture has continued to weaken. Nevertheless, the Popular Party does have this grounding in society that the Socialists, Republicans, Liberals, and Social Democrats lack. Second, its centrist positioning between the PDS on the one hand and the League and the MSI on the other would allow the Popular Party to compete with these parties for votes that the DC once had and that these parties may find difficult to retain, especially if Italy proves ungovernable after the 1994 parliamentary elections and (an even bigger "if") if the Popular Party is seen as actually representing something new and reformed compared to the DC.

The Popular Party — as the successor of the DC — has one major disadvantage that cannot be easily overcome: the DC's substantial share of the responsibility for the massive political corruption and for Italy's serious economic and social problems after nearly fifty years as the permanent government party and the embodiment of the old political system. Surveys have shown widespread dissatisfaction with the DC for more than twenty years, but the end of the Cold War and the uncovering of the pervasive corruption in Italy's political system have unloosened a great number of votes that once went to the DC. A second, related, disadvantage is that the system of patronage that was a key source of the DC's hold on power has been greatly undercut.

The Popular Party faces a series of daunting tasks in overcoming its disadvantages and in exploiting its advantages. In 1993, the DC was unable to resolve these challenges. The Popular Party in early 1994 still has a long way to go both to bring about fundamental reform of the party and to demonstrate to the Italian electorate that it has done so. The Popular Party must also define its mission and a concrete political program. One indication of the deep public cynicism about DC reform efforts that the Popular Party must overcome is found in an early July 1993 national survey of practicing Catholics (a primary source of DC support); fully 71% said they were either "little" (29%) or "not at all" (42%) interested in "the Assembly that will meet in mid-July on the birth of a new party in place of the DC."[20]

The DC in late 1993 was a demoralized, isolated, greatly weakened party as it approached parliamentary elections in 1994. The problems facing it were unprecedented in nature and of a much greater magnitude than ever before. The disastrous losses of the November elections delivered the greatest shock to the DC in its history. Clearly, those municipal elections imposed drastic choices on the DC: They revealed that the DC had to accept and attempt fundamental change if it was to have any hope of continuing to be an important player in the Italian political system. The creation of the Popular Party was the first response. It remains to be seen how different the Popular Party will be from its predecessor and, even if does differ from the DC, whether it can convince sizable numbers of Italian voters, including many within the Catholic world, that the PPI is a new and reformed political force.

Notes

The views expressed herein are those of the author and do not necessarily represent the views of the United States Information Agency or those of the United States Government.

1. Gianni Baget Bozzo, "Politica dello Sturzo," *Panorama*, August 8, 1993, pp. 52-55.

2. See the chapter by Giacomo Sani in this book for further analysis of these elections.

3. Robert Leonardi and Douglas A. Wertman, *Italian Christian Democracy: The Politics of Dominance* (London: Macmillan, 1989), pp. 162-163; Douglas A. Wert-

man, "The Christian Democrats: A Party in Crisis," in Gianfranco Pasquino and
Patrick McCarthy (eds.), *The End of Post-War Politics in Italy: The Landmark 1992
Elections* (Boulder, Colorado: Westview Press, 1993), pp. 19-20.

4. Howard R. Penniman, *Italy at the Polls: The Parliamentary Elections of 1976*
(Washington: The American Enterprise Institute for Public Policy Research, 1977),
pp. 355-363.

5. After the 1992 parliamentary elections, 47% of the DC deputies came from
the South (55% if Rome is included as part of the South).

6. "Real reform" of the DC would have included some or all of the following:
removing all of the DC leaders and members implicated in the corruption scandals;
removing long-time factional leaders from power and eliminating the factional
bases of power in the party; developing a party organization which more easily
allows for an orderly turnover of elites (possibly by eliminating the internal
proportional representation system used for electing the members of party organs); limiting the power of the parliamentary party within the DC organization;
having a more open selection of parliamentary candidates and possibly strict term
limitations; altering the role of the rank-and-file members to encourage active
participation in party life and to enable them to influence key party choices; and
providing for more openness of the party organization to individuals and associations of the Catholic subculture.

7. The reform efforts in the DC in the 1975-1992 period are summarized in:
Wertman, "The Christian Democrats: A Party in Crisis," pp. 12-16; and Leonardi
and Wertman, *Italian Christian Democracy*, pp. 125-136.

8. Information on the membership drive comes from the following sources: *La
Repubblica*, January 15, 1993, p. 11; *Il Messaggero*, January 20, 1993, p. 6; *Panorama*,
April 18, 1993, pp. 36-38; and *Panorama*, September 12, 1993, pp. 57-58.

9. For detailed information on the Assembly, see the *Corriere della Sera*, from
July 23 through July 27, 1993.

10. *Corriere della Sera*, June 12, 1993, p. 5.

11. *La Repubblica*, July 13, 1993, p. 10.

12. Baget Bozzo, "Politica dello Sturzo."

13. *Corriere della Sera*, June 30, 1993, p. 4.

14. *Famiglia Cristiana*, August 25, 1993, pp. 36-37.

15. *Corriere della Sera*, June 15, 1993, p. 5.

16. Leonardi and Wertman, *Italian Christian Democracy*, pp. 181-183.

17. *Famiglia Cristiana*, November 24, 1993, p. 26. For evidence on left-right self-
placement among Italian voters from 1975 to 1985, see Renato Mannheimer and
Giacomo Sani, *Il mercato elettorale* (Bologna: Il Mulino, 1987), pp. 160-169.

18. *Corriere della Sera*, October 10, 1993, p. 7, and October 17, 1993, p. 7.

19. *L'Espresso*, September 26, 1993, p. 50.

20. *Famiglia Cristiana*, July 21, 1993, p. 26.

7

The RAI:
Restructuring and Reform

Gianpietro Mazzoleni

In 1993, in a phase of great transformation of national politics marking the passage from the First to the Second Republic, Parliament approved two laws that decisively influenced the development of the Italian radio and television system. On June 25, the so-called "mini-reform" of the *Radiotelevisione Italiana*, the RAI, was passed (Law No. 206), which revolutionized the criteria for nominating the top management of the public television system. On October 27, another law (No. 422) addressed television licenses, pay television, and advertising. How and why would a political system in its twilight launch a reform of the public radio and television network?

These two legislative measures of 1993, combined with a series of associated administrative acts, put an end to the "period of emergency and urgency in decision making" that began with the approval of the Mammì Law (No. 223 of August 6, 1990, named for the Minister of Posts and Telecommunications at the time). The enactment of the Mammì law opened a turbulent three-year period in the mass communications sector: Since it was devised to address the chaos in broadcasting that fifteen years of non-regulation and unchecked expansion of private television had created, the law dealt with public television only marginally and did not disturb the practice of *lottizzazione*, of subdividing control of public television among parties.[1]

The first logical step in restructuring the RAI was therefore a reform of the Mammì law, which all interested parties urged, if for different reasons. This was an objective of the Ciampi government, which had instituted an ad hoc interministerial committee to formulate a proposal for reform before the end of the year. But other urgent political matters were to prevent the achievement of this aim. And the results of the mayoral elections in Italy's largest cities accelerated steps towards holding early parliamentary elections. Thus, it will be the new Parliament elected in 1994 that — in a radically changed political context — will confront the problem of a global reform of the television system and the new mass media.

The measures that were approved in 1993, however, did begin to resolve several serious political problems that had plagued mass communications — and the RAI above all — for many years, both before and after the passage of the Mammì Law. Of the two laws passed in 1993, the one that attracted the most media attention, probably because of its quite tangible effects on the RAI, was the first, the so-called "mini-reform." I thus direct greatest attention to this law.

The Contents of the Reform

Law No. 206 of June 25 consists of only five articles and for this reason it was identified as a "little law" (leggina) in the jargon of journalists. The first article establishes the juridical nature of the RAI as a joint-stock company of national interest. The second sets the procedures for nominating the Board of Directors of the RAI, the Board's characteristics, and its powers: The number of members is five and they are nominated by the Presidents of the Chamber and of the Senate, as opposed to the previous sixteen who were nominated by a parliamentary oversight committee according to parties' shares of seats in Parliament. The five members can serve no more than two terms and will at any rate be replaced when a new and complete set of regulations for public radio and television services is introduced, which is expected to take effect within two years. The third article stipulates that the Board of Directors nominates the Director-General after having received the non-binding opinion of the IRI (the Institute for Industrial Reconstruction, the giant state holding company in industry and finance and the major shareholder in the RAI); in the past instead IRI had directly nominated the Director-General. The third article also defines the powers, tasks, and responsibilities of the Director-General, who will now report to the Board of Directors and no longer to IRI. In this sense the Board's powers increase and those of the Director-General are reduced, which re-establishes a distribution of power that previous legislation (Law No. 10 of 1985) had abolished in favor of a stronger Director-General. Article Four states that within three months a new agreement between the RAI and the Minister of Posts and Telecommunications must be reached in order to decide the fees for licenses[2] and to raise antenna fees "by an amount not lower than the inflation rate."

The formal, colorless language of the law conceals the truly revolutionary effect of its few but weighty articles. There is no other way to explain why this "little law" had such an arduous journey through Parliament. The story of its passage is full of spectacular scenes, unexpected obstacles, ambushes, showdowns between its opponents and advocates, and thousands of amendments proposed and rejected amid great drama.

The Events Leading Up to Reform

Article 25 of the Mammì Law established that the Board of Directors of the RAI was to be nominated at the start of a legislative term by the parliamentary committee charged with overseeing public radio and television services; and the Board was to serve in office for the duration of the legislature. In other words, the Board's term ended with that of the legislature and each newly elected Parliament was to nominate a new Board. The Parliament that took office after the elections of April 5, 1992, did not proceed to nominate a new Board according to the old rules because of an increasingly evident trend in public opinion: a rejection of the logic and the practices of the old party system.

Signs of this change in public opinion appeared in the debate that preceded the 1991 referendum on the single preference vote and also in the lively expression of views on the corruption scandal and the fall from power of the leaders of the governing parties. The issue of a complete reform of the public radio and television system, which had been left hanging for years, was thus taken up by the new Parliament as the occasion to meet the need to renew the leadership of the RAI. A comprehensive reform would have required an enormous effort and exceptional political will on the part of all parliamentary delegations. And yet, due to a series of dramatic events, it turned out that both effort and will were lacking.

After the April 1992 elections Italy's political parties were increasingly delegitimized by the "Clean Hands" (*Mani pulite*) investigations into corruption.[3] Those political forces that were not involved in the scandals — the Northern League, the Democratic Party of the Left (PDS), and Mario Segni's movement — urged immediate institutional reforms and the holding of new parliamentary elections. Thus, the Parliament dating from April 1992 discovered that, paradoxically, it no longer represented the country that had just elected it. The legislature assumed a provisional and transitional character, both in the perceptions of the public and in the judgment of those political forces most interested in change. In this atmosphere a total reform of the RAI could not realistically be undertaken, and so the Parliament chose a minimalist route: a package of measures addressing the most serious problems, that is, a "mini-reform."

The reform proposals advanced inside and outside Parliament were quite numerous, and they treated other problems in the radio and television system that had been put on hold and were now discussed in Parliament (licenses, pay television and advertising). I do not examine these proposals here, as they have all been superseded by the new law. The ideas put forth included the creation of a guarantee committee that would have contained representatives from the relevant professions (suggested by the USIGRAI, the union of RAI journalists); the partial privatization of the RAI; the naming of a new provisional administrator for the RAI; and the abolition of the parliamentary committee overseeing the RAI.

Whereas most of these proposals did not enjoy success, two bills presented in October 1992 — one by the PDS and the other by the DC — dominated parliamentary deliberations. Each bill stipulated a reduction of Board members to five. The bills differed, however, in their attribution of powers to nominate the Director-General: The PDS proposed that this task be assigned to the Board of Directors, while the DC wanted this responsibility to remain with IRI (for obvious reasons, since IRI was traditionally a DC fiefdom). The two bills, which were soon combined, formed the basis for the long and very arduous parliamentary debate mentioned above. But they became law in June 1993 without substantial change.

This "mini-reform," apparently supported by all political groups, had to face an unprecedented political situation. The RAI, which had always been viewed and used as a crucial resource in party battles, could not be "lost" without its old "owners" (the parties) fighting to prevent attempts at expropriation. The revolutionary aspect of the bill under discussion was in fact its move to deprive the parties of the power to nominate the RAI Board of Directors at the same time that it drastically reduced the number of Board members. In the past the parties' powers of nomination and the large size of the Board had made for an easy partitioning or allotment (*lottizzazion*) of Board posts among party-identified nominees. This bill put the power to nominate the Board of Directors in the hands of the Presidents of the Chamber and Senate, whose institutional responsibilities make them *super partes*. Moreover, the bill stripped IRI — notoriously controlled by the parties — of its power to nominate the RAI Director-General: This was the final blow that severed the traditional and strong umbilical cord between parties and the RAI.[4]

The authority, authoritativeness, and autonomy that the new law grants the Board of Directors render it invulnerable to attacks by the forces inside and outside the RAI who attempt to resist change and reorganization.

The Start of a New Era

Only five days after the approval of Law No. 206, the Presidents of the two Chambers nominated the new Board of Directors. The new rules required that Board members be "chosen from among men and women of recognized professional prestige and of noted independence of conduct, who should be distinguished in business and economics, science, law, the humanities, or in the media, and who bring significant managerial experience to their new post" (Article 1, Section 1). The five names put forward were in perfect accord with these requirements: economist Claudio Demattè, jurist Feliciano Benvenuti, philosopher Tullio Gregory, journalist Paolo Murialdi, and publisher Elvira Sellerio.

Notwithstanding their diverse backgrounds and expertise, the five new Board members had one trait in common: None of them had ever been associated with the RAI in the past. Although all the nominees were officially recognized by the highest institutional powers for their independence from any particular party, it was to be expected that many political commentators in various newspapers indulged themselves in searching for some sort of connection to, or sympathy with, those political parties who had, until the day before, divided the RAI among themselves. The RAI's central place in the national political landscape explained why the nomination of the new Board, of its President Claudio Demattè, and of the Director-General Gianni Locatelli, along with their first acts in office, should have commanded the attention of the mass media for many months.

Without delving into the minute details of the many surprises, reactions, and controversies that followed the "mini-reform" (debates that were far from settled at year's end), the most significant factors that characterize the new era at the RAI can be identified as: (1) the nomination of Locatelli; (2) the presentation of the RAI restructuring plan; (3) the nominations of the directors of RAI channels and of other managers; and (4) the exacerbation of financial problems at the RAI.

Before the Board of Directors nominated the new Director-General, a wide range of players joined an impassioned game of "Director-General Lottery," as the press came to call it. The potential candidates listed for weeks by politicians, journalists and commentators from all camps covered the entire spectrum of Italian public and private entrepreneurs; yet the best qualified was Gianni Locatelli, the manager of the business newspaper *Il Sole 24 Ore* whose candidacy had already been discussed a year before when it seemed possible that an outside emergency administrator would be named to manage the RAI. The choice of Locatelli proved wrong the idea that the winning candidate would be an "insider," that is, a RAI manager promoted to the top, which would have pleased many within the RAI. But what became known as the "Locatelli case" developed after the nomination. The new Director-General soon faced two weighty accusations: that he had engaged in "insider trading;" and that, before the editorial board of *Il Sole*, he had denied his (and his wife's) involvement in the Lombardfin affair.[5]

Apart from the gravity of these charges, which were examined by the appropriate bodies (the Association of Journalists and the Public Prosector of Milan), the Locatelli case threatened to compromise seriously the credibility and authority of the entire RAI leadership. After several weeks, however, the storm seemed to have calmed and the media turned its attention to other matters.

At the end of September, the President of the Board of Directors, Demattè, presented the "Programmatic Guidelines for the Plan to Restructure the RAI." The 65-page document illustrated in detail the operating philosophy and overall themes that were to guide the RAI for the next two years. The declared objective was to strengthen and expand the public television and radio system, after having corrected its malfunctions, some of which are "constitutional" and need to be addressed by more comprehensive reforms. Indeed, the Demattè guidelines gave this lucid definition of the juridical paradox of the RAI as a public service: "The RAI is a singular institution: It is a joint-stock company, but its primary shareholder is deprived of the typical powers of a shareholder; it must obey the civil code, but is subject to the rulings of the Court of Accounts; it administers a public service, but operates in a competitive system; it is exposed to market risks, but the bulk of its profits result not from market dynamics but instead from political decisions."[6]

After providing a broad survey of the problems facing public and private radio and television systems in Italy and abroad, the Demattè document addressed the serious situation at the RAI: the imbalance between its costs and its profits, the crisis of its legitimacy in the public eye, and its lack of an "organizational culture." The document then outlined courses of action, emphasizing the objectives of revitalizing the RAI, as highlighted by the repeated use of the terms to "reconstruct" (the RAI's strategy), to "redefine" (the mission of public communications services), to "reposition" (the RAI in the political arena), to "reframe" and "reorient" (the RAI's strategy), to "reorganize" (radio broadcasting and televised news and current events programming), to "restructure" (production and the various regional headquarters), and to "reorder" (shareholdings).

This language, suggestive of some sort of manual for company reorganization, obscured the concrete restructuring of the entire apparatus of the RAI. The three RAI networks now became "channels" with their own specific objectives. In addition to the three existing television news programs, a regional-national newscast was added as a cultural link between center and periphery and an inter-channel sports news program was to be developed. The three radio channels were also assigned specialized programming (news and music, family entertainment, and cultural programs), while the three radio newscasts were unified into one. Both radio and television channels, contrary to past practice, would no longer enjoy financial autonomy, but were now required to turn to different budgeting departments for films, series and mini-series, acquisitions and sales, and light entertainment. Finally, a set of proposals was designed to improve the RAI's financial status. The proposals addressed recapitalization, a campaign for new shareholders, an increase in antenna fees, a reduction of license fees, and drastic spending cuts in all sectors.

On October 22, only a few weeks after the presentation of the Demattè plan, the Board of Directors approved a package of nominations that renewed the RAI top management. The RAI-1 television channel would be headed by an "outsider," Nadio Delai, the sociologist and director of CENSIS,[7] and would have as its vice director an "insider" with substantial experience in television. Demetrio Volcic had just been nominated as the chief of the RAI-1 news program (Tg1, or *Telegiornale-1*). The RAI-2 channel would have insider Giovanni Minoli as its head and its news program, Tg2, would be directed by a print journalist, Paolo Garimberti. Angelo Guglielmi was confirmed as head of RAI-3 and another internal candidate, national editor-in-chief Andrea Giubilo, was chosen to manage the Tg3 news program. The Board of Directors selected the editorial secretary of Tg3, Barbara Scaramucci, as the chief of the regional news broadcast, Tgr (*Telegiornale regionale*). Aldo Grasso, an expert on the mass media and the television critic for the *Corriere della Sera*, was nominated director of radio programming and the three radio newscasts were combined under the leadership of Livio Zanetti, who had served until then as the director of the Gr1 (*Giornale radio-1*) newscast. Beyond these channel-specific nominations, the Board appointed other managers to head up sections of the coordinating structures established in the plan for the RAI's renewal: Franco Iseppi became coordinator of television programming and Andrea Melodia took charge of the key sector of television series and mini-series.

This package of nominations immediately became the object of commentary and controversy, as could be expected. The Left in particular raised a chorus of strong criticism and accused the RAI leadership of having favored a Christian Democratic faction.[8] But what received the most press for days, both before and after the nominations were announced, was the case of Sandro Curzi, the outgoing director of the Tg3 news program who was unanimously recognized as responsible for the success of the newscast on what had been "the PCI/PDS channel."[9] Curzi would not resign himself to the fate suffered by his colleagues who fell victim to the process of detaching the RAI from previous practices of *lottizzazione*. In fact, he saw his dismissal as a humiliation and publicized via newspapers, weeklies, and television his spirited criticisms of the President and the Director General of the RAI. Replaced as head of the program he had created, Curzi left the Tg3 in anger and traveled to the

Telemontecarlo station, where he hoped to repeat the record of success he had built at the Tg3.

But the financial rehabilitation of the public radio and television agency was the single most salient issue that preoccupied RAI leaders, triggered protest on the part of RAI employees, received an ambiguous response from the government, and drew comprehensive coverage in the media. The theme of the "budget debacle," as Director-General Gianni Locatelli called it,[10] not only achieved media notoriety in December 1993: The RAI's ruinous financial situation was on the agenda from the moment the new Board of Directors took office. Towards the end of the year, however, the budget problem took on unprecedented urgency and a rapid succession of events brought this crisis into the public eye. The election of Claudio Demattè, economist in the School of Management at the Bocconi University, as President of the RAI Board sent a clear message about the intentions of the new Board of Directors: Restoring financial health was a top priority. And in fact the new leadership had already instituted a series of cuts and savings at all levels of the RAI, from large items to such minute ones as an abolition of the use of "blue cars" (the chauffeur-driven Alfa Romeo sedans that are well known in Italy as the transportation of choice for politicians and public officials), a reduction in the number of daily newspapers delivered to managers, and a tighter control of journalists' expense accounts, stimulated in part by several cases of purported fraud. "In six months," Claudio Demattè declared, "we have attempted to cut where cuts could be made, 'pruning' expenses by nearly 240 billion [lire]. ...Cuts in 1994 should reach 305 billion and 1600 jobs will be eliminated."[11]

But the savings of the new management did not suffice. The RAI was losing one billion lire per day.[12] If broader steps were not taken, the RAI deficit would remain quite serious and could even bring about the liquidation of the company. This was the judgment that emerged during the meeting of November 29 that was called to examine RAI assets and liabilities. At this meeting it was revealed that RAI losses totalled 307 billion lire, not much less than total assets in reserve (316 billion): Only this small margin kept Demattè from declaring bankruptcy that very day. The RAI had to be recapitalized by the end of the year if it was to be saved. According to Demattè, the RAI required an influx of 350 to 400 billion lire. Unfortunately, its major shareholder, IRI, was without resources, and it was therefore up to the government to intervene to guarantee the survival of the public radio and television system. Thus began the wrestling match between RAI executives and government ministers as they attempted to secure approval of the measures needed to save the RAI by December 31, 1993. Demattè asked for a series of provisions: a 15 percent increase in antenna fees, a drastic reduction in license fees, the cancellation of roughly

320 billion lire due as license fees for 1992 and 1993, and the reassessment of RAI real property holdings.

In the meantime, the Board of Directors hoped to pressure the government by making an unpopular decision: It announced that it would suspend payment of year-end bonuses to RAI employees. The maneuver worked: The entire RAI mobilized in strikes, assemblies, special television broadcasts, and appeals to the President of the Republic. The government, finding itself in difficult straits, overcame its internal uncertainties and differences and finally issued the so-called "save-the-RAI decree."

According to this decree, antenna fees increased by 12 percent, from 148,000 to 156,000 lire. The license fee paid to the Ministry of Posts and Telecommunications for use of frequencies dropped from 160 to 40 billion lire. The 350 billion that the State was due to receive in fees from 1992 and 1993 would be transferred to the Ministry of the Treasury, which thus became owner of a part of the RAI's capital. Finally, RAI assets would be reassessed and the reduction of other financial obligations would bring an additional 300 billion lire into the RAI's coffers.

But if the government's decisions resolved the RAI's immediate financial crisis, other pressing problems of a political nature would serve to keep alive the long-standing debate on the fate of Italian public telecommunications and on the appropriate structure for such a system. The electoral campaign for the new Parliament was already on the horizon, a campaign that for the first time featured a party led by the father of commercial television, Silvio Berlusconi. Unprecedented events thus ushered in the new year of 1994.

The "Mini-Reform" and the Evolution of the Italian Radio and Television System

The so-called "little law" that launched the mini-reform of the RAI, together with the "little law" on local broadcasting, proved to be last-ditch efforts made by a largely delegitimized party system that for two decades had failed to frame and put forward a comprehensive plan for the development of the Italian mass media system.

The very law that sought to reform the RAI in 1975 (No. 103) created the difficulties that would soon threaten to overwhelm the public radio and television system. In 1975 no one was able to see the risks that Law No. 103 posed. This reform transferred control of the RAI from the executive to the directly elected Parliament, which seemed formally more democratic. The good intentions of the champions of this law were not followed, however, by equally admirable actions. In fact, as subsequent developments would show, effective control of the RAI soon passed into the hands of the parties of the governing majority and later to the opposition as well.

From 1975 to 1990, in a legislative vacuum that seems inexplicable even today, the Italian media system experienced the most turbulent period in its history. In the same time span, the other major member countries of the European Community confronted the challenge of commercialization and global competition by launching comprehensive reforms and planning for the future. In Italy, the story was quite different. In 1976, private television was introduced, but was confined to the local level by a Constitutional Court ruling. Yet within a few years large private networks began to appear on the scene, founded by major publishing houses such as Rizzoli, Mondadori, and Rusconi, and even by Berlusconi, an almost unknown businessman at the time. The latter, without doubt a gifted entrepreneur, quickly built a television empire, thanks in no small part to the failure of his partners, who ceded their networks to him. In the absence of even a rudimentary regulatory framework, Italian commercial television saw explosive growth.

At the RAI during the same period the system of "partitioning" spoils among party loyalists solidified. All positions — from the appointment of the Board of Directors, to the hiring of journalists, to the promotion of managers, on down to the lowest levels — were divided among parties, large and small, according to the "Cencelli Manual"[13] In 1985, with the approval of the "Berlusconi decree," as it was called (Law No. 10), even the PCI obtained an "allotment:" Its sphere of influence became the RAI-3 network, including the RAI-3 news broadcast. This law, vigorously pushed by the Socialist Premier Craxi, also protected Berlusconi's networks from any potentially unfavorable court rulings.

The RAI, held back by legal and political constraints, was ill prepared to compete in the increasingly commericalized television system that emerged. The RAI allowed itself to be dragged into a dramatic battle for higher ratings and advertising funds. The effects of this uneven competition have been repeatedly analyzed and the RAI has been criticized in many political and cultural sectors for lowering the quality of its programming, capitulating to market pressures, and losing sight of its role as a public service.[14]

Fifteen years after Law No. 103 was approved, Parliament finally acknowledged the failure of that reform. The Mammì law of 1990 addressed a state of affairs that the political parties had not been able or willing to manage in the public interest. Even so, as already observed, the Mammì law did not initiate reform of the public radio and television system, which continued to be permeated by party influence. Public opinion in Italy would come to reject the system of party partitioning of the

RAI only with the political upheaval wrought by the "Clean Hands" investigations and by the growth of the Northern League.

The "mini-reform" is the product of this new climate. One could well ask why a law that eliminated the parties' control of the RAI could be approved by these same parties, against their interest. The "Clean Hands" revelations played some role, of course; without a doubt, as well, the parties knew that the disarray at the RAI was so serious as to endanger its very existence. No political actor wished to be responsible for the RAI's demise. The parties therefore made virtue out of necessity, rescuing a corporation that they had helped to undermine. Another explanation is that the old and new party system could not, on the eve of a historic appointment with the electorate, permit the RAI to fail. Long deployed as an instrument of political pressure, the RAI could, even if reformed, still be useful during the spring electoral campaign. The parties of Left took the forefront in the salvation of the RAI. The collapse of the RAI would have given greater political weight to the private television and radio system.

As noted above, the "mini-reform" ended a phase of urgency in decision making. And yet the state of emergency within the television system is far from over, as shown by the battle at the end of the year between RAI executives and the government to stabilize RAI finances. Furthermore, it is not yet clear how the entry of media magnate Silvio Berlusconi into the political arena will influence Italian radio and television. This last development, which was set in motion during the closing weeks of 1993, raises unprecedented problems. At this point the Mammì law looks like a remnant of the past. In the face of the events and phenomena that have defined a new national political context, that law will have to be completely rewritten, for in its current form it lacks the instruments needed to solve problems that are above all political in nature. The difficulty is that the RAI is inextricably linked with the private television sector and only politicians can untangle and reorder these relationships. In Italy the history of ties between political interests and the mass media is one in which collusion has prevailed.[15] Even though the mass media have been quite active in publicizing the "Clean Hands" investigations, the media's regulatory framework is still largely unsettled and thus is vulnerable to changes in the political climate. If these Italian specific variables are combined with general ones, such as the challenges to national public radio and television services caused by the rise of a worldwide market for multimedia products, it is obvious that a simple reform of the Mammì law or a reform of the RAI alone is utterly insufficient.

The fate of the RAI and of Berlusconi's networks depends now more than ever on the political system that will emerge from the spring 1994 elections. The Italian mass media could be rebuilt on completely new foundations, so as to take into account advances in technology and the evolution of mass-media markets. On the other hand, the media might reproduce the old vices that in the past were elevated to a creed and applied in practice. In the first case Italy would join other countries that have begun to address the challenges of contemporary mass communications; in the second case the media would again be subject to sporadic policy initiatives designed to serve the political logic and equilibrium of the moment. If the second scenario materializes, the Italian radio and television system will remain at an impasse, blocked by government policy making that still moves forward by the tiny steps of "little laws" and "mini-reforms" such as the law of June 25, 1993.

Chronology of RAI Reforms

June 25.   Parliament approves the mini-reform of the RAI (Law No. 206), "Rules for the company licensed to provide public television and radio service."

June 29.   The Presidents of the Chamber and the Senate nominate the members of the new Board of Directors of the RAI.

July 13.   The Board of Directors of the Rai nominates Claudio Demattè as President.

December 31. The government issues the decree that allows for the financial rescue of the RAI.

Translated by Claire Holman and Carol Mershon

Notes

1. The term *lottizzazione* refers to the practice of distributing political resources according to the balance of power among parties. This practice of allotment or partitioning, endemic to the Italian political system, had by the early 1990s assumed extreme forms in many sectors of national life and was seen as a symbol of the deep flaws of the old party system. One example of *lottizzazione* was found in the so-called "Cencelli Manual," named for an obscure functionary of the DC. This manual established the precise weight of every faction within the DC and distributed party and government posts on the basis of those weights. The Italian press quickly identified the manual as a model for the division of spoils among the various parties in government coalitions. *Lottizzazione* produced visible results in appointments at the three RAI television channels. From the late 1970s until 1993, RAI-1 was controlled by the DC, the smaller RAI-2 by the Socialists, and the smallest RAI-3 by the Communists (today the Democratic Party of the Left).

2. Until 1993 the RAI paid 165 billion lire per year for licenses, as opposed to the 400 million lire charged to private television networks.

3. "Clean Hands" is the label given by the Italian press to the series of sensational investigations begun in February 1992 by the *Procura* (Public Prosecutor) of Milan. These investigations have uncovered systemic corruption regarding illicit financing of political parties and have produced accusations against virtually the entire political class governing Italy since World War II. As a result the old political class has undergone an irreversible decline.

4. In March 1993, the *Garante* for radio broadcasting and publishing (the person charged with assuring fairness and enforcing rules in the sector) made a report to Parliament on the implementation of the Mammì law. He emphasized that the "mini-reform" could be viewed positively for the following achievements: "a) breaking the hold of 'partitioning' (*delottizzazione*) on nominations for executive bodies...; b) redefining the power relationships between the two fundamental corporate organs (Board of Directors and Director-General), thus ... giving greater weight to the collective body; c) improving the use of financial resources and personnel, according to criteria of efficiency and economization." "La Relazione del Garante al 31 Marzo 1993," Roma, Presidenza del Consiglio dei Ministri, 1993, p. 9.

5. In brief, the accusation charged that Locatelli, when he was still Director of the Confindustria-owned newspaper, attempted to realize substantial gains through the use of inside information on speculative trading of Lombardfin stock. Locatelli's wife, a client of a Lombardfin broker, was an instrumental actor in the affair.

6. "Indirizzi programmatici per il piano di ristrutturazione Rai," September 1993, p. 9.

7. CENSIS, the Centro Studi Investimenti Sociali, is a prestigious center for social research headquartered in Rome.

8. A few brief quotes reported in newspapers on October 23 convey the tone of the controversy: "This is a huge Christian Democratic pig-out [*abbuffata*]" (Mauro Paissan of the Greens); "From partitioning among parties we have moved to a single party" (Lucio Magri, Communist Refoundation); "A critical step backwards" (Vincenzo Vita, PDS).

9. See note 1.

10. *Corriere della Sera*, December 4, 1993.

11. *Corriere della Sera*, December 14 and 16, 1993.

12. Declaration of President Claudio Demattè in an interview published in *Corriere della Sera*, October 21, 1993.

13. See note 1.

14. For recent examples of such critiques, see the analyses of G. Giulietti, G. Mazzoleni, P. Murialdi, V. Vita, and R. Zaccaria in J. Jacobelli, ed., *Per una nuova riforma della Rai* (Bari: Laterza, 1992); P. Martini, "Tv: Il duopolio stringe," *Problemi dell'Informazione*, No. 1, 1991, pp. 83-90; and S. Balassone and A. Guglielmi, *La brutta addormentata. Tv e dopo* (Rome: Theoria, 1993).

15. See G. Mazzoleni, *Communicazione e potere* (Naples: Liguori, 1992), pp. 11-21.

8

Politics, the Mafia, and the Market for Corrupt Exchange

Donatella della Porta and Alberto Vannucci

Consideration of Mafia connections should not focus only on the 'lower branches' of politics. It is unthinkable that the vast phenomenon of collusion with the Mafia in communities of the South could have developed as it has without some sort of participation of political actors at a higher level. This collusion tends to spread beyond local circles because Mafia heads, who control votes and direct them towards local politicians, are also willing to support regional and national candidates, who in turn are linked to local politicians by party loyalties or, more often, faction or group loyalties.[1]

This assessment appears in the April 1993 report of the Parliamentary Anti-Mafia Committee on relationships between Cosa Nostra and politics. The Committee decided in October 1992 to focus on the ties between the Mafia and politics, after the order was issued that the defendants charged with the murder of the Hon. Salvo Lima[2] should be placed in preventive custody. In the Committee's report, the judge conducting preliminary investigations in the Lima case "indicated several elements from which one could draw the conclusion that stable relationships had existed between the murder victim and Cosa Nostra figures, relationships that had as their object the delivery of political support in exchange for favors of a judicial nature or of other types."[3] This report, as we show, clarifies many aspects of the relationship between institutional and hidden powers. Alongside these revelations are others, just as illuminating, that have emerged as a result of judicial investigations into organized crime and corruption in southern Italy, investigations that have relied on the testimony of more than 300 collaborators with justice. Indeed, the "Clean Hands" investigations that had begun in Milan in 1992[4] were extended in two directions in 1993: toward "the top," upsetting the leadership of the largest national companies (from the National Hydrocarbons Agency, ENI, to the Institute for Industrial Reconstruction, IRI, to the chemicals conglomerate Montedison); and towards the South, ending the careers of many local and national political bosses.

In this essay we depict the *Tangentopoli* (Bribe City) of the South. Using the judicial and parliamentary materials we have already cited, we address several questions raised in the political debates of 1993. Have the investigations into political corruption revealed — as many southern politicians would like to think — that "it's the same all over the world" (*tutto il mondo è paese*)? Or have the investigations instead established that substantial differences still distinguish the regions of Italy? Do politicians become corrupted in the same way in Milan as in Palermo? Or do the characteristics of political corruption vary according to the relationships existing between the political class and organized crime? The evidence that we present below indicates that the traditional divide separating (at least) two Italies has been reflected in the development of (at least) two kinds of *Tangentopoli*. Whereas in the North, in fact, the political parties seem to have exerted a certain degree of control over hidden exchange and over the illicit gains that flowed from it, in the South the parties have had to share power and money with an increasingly prominent actor: large-scale organized crime. According to the detailed reconstructions of the magistrates, in the Mezzogiorno the Mafia, the Camorra and the 'Ndrangheta[5] have actively participated in organizing the market for corruption, building complex networks of exchange with politicians (examined in section one of this chapter), with businessmen (section two), and with both (section three).

The Corrupt Politician and Organized Crime

It is not the Cosa Nostra that contacts the politician; instead a member of the Cosa Nostra says: that president is *mine (è cosa mia)*, and if you need a favor, you must go through me. In other words, the Cosa Nostra figure maintains a sort of monopoly on that politician. Every family head in the Mafia selects a man whose characteristics already make him look approachable. Forget the idea that some pact is reached first. On the contrary, one goes to that candidate and says, '*Onorevole*, I can do this and that for you now, and we hope that when you are elected you will remember us.' That candidate wins and he has to pay something back. You tell him, 'we need this, will you do it or not?' The politician understands immediately and *acts* always.[6]

This quotation, chosen from among the many that are available, vividly portrays the hidden exchanges that link politicians and organized crime. The Mafia and the politicians invest different types of resources in these exchanges. And each side derives numerous advantages from these exchanges.

Resources: Violence and a Reputation for Dangerousness

There are elements ... that indicate that ... the Hon. Pomicino ... has used Engineer Greco as his technical instrument ... and Carmine Alfieri as his reference point in the Camorra capable of assuring him every type of coverage, assistance, and protection in the areas he controls and in all sectors with which he might interact: political factions different from his own, aggressive groups in the Camorra, timid or enterprising city officials, or whoever might not recognize his power.[7]

The first resource that organized crime can offer politicians is physical violence: the elimination of adversaries in extreme cases, but also, and more often, attacks upon property or threats against political opponents or personal enemies. Investigations into political corruption have revealed episodes of violence against people who refused to pay kickbacks and bribes or who attempted to negotiate the amount to be paid, as well as against potential witnesses in criminal trials. If occasional relationships between politicians and organized crime have been documented in other regions of Italy,[8] the investigations into political corruption in the South have uncovered generalized mutual protection linking some politicians and important organized crime bosses. In this situation the politician's "flaunting" of his privileged relationship with a Mafia boss is intended to create a reputation for dangerousness.

Organized crime in the South has at its disposal an enormous potential for intimidation, for it can credibly threaten the use of force. In the words of Antonio Calderone, a Mafia figure turned State's witness: "Any *mafioso* understands perfectly, when all is said and done, what the source of his power is. People are afraid of being physically attacked and no one wants to run even a minimal risk of being killed. The *mafioso* instead is not afraid to take risks and so he puts the lives of others at risk."[9] According to Diego Gambetta, the characteristic activity of the Mafia is to produce and sell a particular commodity: private protection.[10] In Gambetta's perspective, violence constitutes a resource that can be used to settle or override controversies in those markets in which transactions are dominated by mutual distrust and uncertainty — and especially in those contexts in which the protection elsewhere supplied by the State as a public good is either unavailable or ineffective. This is the case, for example, in black markets. Even though an ability to use force is indispensable when providing credible protection, the two resources need not coincide. Violence will be used only to the extent necessary and, when possible, it will be "economized on." As Judge Giovanni Falcone observed, "In these organizations violence and cruelty are never gratuitous but instead represent the last resort, to be used when all other methods of intimidation have failed or when the gravity of the behavior requiring Mafia 'correction' is such that it must be punished by death."[11] For the Mafia, violence is tied to another resource, reputation, which with time can become a substitute for violence. If individuals expect that the *mafioso* is capable of deploying effective and violent instruments of dissuasion, his need to turn to actual violence declines: "A reputation for credible protection tends to coincide with protection itself. The more solid the reputation of an enterprise in the protection business, the less need there will be to use the resources on which the reputation is founded."[12]

The resources of violence — or the reputation of being able to use violence — help politicians in their careers in several ways. The reputation that a politician enjoys the protection of organized crime, which is often reinforced by using bodyguards with a clear Mafia stamp, generally offers an advantage in electoral terms. As reported by the Parliamentary Anti-Mafia Committee, "Support from the Cosa Nostra can also involve supplying a constant 'supervision' of the candidate, who, as he makes his rounds in his electoral constituency together with members of the [Mafia] family, is not only protected in terms of personal safety, but shows voters that he is backed by 'men who count.'"[13] Second, these resources of violence can be activated in attacks against political adversaries, so as to put them out of the running or "soften" their positions. Third, in the market for bribes and kickbacks, access to resources of violence strengthens the position of the politician expecting payment and discourages any attempt to avoid paying him. According to the Tribunal of Palermo, for example, the career of Christian Democrat Vito Ciancimino was repeatedly favored by the support of several Mafia families. Thanks to the forces of intimidation marshalled by his Mafia allies, "not only could one never fail to consider Ciancimino's requests, but he never needed the least bit of documentation to claim his money, since it was unimaginable that anyone could have betrayed his trust."[14]

Mafiosi can also offer their services of violent protection in the more general area of political agreements and exchanges. Before the new municipal electoral laws were approved in March 1993, city-level government and administration almost always required the formation of coalitions among multiple parties, each of which was subdivided into factions in lively competition against each other. Often, especially in the South, these political coalitions were extremely precarious and unstable and thus blocked the distribution of public resources. In some of these cases, the guarantee of Mafia bosses served to restore stability to the managing boards of municipal agencies, so that the obstacles to the flows of public spending were removed. One example of a Mafia guarantee of a municipal coalition was described during the investigations into the murder of Ludovico Ligato, a powerful Christian Democratic boss in Reggio Calabria. According to a repentant State's witness from the local Mafia,[15] "The two parties, DC and PSI, competed against each other to divide up between them (*lottizzarsi*) all the positions of power and all the economic interests in the city of Reggio. But Ligato, who was determined to take up the management of local politics himself, from the top, found all doors closed to him. At this point he chose the strategy of threats. This was the overall situation that resulted in Ligato's physical elimination." The murder had the effect of consolidating the nascent political coalition in Reggio, according to the investigating judge in the case: "The stagnation that preceded Ligato's murder was followed, after the tragic act of violence, by a perceptible renewal of municipal politics, and a new mayor was elected."[16] Any element that might have disrupted the coalition and its plans for sharing out public resources was thus eliminated through the use of violence and intimidation. The State's witness observed: "The problem became most dramatic once billions of lire were about to arrive in Reggio (through the so-called Reggio decree), because it was clear that whoever held political power in the city would also control these funds."[17] Thanks to this forced "pacification," the market for corruption could expand undisturbed and benefit Reggio's "illicit, Mafia-type structure, which was called the 'business committee'" and was composed of "prominent figures in the dominant political class, who were able to influence the choices of local and central public agencies," of "'favored' national companies that routinely received public contracts," and of "local entrepreneurs who acted in symbiosis with local organized crime and were thus the actual executors of the work."[18] We further discuss this sort of tripartite alliance below.

The Vote of Exchange

I do not solicit politicians. They solicit me at election time. They need me, I don't need them.[19]

Along with physical protection — which, as just observed, can by itself strengthen the electoral position of a candidate — organized crime also offers packets of votes to corrupt politicians. Electoral exchanges between politicians and the Mafia, penalized by Article 11/Supplement of Decree Law 306/92 (passed as Law No. 36 of August 7, 1992)[20] seem to have assumed especially noteworthy proportions in Campania, Calabria and Sicily. The activity of Mafia groups in these regions can explain the spread and efficiency of the market for votes there — an illicit market that, given its characteristics, has a particular need for outside guarantees. Mafia groups are well equipped to supply such guarantees. The Parliamentary Anti-Mafia Committee has learned that organized crime has several ways of controlling packets of votes:

> The Mafia makes it known in the environment in which it operates that it is able to control the vote and it thus makes voters fear reprisals. Intimidation of this type is rather widespread and so also is the surveillance of polling places. In various cases elections have been rigged. More often no outright intimidation is needed. Advice is sufficient. The absence of political energy and passion, the notion that a vote serves only to mark one's adherence to a clientele group and not to indicate a choice of ideas, and the levelling of political traditions among the different parties all lead [voters] almost naturally, without any forcing, to respect the 'racing orders' [given by the Mafia].[21]

Mafia groups can also organize the consensus of their affiliates, relatives and friends. The block of voters that *mafiosi* are able to mobilize directly is indeed impressive in both size and discipline. For example, according to former Mafia affiliate Antonio Calderone:

> The family of Santa Maria del Gesù is the most numerous and has about 200 members. ...We are talking about a terrifying, massive force, if you keep in mind that every *uomo di onore*, between friends and relatives, can count on at least forty to fifty people who will blindly follow his directives. ...If we think that in Palermo, in my time, there were at least eighteen administrative districts, and that each of these areas included not less than two or three [Mafia] families, we can readily understand the significance of Mafia support in electoral competition.[22]

It should be noted, finally, that the electoral strategies of organized crime reflect quite pragmatic considerations: "It is natural for the Cosa Nostra to influence votes. Its influence results not from an ideological choice but instead from a search for advantage, from exploiting fully its roots in the society and territory."[23] Organized crime directs the votes it commands toward the candidates that it maintains are both useful (in resources controlled and expected permanence in power) and reliable (in respecting illegal agreements). As one State's witness has revealed, "It is important to know which political figures receive electoral support from the Cosa Nostra, because, if that is the case, it is possible to turn to them for favors in compensation for the electoral backing already given."[24]

In exchange for protection and electoral support, organized crime asks politicians for what one State's witness has called "small favors" — that is, above all, protection from judicial investigation. We now turn to this issue.

Impunity

> The unanimous belief was that one could usefully influence the action of the courts through politicians and that, further, the function of Sicilian politicians was critical for 'Roman politics' [or national-level political decisions] with regard to Sicilian matters involving the Cosa Nostra.[25]

Impunity for crimes committed is a resource of prime importance for *mafiosi*, who live in a situation of illegality, often as fugitives or in jail.[26] According to several judicial documents, the relationships between Mafia and Camorra members, on the one hand, and political figures of national prominence, on the other, were in fact primarily directed towards obtaining protection in investigations and acquittals in trials; these ends were achieved as political "patrons" pressured the forces of order and magistrates.

The cases range from the politician who sees that house arrest is arranged, to the politician who works to hinder investigations of people improperly certified to receive disability payments, to the politician who negotiates the transfer of particularly disagreeable public officials.

For this type of organized crime, impunity not only has an instrumental value but is also particularly important in a symbolic sense. As the Parliamentary Anti-Mafia Committee has asserted,

> Impunity for the Cosa Nostra has a relevance far greater than the natural hope of criminals that they may escape punishment for crimes committed. Beyond its effect on individuals, immunity from punishment confirms the overall power of the criminal organization, legitimizes the organization in the eyes of citizens, and mocks the function of the State. Thus, impunity is a structural necessity for the organization that confers the aura of 'de facto legality' to its operations. Impunity is the principal concern of the Cosa Nostra.[27]

Along with the concrete advantage of sparing the *mafioso* from legal penalties, immunity from judicial action has a crucial demonstrative effect that enhances his reputation for force and power.

Organized Crime and Business

In addition to its relationships with politicians, the Mafia maintains a dense web of interactions with several business sectors, exchanging resources of various types. We focus first on how the Mafia supports illicit business cartels through threatened or actual violence.

Violent Sanctions and Privileged Information

We started out by helping the various businesses involved to come to agreement, in the sense that we formulated bids so that the contract would be awarded with a minimal 'discount' that allowed for the payment of a kickback of the proper amount. The person who acted to assure coordination among the various companies was Siino; and I remember that in this first phase those of us from the Cosa Nostra had the task of presenting his qualifications to different businesses and to the *uomini di onore* in the areas in which he was operating.[28]

The formation of collusive agreements can permit businessmen who compete for public contracts or subcontracts to realize huge profits. Concealing the coordination of their respective bids, these entrepreneurs are able to fix in advance both who will win the competition and how much will be paid by public officials. The company awarded the contract can then compensate the others with a share of its profits or the promise of letting another company take its turn in the future. As a result of the "Clean Hands" investigations into corruption, multiple collusive agreements involving at times numerous groups of businessmen have been discovered in northern and southern Italy.[29] These agreements followed different criteria for the division of spoils: drawing lots, moving down a list, taking into account the public agency issuing the contract, or considering geographic area (the company due to win the contract is the one with the plant nearest the work site). The participating companies had to resolve the problem of potential defection, however. A business obtaining a contract might find it convenient to "forget" to return the favor. In these cases agreement rested on strategies of conditional cooperation in repeated interactions: If a player did not keep his word, the only feasible sanction was to deny him the future benefits of collusion.

In the South several factors have contributed to the success of such agreements. Local businesses are few and they depend almost entirely on demand from the public sector, given the scarcity of opportunities in the private sector. The prospect of frequent and prolonged interaction with other companies fosters stability in cartel agreements. But it is above all the presence of Mafia-type organizations that makes such cartels so strong and durable. In this context, too, organized crime offers the service of preventing or resolving controversies. The agreement is upheld or revised under the threat or use of force. Any businessman who defects from the collusive agreement or refuses to take part in it exposes himself to violent retaliation from a Mafia protector. Naturally these cartel agreements are not limited to the sector of public contracts. In many other markets conditions may be such that a forced regulation of competition is highly desirable. Mafia protection allows a firm to keep dangerous rivals at a distance or acquire other competitive advantages.[30] Mafia repentant Antonio Calderone has stated that

> Almost all Sicilian firms of a certain size and importance turned to the Mafia so as to be able to work undisturbed (*lavorare in pace*) and to keep firms from the North out of their market. ...Having the Mafia on your side meant ... that you could work undisturbed and make a lot of money without the risk of seeing your machinery damaged, without the fear that strikes might stop your job half-way through, without the requests for payments that even the least important *mafioso* thinks he has the right to demand from anyone who makes an investment in his territory.[31]

The proven method for successfully dividing up the market was as follows:

> After a request for bids is announced, the cartel's allies in the agency contracting out the work reveal to Mafia personnel the list of companies that have officially communicated their intent to bid. The firms on the list are then contacted and (with a mixture of veiled threats and promises of future benefits) are invariably persuaded not to present bids or to present their bids in a way that assures that the contract is awarded to whatever company the [Mafia] organization has selected.[32]

Once firms have effectively established collusive agreements, they can in some cases do without attempts to corrupt politicians and public officials. Access to privileged information — such as the identity of companies invited to bid for contracts — can suffice for collusion to work. The firms in the cartel can receive this confidential information from the *mafiosi*, who in turn can obtain it from their "reference points" among politicians and bureaucrats in public agencies.

Palermo magistrates have found that at the end of this process, when the cartel protected by *mafiosi* has consolidated its operations and reputation, every local businessman finds himself forced to choose among the following alternatives: "(1) accept the rules of the game and thus enter into an arena in which each player will eventually be awarded the contracts assigned to him under the discretionary rule of the Mafia organization; (2) reject those rules but still compete for contracts, which means meeting retaliation from the [Mafia] organization; (3) abandon the Sicilian market."[33] We would also identify a fourth course of action that is surely the most dangerous of all: denounce the facts publicly or to investigating authorities. The presence of Mafia groups tends to make collusive agreements very stable, which in turn makes the first option more attractive and the second and fourth alternatives, more risky.[34]

It should be noted that businessmen are not always passive victims of the *mafiosi* who foster the success of these agreements. As the Palermo judges discovered in some instances, "after the businessman is contacted by the [Mafia] organization and accepts its rules, he gradually begins to participate actively in manipulating competition for contracts, deriving repeated benefits from doing so."[35] Investigations in Palermo further indicate that "the entrepreneurs involved do not seem to require intimidation any longer. This explains why crimes against property and persons are much rarer than the number of illicit agreements in effect. ...Those who operate in the sector have no need to be explicitly reminded of the rules of the game. A tacit and clear understanding of these rules is in place."[36] By rotating access to contracts over time, all participating companies share the gains of collusion and carry out a perverse sort of "distributive justice."

Some entrepreneurs can thus find it individually advantageous to build ties with *mafiosi* in order to give power and pervasiveness to the cartels set up to subdivide the market. By delivering a portion of their earnings to the Mafia, firms receive from the Mafia the guarantee that collusive commitments will be binding for all and that politicians will not obstruct the cartel.

Bribery and Intermediation

In return for their services, *mafiosi* receive different types of resources from businessmen. First, as might well be imagined, they get money. The Mafia's "cut" (*tangente*) is often just that, a percentage of the value of the contract that parallels the "cut" paid to corrupt politicians, as discussed below. The Parliamentary Anti-Mafia Committee has observed that

> in Sicily a committee for managing contract competitions exists, a sort of executive board composed of businessmen — the most important Sicilian entrepreneurs and a few of national stature — who decide *a priori* (and regardless of the choices that might be made by public bodies) how the contracts will be awarded to firms. This committee can operate only with the Cosa Nostra guarantee behind it: This [Mafia] presence explains why Sicilian businessmen remain silent about corruption. The Mafia does not intervene to settle which company should win the contract, unless it happens to have a special interest in some company or unless it must use threats to demand that the criteria for allocating benefits be respected. Whatever company wins, the Mafia's share of the gains is assured.[37]

Another resource that businessmen can use in their exchanges with organized crime is the acceptance or instead the boycotting of companies protected by the Mafia or, within some markets, of Mafia-owned companies.[38] Not even belonging to the Cosa Nostra or enjoying the protection of a *mafioso* permits a businessman to dictate to his competitors. One Sicilian manager describes the local market as follows:

> You need to keep your word, but other than that things work here the same as in other places. Along with ordinary business risk you have to add the risk of reprisals against property and people. Suppose a businessman is also a *mafioso*; this is not necessarily an advantage for him. He too must uphold agreements, he cannot win all the contracts he would like, he will not always find a public official or politician ready to cover him, and if he breaks an agreement, he could find himself facing thirty or forty companies united in a pricing war against him.[39]

No statement more clearly conveys the nature of the exchange between *mafiosi* and businessmen. Like anyone else, the *mafiosi* are constrained by the commitments they make. Businessmen retain some capacity to oppose the Mafia or to discourage defection even without turning to violence. If they were to abandon or boycott a collusive agreement, they would damage the *mafiosi* and those with Mafia protection.

As already noted, a crucial asset for *mafiosi* is protection from measures taken by investigative bodies and the magistrature. A company that has already established hidden contacts to secure such protection can, at rather limited expense, pay the same public officials to extend the benefit of protection to *mafiosi*. Thus, as a further means of compensating the Mafia, an entrepreneur can serve as an intermediary between the Mafia and the political authorities to be corrupted. Mafia repentant Calderone recalls that

> We were well protected and well informed. We protected the biggest businessmen from being disturbed by petty criminals and by non-Catanian Mafia families, and they in turn protected us from any trouble we might have had with the forces of order or the magistrature. The Costanzo company had a lot of magistrates in hand. Costanzo cultivated them for his own reasons, because he had constant problems with the courts. Any large company has some complication in court practically every day: a fine, an accident on the job site, a dispute with another company. And since Costanzo had these contacts, he used them to help us with trials and other things.[40]

Corruption, the Mafia, and Contracts

On the subject of Mafia earnings, we should not forget contracts and subcontracts. Indeed I wonder if this might be the most lucrative business of the Cosa Nostra. The control of competition for contracts dates back many decades, but today it has reached impressive dimensions. It doesn't matter whether the company awarded the contract is Sicilian, Calabrian, French or German: Whatever its origins, the company that wants business in Sicily must submit to certain conditions, submit to Mafia control of the territory.[41]

Along with those resources analyzed in section one above, control of public contracts is another resource that corrupt politicians can furnish to organized crime and "protected" businessmen. In general, the influence that corrupt politicians exert on local public agencies allows those politicians to administer at their discretion a range of public resources, such as contracts, licenses, permits, and jobs in the public sector. For example, the sentence of the Court of Palermo in the case of Vito Ciancimino cites a long series of favors given by the Sicilian politician to various associates of Mafia families: from assigning subsidized housing to people not eligible for it, to issuing permits to build on land set aside for public parks and gardens, to granting construction licenses as a result of illegal pressure.[42] As the Palermo judges observe, "Access to a political contact capable of decisively shaping the life and policy choices of municipal government in Palermo has done much to strengthen Mafia control of economic activity and to strengthen the Mafia itself."[43]

In this hidden market for contracts, triangular exchange relationships often form that bring together politicians, businessmen, and members of organized crime. As one repentant *mafioso* remarks, "There is an agreement between politicians and businessmen, then between businessmen and the Cosa Nostra, and finally between politicians and the Cosa Nostra. The function of the Cosa Nostra is to control everything, every step of the way."[44] As noted above, in the South the system of public contracts offers particularly attractive economic opportunities, given both the magnitude of public expenditure and the weakness of private demand. The specific activity of the Mafia in this context, again, consists of backing and guaranteeing corrupt agreements that have as their object the subdivision of these resources. As the judges investigating collusion between criminals and politicians in Naples have recently found, the availability of funds from illicit sources makes firms protected by the Mafia especially competitive and allows them to influence "a political-administrative apparatus that is by now ... permeated by widespread illegality and is thus, in many instances, quite sensitive to the call of money or simply open to blackmail." Beyond vast funds, businesses with Mafia protection "also have an enormous capacity for intimidation, which they do not hesitate to display brutally whenever they encounter any resistance from 'honest folk' or, worse, from institutional or business actors believed to be infiltrated by rival [criminal] organizations." The support of a criminal boss able to guarantee that promises will be upheld and that bribes paid will elicit the behavior desired often represents a crucial advantage for businesses.

The consequence is a "conquest of the market achieved through corruption or intimidation as well as economic assets that beat the competition (in the realm of prices, for example, or in the duration of deferrals of payment)."[45]

The focus of criminal interests on public contracts tends to stabilize relationships among crime, politics, and business, producing alliances among individual Mafia bosses, politicians, and entrepreneurs, alliances nourished by reciprocal protection. In other words, the supply of Mafia guarantees can find interested customers among corrupted politicians, who in this way receive certification of the reliability of corrupting businesses. The turning point in the relationship between the Mafia and politics may be located at the end of the 1950s when the Mafia of the countryside turned into the Mafia of the city and developed new ties to politics in the process. During the years of the so-called "sack of Palermo," with Lima as mayor and Ciancimino as assessor of public works, "a pact was forged among the Mafia, the municipal administration, and construction companies that became a model for crime in many areas of the South. Many teams of *mafiosi*, entrepreneurs, and individual politicians emerged then, which eventually perverted the nature of public functions, destroyed the market, and made a mockery of administrative legality."[46]

These tripartite agreements are cemented by the expectation that, if internal disputes or external obstacles arise, the criminal component will see to a prompt resolution of the problem. In this way the Mafia contributes decisively to the vertical expansion of the market for corruption. The Palermo judges assert:

> the criminal organizations making up the Cosa Nostra attempt to gain full control of public contracts in four phases: (1) intruding into the selection of public works to be financed, via technicians (planners, engineers, professionals, 'meddlers') who act as illicit mediators among the public agencies financing the contract, the companies competing for the contract, and the public agencies receiving funds under the contract...; (2) completely manipulating the bidding competition, through 'combination' techniques that are forced on participating companies with intimidation when needed; (3) managing subcontracts, which in the new system of Mafia control no longer constitutes simple parasitic interference, as in the past, but rather serves as a strategy for balancing the involvement of local Mafia groups; and (4) expecting 'courtesies' and allowing 'mistakes' during the execution of work and during the final inspection stage.[47]

As observed above, companies that strike cartel agreements are able to eliminate all competition in the assignment of puolic contracts. Politicians, who would be cut out of the market if they did not act, have different ways of re-entering the game. Under Mafia supervision they can provide "accessory services" (such as confidential information about the bidding competition or "steered" invitations to bid) that favor the cartel. Or they can get leverage by exploiting their power to solicit public financing, by adopting criteria for choice that leave great discretion to decision makers (and are thus more difficult to "maneuver" from the outside), or by carrying out especially close checks on the contracting process.

In some regions of Italy, then, aggregates of interests from the political, business and criminal worlds have solidified around public contracts. As one Camorra repentant has described, a complex division of roles and functions has been established among the actors:

> The politician who directs the financing of the contract, and thus its assignment or concession, acts as a mediator between the company (which is almost always from the North or Center and is quite large) and the Camorra. This mediation occurs by forcing the company to pay a kickback to the politician or his direct representatives, and to accept that subcontracts be assigned to [local] companies directly controlled by the Camorra. The relationship becomes more complicated since the local companies flank the principal company as equal partners in the job: In this case an overall management of the operation emerges that involves politicians, business-men, and *camorristi*, in complete fusion.[48]

Even though both the Mafia and politicians supply "protection" to businesses in the market for corrupt contracts, it seems that the power of the politician tends to decline progressively as the relationship among the actors evolves. This is evident, for example, in the distribution of payments for protection, that is, bribes. The Palermo judges write, "Until the early 1980s, the politicians decided to whom they would assign a contract and pocketed as much as 50 percent of the kickbacks. This all changed when the Cosa Nostra changed. ...The largest share in recent years ended up with the heads of the Cupola [the Mafia's multi-family committee], then came the local 'family' directly involved in the contract, and the politicians were last."[49]

Conclusion:
Organized Crime and Politics

The most recent judicial investigations into organized crime and political corruption have revealed, for southern Italy, continuous and system-atic exchanges between organized crime and members of the political class. As judges in Naples have observed, "It must be emphasized in the strongest terms possible that a constant relationship of functional interchange exists ... between the political-electoral system, on the one hand, and the system of criminal interests, on the other, each aggregated around representative and charismatic individuals, interacting among themselves both directly and through their respective representatives."[50]

In this situation a series of vicious circles seems to have been activated, in which political corruption and common crime have reinforced each other and weakened the market, the State, and civil society. Organized crime has strengthened corrupt politicians with its packets of votes and resources of violence, and in turn corrupt politicians have used their power to enhance the power of the organized crime families supporting them. Through the guarantee of impunity and the control of territory assured through manipulation of public contracts, corrupt politicians have further buttressed the underworld.

The ties between organized crime and corrupt politicians have been favored by the presence of incompetent local government and have in turn helped to undermine governmental performance. Given the defects of local government, the dependence of citizens on organized crime has increased. As the Anti-Mafia Committee warned,"Where local government is inert or inept, where administrative controls fail to operate, an environment favorable to the intertwining of politics and the Mafia is almost automatically created. ...In these areas ... a Mafia microsystem has developed that affects the daily life of citizens in a particularly oppressive way; the degradation is profound and no civil right of any importance exists that can be exercised without Mafia mediation."[51]

The vast spread of govermental and administrative inefficiency, encouraged by political corruption, has led citizens to distrust public procedures and decisions and to be pessimistic about the State's ability to furnish authentic and impartial public protection. Some citizens have thus turned to providers of a "surrogate" for public protection, boosting the demand for services of private protection supplied by *mafiosi*. Moreover, the agreements that corruption entails are often backed by Mafia groups, which are able to "persuade" the actors to maintain their commitments. By reducing the costs of hidden transactions, the Cosa Nostra has contributed to the expansion and strengthening of the market for bribes. Hence the conditions have been created such that governmental inefficiency, the Mafia, and political corruption feed each other.

As we compare the *Tangentopoli* of the South and corruption as practiced in the Center and North of Italy, we find that the search for protection in illicit exchange and in relations with public agencies has produced partially different patterns. In the Center and North, several centers of power have often supplied political protection, and citizens and businesses have turned to those centers to defend themselves against possible instances of nonfulfillment on the part of the public administration or partners in corrupt exchanges.[52] In many of the cases of corruption that have come to light in north-central Italy, it was discovered that organizations of corrupt politicians coordinated and managed illicit transactions. These organizations handled the important task of guaranteeing respect for hidden agreements in the system of corruption. In fact, as Alessandro Pizzorno has contended, these organizations assured repeated plays of the game: "It is advantageous for the actors who enter into such transactions to foresee a certain regularity in their ties. The collective actor that is created out of them will be more able than isolated individuals to both inflict punishment (or better, when obligations are accepted, to transmit credible warnings of punishment) and assure continuity, creating expectations that the game will be reiterated."[53] This explains why a portion of the bribes collected has been directed to the central offices of the political parties or to other decision-making centers that are apparently extraneous to the transaction.

In contrast, in the episodes of corruption that have emerged to date in the South, groups of corrupted politicians have been much smaller in size and the role of political parties in the subdivision of bribes more limited. Even though we must await the further evolution of judicial investigations to have a more detailed understanding, we can now advance the hypothesis that these geographic differences in corruption reflect different structures of the market for protection. Where organized crime provided effective private protection, the formation of informal groups of politicians aiming to endorse and sustain hidden exchange would have been superfluous. Each individual corrupt politician could, in fact, obtain the desired guarantees of compliance and reliability simply by giving up, and handing over to the Mafia, a cut of the bribe.

Translated by Claire Holman and Carol Mershon

Notes

This article presents the first results of a research project on Italian public administration funded by the Italian National Research Council (CNR).

1. Parliamentary Anti-Mafia Committee (PAC), "Relazione sul tema dei rapporti tra 'Cosa Nostra e politica,'" supplement to *La Repubblica*, April 10, 1993, p.2.

2. Long the Sicilian head of the DC faction led by Giulio Andreotti, Salvo Lima was mayor of Palermo, member of the Italian Parliament, and member of the European Parliament before he was killed in March 1992.

3. PAC, "Relazione sul tema dei rapporti tra 'Cosa Nostra e politica,'" p. 2. For an excellent selection of parliamentary documents on the Mafia, see N. Tranfaglia, *Mafia, politica e affari. 1943-92* (Bari and Rome: Laterza, 1992).

4. On the evolution of the "Clean Hands" investigations during 1992, see D. della Porta, "Milan: Immoral Capital," in S. Hellman and G. Pasquino, eds., *Italian Politics*, Vol. 8 (London: Pinter, 1993), pp. 98-115.

5. In Italy the terms Mafia and Cosa Nostra, in the narrow sense, refer to Sicilian families engaged in organized crime. Both terms are also used more loosely as labels for organized crime in general. The Camorra and the 'Ndrangheta are more specific terms, referring to organized crime in the regions of Campania and Calabria, respectively.

6. Tommaso Buscetta, quoted in *La Repubblica*, November 18, 1992, p. 2.

7. Public Prosecutor (*Procura*) of the Republic in the Court of Naples, "Richiesta di autorizzazione a procedere pervenuta il 7/4/1993," supplement to *La Repubblica*, April 15, 1993, p. 20.

8. D. della Porta, *Lo scambio occulto* (Bologna: Il Mulino, 1992).

9. Quoted in P. Arlacchi, *Gli uomini del disonore* (Milano: Mondadori, 1992), p. 200.

10. D. Gambetta, *La mafia siciliana* (Torino: Einaudi, 1992).

11. G. Falcone (in collaboration with M. Padovani), *Cose di Cosa Nostra* (Milano: Rizzoli, 1991), p. 28.

12. D. Gambetta, *La mafia siciliana*, p. 48.

13. PAC, "Relazione," p. 16.

14. Tribunale di Palermo, "Sentenza n. 411/90/R.G.," January 17, 1992, p. 194.

15. In Italy, members of organized crime families who turn State's witnesses are termed *pentiti*, or "repentants."

16. Both quotes in *Panorama*, December 13, 1993, pp. 52-53.

17. Quoted in A. Galasso, *La Mafia politica* (Milano: Baldini & Castoldi, 1993), p. 198.

18. Camera dei deputati, "Domanda di autorizzazione a procedere in giudizio nei confronti del deputato Misasi," Document IV, No. 256, 1993, p. 2.

19. Quote from the interrogation of the Camorra boss Francesco Alfieri, in Public Prosecutor of the Republic in the Court of Naples, "Richiesta di autorizzazione a procedere pervenuta il 7/4/1993," p. 8.

20. On the anti-Mafia legislation of the 1990s, see PAC, "Relazione," p. 2.

21. PAC, "Relazione," p. 16.

22. Tribunale di Palermo, "Richesta di autorizzazione a procedere contro il senatore Giulio Andreotti," March 27, 1993, supplement to *Panorama*, April 11, 1993, p. 39. The term *uomo di onore* (man of honor) refers to a member of the Mafia.

23. PAC, "Relazione," p. 16.

24. Tribunale di Palermo, "Richesta di autorizzazione a procedere contro il senatore Giulio Andreotti," p. 39.

25. Interrogation of Gaspare Mutolo in *ibid.*, p 24.

26. The same argument has been made for the American context: "The gangster depends upon political protection for his criminal and illicit activities. He, therefore, has a vital business interest in the success of certain candidates whom he believes will be favorably disposed to him." J. Landesco, *Organized Crime in Chicago* (Chicago: University of Chicago Press, 1968), p. 183.

27. PAC, "Relazione," p. 9.

28. Testimony of Baldassare di Maggio, cited in *Panorama*, April 11, 1993, p. 61.

29. See, for example, the declaration of public sector manager Alberto Zamorani: "For many years at ANAS [the National Roads and Highways Agency] there has been a cartel of about two hundred companies that periodically meet to examine the roster of the projects that have been or will be presented to the ANAS Board; and these companies decide among themselves who will receive the contract." Camera dei deputati, "Domanda di autorizzazione a procedere in giudizio nei confronti del deputato Craxi," Document IV, No. 166, 1993, p. 28.

30. The Mafia-owned company described by Arlacchi with reference to Calabria combines three elements that give it a privileged position in the market: discouragement of competitors through intimidation, lower salaries and evasion of social security and insurance contributions, and greater financial solidity and flexibility given access to funds from illegal activities. P. Arlacchi, *La mafia imprenditrice* (Bologna: Il Mulino, 1983), pp. 108-125.

31. P. Arlacchi, *Gli uomini del disonore*, pp. 195, 189. According to Mafia repentent Messina, "there are businessmen who pay a monthly stipend to the Cosa Nostra. Not only for protection. We also intervene to give them advantages in the market." PAC, "Verbale delle deposizioni di Tommaso Buscetta, Leonardo Messina e Gaspare Mutolo davanti alla Commissione," in *Mafia e Potere*, supplement to *L'Unità*, April 15, 1993, p. 79.

32. Public Prosecutor of the Republic in the Court of Palermo, "Richiesta per l'applicazione di misure cautelari," No. 2789/90N.C., 1990, p. 7.

33. *Ibid.*, p. 8.

34. The power of the Mafia to deter and intimidate is tremendous. In Palermo alone 34 entrepreneurs and 78 shopkeepers were assassinated by the Mafia between 1978 and 1987, according to the "Giuseppe Impastato" Research Center in Palermo. U. Santino and G. La Fiura, *L'impresa mafiosa* (Milano: Angeli, 1990), p. 413.

35. Public Prosecutor of the Republic in the Court of Palermo, "Richiesta per l'applicazione di misure cautelari," p. 9.

36. Carabinieri Legion of Palermo, "Rapporto giudiziario di denuncia contro Cosentino Francesco + 73," R.G. No. 2215/11-1-1988, February 23, 1989, pp. 123-124.

37. PAC, "Relazione," p. 18.

38. Some *uomini di onore* also are engaged in legitimate business activities. Mafia repentant Calderone has recalled, for example, that "there have always been merchants, shopkeepers, and agricultural exporters in the Cosa Nostra, as well as an infinite number of contractors and builders" (quoted in Arlacchi, *Gli uomini del disonore*, p. 28).

39. Quoted in *Panorama*, May 23, 1993, p. 55.

40. Quoted in Arlacchi, *Gli uomini del disonore*, p. 28.

41. Falcone, *Cose di Cosa Nostra*, p. 142.

42. Tribunale di Palermo, "Sentenza No. 411/90/R.G.," pp. 88, 151.

43. *Ibid.*, p. 202.

44. PAC, "Verbale delle deposizioni," p. 70.

45. Public Prosecutor of the Republic in the Court of Naples, "Richiesta di autorizzazione a procedere," p. 7.

46. *Ibid.*, p. 15.

47. Public Prosecutor of the Republic in the Court of Palermo, "Richiesta per l'applicazione di misure cautelari," pp. 5-6.

48. Public Prosecutor of the Republic in the Court of Naples, "Richiesta di autorizzazione a procedere," p. 9.

49. *La Repubblica*, May 27, 1993, p. 8.

50. Public Prosecutor of the Republic in the Court of Naples, "Richiesta di autorizzazione a procedere," p. 7.

51. PAC, "Relazione," p. 18.

52. A. Vannucci, "Scambi e collusioni: analisi di un caso," *Il Progetto*, 74, 1993, pp. 75-86.

53. A. Pizzorno, "La corruzione nel sistema politico," Introduction to D. della Porta, *Lo scambio occulto*, p. 30.

9

Eppure Si Tocca: The Abolition of the Scala Mobile

Richard Locke

Introduction

Over the last two decades, the single most important and contentious issue in Italian industrial relations has been the nationwide cost-of-living escalator known as the *scala mobile*. Two recent agreements between the *Confindustria* and the unions (signed on July 31, 1992, and July 3, 1993) have abolished the *scala mobile* and rationalized Italy's complex and often incoherent collective bargaining arrangements. Both of these accords seek to contain wage and price increases and thus contribute to the revival of the Italian economy. Why, after years of controversy, did disagreements over the *scala mobile* reach an apparently definitive settlement in 1992? Why would the unions, after insisting for so many years that *"la scala mobile non si tocca"* (don't meddle with the *scala mobile*), abandon such a powerful institution? How will the end of nationwide indexation affect other industrial relations arrangements (e.g., collective bargaining) and the strategies of the Italian unions?

This essay seeks to address these questions by analyzing the recent accords on the cost of labor. The first section of the essay provides a highly synthetic historical sketch of the 1975 *scala mobile* accord and of various subsequent events in order to illustrate the *scala mobile*'s significance for Italian industrial relations. The second section then describes the negotiations that led to the 1992 and 1993 accords and details the content of these agreements. I conclude by pondering the lessons these recent agreements may have for the way we think about industrial relations reform in Italy and elsewhere.

Why Was the *Scala Mobile* So Important?
A Brief Historical Sketch

Introduced initially in the national contracts of 1945 and 1946, the *scala mobile* was a cost-of-living adjustment escalator aimed at safeguarding workers' real wages against inflation. Price increases were periodically calculated in relation to an "average" working family's "shopping basket" of goods. An increase in the cost of the basket translated automatically into a proportional rise in workers' wages.

In 1975, in an attempt to moderate labor conflict, control inflation, and stabilize Italian industrial relations, Italy's leading business association, the *Confindustria*, and the major union confederations (CGIL, CISL, UIL)[1] negotiated an accord that enhanced the *scala mobile*'s benefits, especially for lower-paid, semi-skilled workers. The main aspects of this accord were a 100 percent indexation[2] of the *scala mobile* and a secondary agreement guaranteeing 80 percent of workers' wages in the event of lay-offs. Together, these accords would provide industrial workers in Italy with significant wage guarantees against both high inflation and industrial restructuring. The *Confindustria* hoped this accord would also shift the center of gravity in bargaining to the national level, and in doing so shift the power away from the militant industrial unions and toward the more moderate peak-level confederations.

Initially, it appeared as if the 1975 accord would provide benefits for both sides. For the unions, it not only protected workers in their already established bastions (primarily large, well-organized plants in the North) but also extended this bargain to workers in smaller, less organized plants. Together with the *inquadramento unico* of 1972 (unification of blue- and white-collar job classifications), the 1975 *scala mobile* agreement defined Italian union strategy for over a decade. Major Italian firms gained as well. Given that compensation for price increases would be paid by large firms in any event (because of the strong union presence within their plants), the agreement imposed the same terms on smaller potential competitors. Moreover, by removing disputes over price-related wage increases, this accord would eliminate a primary source of conflict within large plants, thereby reducing the power of the factory councils as well.[3]

But there was also an ideological component to the 1975 accord. For the unions, the egalitarianism of the *scala mobile* accord, like the *inquadramento unico*, resonated with the goals and achievements of the "Hot Autumn" of 1969 that had brought skilled and unskilled workers together to seek radical change in labor politics.[4] For the *Confindustria*, the aim was to create a privileged sector of industrial workers with job and wage security who would see the long-term benefits of moderation in terms of increased real wages and better working conditions and who could also be enlisted in the private sector's fight against the inefficient and bloated public sector.

In short, the *Confindustria* hoped to accomplish several things in this one sweeping agreement. First, like its Swedish counterpart in the 1930s, it hoped that a single official agreement would simultaneously bring about the centralization and domestication of the national union movement. By shifting the center of gravity of bargaining to the more moderate confederations, and by taking price-related wage increases and job security out of the bargaining arena, it hoped to restructure Italian industrial relations along more predictable and quiescent lines. Second, this centralization of wages would also, in the long run, enhance the competitiveness of Italian exports by tying wages in the export-oriented industrial sector to moderate price increases in the Italian economy as a whole.[5] Finally, by enlisting the industrial working class in a "producers' alliance" against the public sector, the *Confindustria* was sending a clear signal to the Italian state that it was prepared to do battle if the government continued to encroach on its terrain.

Yet this effort at controlling price increases and moderating labor relations through indexation backfired in several ways. First, due to Italy's high inflation rates, the 1975 agreement over wage indexation gained massive weight in the determination of wages. By the early 1980s, it was estimated that the *scala mobile* accounted for over 60 percent of annual wage increases.[6] This not only caused problems for management, which had to pay for these increases, but also for the unions, whose control over wage determination through collective bargaining had been severely reduced by indexation. The government, too, wanted a reform of this system since it confounded all policies aimed at reducing inflation.

Second, public sector workers mobilized to protect their wages. Where the confederal unions (CGIL, CISL, UIL) failed to articulate these demands, new rival organizations (autonomous unions or *sindacati autonomi*, and rank-and-file committees, *COBAS*) emerged to fill this representational void. As a result, not only was indexation extended to all sectors of the economy, thus undermining the economic logic of the accord, but also strike activity increased dramatically, and for the first time in Italy's history the increase was concentrated in the public and service sectors.[7]

Finally, because of the particular formula used in calculating wage increases, and given that indexation during the high inflation years of the 1970s accounted for over half of all wage gains, wage differentials based on different skill levels were significantly reduced (as shown in Table 9.1). As a result, the unions found themselves criticized, and in some cases simply abandoned, by their more skilled members who felt under-protected and insufficiently appreciated by the unions' leadership.

Far from providing mutual benefits for both organized labor and big business, the 1975 *scala mobile* accord instead generated a series of organi-

TABLE 9.1   Wage Differential Indexes Related to Metalworkers' Job Classification in Selected Years

	1978	1980	1981	1982	1983	1984	1985	1986
Blue-Collar Skill Levels								
1	100	100	100	100	100	100	100	—
2	128	106	108	109	105	107	106	100
3	115	113	116	114	111	113	112	106
4	122	117	121	122	119	119	118	112
5	132	126	131	132	127	127	126	119
White-Collar Skill Levels								
2	104	105	107	108	106	109	—	—
3	117	117	118	118	114	116	114	114
4	127	124	127	127	123	125	120	120
5	148	138	139	140	135	139	132	132
5 Super	161	151	151	157	149	152	145	145
6	195	174	172	183	172	174	164	164
7	248	227	227	224	215	220	209	209

Source: Elaboration of Centro di Studi Sociali e Sindacali (1982, 1983, 1985, 1987) data.

zational and economic disasters for both parties. It fueled rather than contained inflation and it further weakened the unions by provoking dissent within their own ranks and defections to rival organizations, triggering conflict with previously friendly political parties, and renewing antagonism with big business.

Because of these problems, the unions, organized business, and the government have repeatedly struggled over the *scala mobile*. Organized business and the government first sought to modify and later abolish this cost-of-living adjustment escalator. The unions, in turn, have long fought to preserve its key features. As a result, since the late 1970s, numerous accords and several key battles between the unions and organized business (as well as among the three major confederations) have revolved around this issue.

In 1983, for example, the government brokered an agreement, heralded as the Italian functional equivalent of neo-corporatist bargaining,[8] aimed at revising the *scala mobile*. The agreement eliminated bracket creep, improved family allowances, established a special investment fund (*Fondo di Solidarietà*), banned plant-level bargaining for 18 months, and reduced the coverage provided by wage indexation by 15 percent.[9] Disagreements over certain clauses of the 1983 agreement erupted and it was not automatically renewed the following year. As a result, in 1984 the government presented its own proposal to fix wage indexation at a set amount, regardless of the actual rate of inflation. The Communists in the CGIL rejected this proposal and used their majority on the CGIL Executive Committee to oppose it. The CISL and the UIL went along with the government in February 1984 and the union movement subsequently split over this so-called "*Disaccordo di San Valentino.*"

The government implemented its policy through an executive decree and the Communists promoted an electoral referendum aimed at abrogating the policy the following year. The very bitter campaign pitted various factions of the union movement against each other. The results of the referendum, held on June 9, 1985, favored the government and the moderate union forces that supported the 1984 accord.[10]

But the 1984 government decree and the 1985 referendum did not end the controversy over the *scala mobile*. In fact, numerous accords aimed at modifying or restricting various aspects of the mechanism continued to be negotiated (almost yearly) by the social partners and the government.

A "New Beginning" or the Beginning of the End?
Repeated Negotiations
over the Cost of Labor in the 1990s

Negotiations over the *scala mobile* underwent a marked change in 1990. As the economic boom years of the mid to late 1980s came to an end, the unions and the *Confindustria* began to work together to reduce the overall costs of labor, hoping in this way to restore the competitiveness of Italian goods on export markets. Initially, the objective of this collaboration was *not* to reform the *scala mobile* but rather to reduce indirect costs (such as social security payments and taxes), which, when added to wages, rendered Italian workers among the most expensive in Europe (as Table 9.2 reports). In January 1990, the unions and the *Confindustria* began to collaborate on a proposal aimed at convincing the government to reduce social security payments for employers and payroll taxes for salaried workers (i.e., the core of the unions' membership). These negotiations did not lead to any major changes. Instead, in July 1990, the social partners signed a letter of intent in which they agreed to continue to work together to reach a new accord on labor costs and the structure of collective bargaining by June 1991.

The 1991 negotiations were quite drawn out and (not surprisingly) no accord was signed by June. But in December 1991, a new, partial agreement was finally signed by the unions and the *Confindustria* that committed the social partners to a comprehensive overhaul of the collective bargaining system by June 1992, and in the meantime, declared "superseded" the current system of wage indexation (i.e., the *scala mobile*). As

TABLE 9.2   Indexes of Hourly Compensation Costs for Production Workers in Manufacturing, 1975-1992 (Foreign compensation costs converted to U.S. dollars at prevailing market exchange rates. Index US = 100.)

Country	1975	1980	1985	1990	1991	1992
U.S.	100	100	100	100	100	100
Canada	94	88	84	107	110	105
Japan	47	56	49	85	93	100
France	71	91	58	102	98	104
W. Germany	100	125	74	147	145	160
Italy	73	83	59	117	117	120
Unit.Kingdom	53	77	48	85	88	91

Source: U.S. Bureau of Labor Statistics, Office of Productivity annd Technology, June 1993.

Italy's macroeconomic situation deteriorated steadily over the course of 1992, the social partners were pushed by the new Amato government to sign a new agreement on July 31, 1992.

The July 31, 1992, Accord

Seen by many at the time as a revolutionary break with recent industrial relations practices, the July 31, 1992, "Protocol on Incomes Policy, the Struggle against Inflation, and the Cost of Labor" was not strictly speaking a collective agreement but rather a document in which the Italian government outlined its future economic policies. The "social partners" were called upon to underwrite this document and to conduct themselves within the parameters established by the document. The main features of the agreement included :
1. the abolition of the *scala mobile;*
2. a one-year moratorium on firm-level wage negotiations;
3. a lump-sum (20,000. Lire) wage increase to be paid in lieu of indexation;
4. a freeze in industrial wages for the rest of 1992; and
5. a freeze in government rates, administrative fees, and salaries.

The July 1992 accord was a central element in the Italian government's radical reorientation of economic policy. The new policy sought simultaneously to lower inflation rates, reduce government expenditures, and improve the country's trade balance. In return for the unions' concessions, the government committed itself to three major reforms. First, the government reformed the pension system by raising the minimum retirement age (from 60 to 65 for men and from 55 to 60 for women) and eliminating certain benefits for public sector employees (e.g., the so-called "baby pensions" in which public sector workers became eligible for retirement after only twenty years of service). Second, the government completely redefined the nature of public sector employment by abolishing previous administrative and legislative rules governing public sector employment and introducing collective bargaining arrangements instead. Finally and perhaps most important, the Amato government sponsored the first major tax reform in the postwar period, aimed at eliminating various inequalities in the system of taxation and reducing tax evasion through the introduction of the "minimum tax" to be paid by all independent workers and small business owners.

The July 1992 accord provoked a major crisis within the Italian unions, especially within the CGIL. Sergio D'Antoni, Secretary General of the CISL, and Bruno Trentin, Secretary General of the CGIL, were both assaulted by protesters at open rallies, and Bruno Trentin was harshly criticized by a large share of the CGIL's leadership. Notwithstanding the CGIL's commitment to "codetermination" and the democratic governance of the economy following its 12th National Congress in 1991,[11] a significant minority within the confederation, closely linked to the left-wing faction *Essere Sindacato*, opposed the July 31, 1992 accord. Because of this internal organizational turmoil, Trentin offered (but later retracted) his resignation. Trentin claimed that he was compelled to sign the agreement, both out of a sense of "responsibility" toward the nation, and because he did not want to see a repetition of the 1984 union split along partisan lines over an analogous austerity package.

The following autumn witnessed numerous demonstrations against the accord. Various factory councils in the North even established a movement of the so-called *"autoconvocati"* to contest the July 1992 accord. Interestingly enough, prominent within these demonstrations were not only members of the militant metalworkers unions but also large numbers of chemical workers, often seen as more moderate union members. Moreover, several local business owners in the North defected from the agreement and signed firm-level contracts providing wage increases since they pre-ferred to pay higher wages rather than endure persistent industrial conflict.

Between July 1992 and July 1993 there was much debate between the *Confindustria* and the unions over the final terms of the agreement. The debate centered less on the demise of the *scala mobile* (which appeared to be certain) and more on the future structure of collective bargaining. According to the *Confindustria*, wage levels and salaries should be determined only through the national industry agreements (*Contratti Nazionali di Categoria*). The unions, however, wanted wage bargaining to take place at both the industry and company levels (or territorial level for small and medium-sized companies). After a series of delays, due in part to the fall of the Amato government and the formation of a new government of "technicians" headed by Ciampi, a new agreement over the structure of collective bargaining was reached on July 3, 1993.

The July 3, 1993, Accord

As with the previous accord of July 1992, this agreement contained a number of policy measures concerning vocational training, technological innovation, government fees, and various labor market policies. The parts of the 1993 accord explicitly devoted to industrial relations included the following provisions.

1. The agreement confirms the abolition of the *scala mobile* but leaves space for some indexation (the equivalent of 30 percent if the national industry contract has expired for over three months; and 50 percent if the national industry contract has expired for over six months).

2. Wage guidelines and the rate of increases in nominal wages are to be determined through periodic tripartite negotiations and must be consistent with the government's macroeconomic predictions as stated in its yearly budget.

3. The structure of national industry contracts is modified so that the contracts resemble those in Germany: The normative clauses, i.e., those clauses of the national contract that govern hiring and firing practices, job classifications, career trajectories, etc., will be negotiated every four years, whereas more strictly economic (wage) clauses will be renewed every two years.

4. Bargaining will take place at both the industry and company (or territorial) levels. Wage bargaining at the firm level will be tied to firm-level productivity.

5. Employees will pay a greater share of their benefit contributions, hence reducing indirect labor costs for employers.

6. Other aspects of the accord include increased labor market flexibility, including provisions for paying slightly lower wages to new entrants, and a restriction in the use of Cassa Integrazione Guadagni (the government-financed redundancy fund).

The July accord also outlines a new structure for firm-level worker representation. Existing plant-level union structures (*Rappresentanze Sindacali Aziendali*), which have historically been dominated by the three confederal unions (CGIL, CISL, UIL), are to be reformed and replaced by unitary union structures, *Rappresentanze Sindacali Unitarie* (RSU), consisting of any union organization that can obtain the support of at least 3 percent of the work force. Two-thirds of the shop stewards involved in these new firm-level union structures will be elected directly by all workers in the production unit whereas one-third of the stewards will be appointed by those unions that have signed the relevant national industry contract. Through this reform, the social partners hope to both revitalize the plant-level union structures and to eliminate a major grievance of, and source of conflict among, the autonomous unions and the *COBAS*.

Interestingly enough, the future destiny of this accord and of the new collective bargaining arrangements will depend upon the success of these new organs of worker representation. If the RSU are able to aggregate the interests and gain the loyalty of diverse kinds of workers, then the "non-overlapping" and "functional specialization" clauses of the July 1993 accord will hold. If, on the other hand, these new firm-level union organs fail to gain legitimacy and the confederal unions continue to suffer a crisis of representation, then the accord and its elaborate new architecture for collective bargaining will collapse due to labor unrest, as was the case for an analogous reform, the "*clausole di rinvio*" of the early 1960s.

Questions about the implementation of this accord point to a broader concern about the possibilities for significant reform in Italian industrial relations, an issue to which I now turn in the conclusion.

Conclusion

Italian industrial relations have often been characterized as highly conflictual, overly politicized, and poorly institutionalized. They were thus seen as a major source of Italy's political and economic woes. In fact, many Italian business, government, and even labor leaders came to believe that before Italy could ever hope to join the ranks of the other, supposedly more stable advanced economies, it would need to reform its system of labor relations.

During the 1970s and 1980s, there were numerous efforts aimed at constructing a new, more "mature" system of industrial relations in Italy. These efforts included the introduction of a comprehensive labor code, the *Statuto dei Diritti dei Lavoratori* (1970), several attempts at building neo-corporatist-like arrangements in the late 1970s and again in the early 1980s, and organized business's desire to negotiate a Swedish-like "Basic Agreement" with labor through the *scala mobile* agreement of 1975. As exemplified by the *scala mobile* agreement, most of these reform efforts failed to produce the intended benefits. And in many ways, the unintended consequences of these failed reforms actually exacerbated the organizational fragmentation, political divisiveness and institutional weaknesses already plaguing the Italian system.

The July 31, 1993 Agreement can be interpreted in two contrasting ways. On the one hand, it might be viewed as a continuation of this never-ending, ad hoc institutional reform process. On the other, some observers see the 1993 accord as a fundamental break with the past — planting the seeds of the renewal of labor relations in Italy. In this accord, the unions have given up what was once seen as a major victory following the Hot Autumn struggles — extensive wage indexation and protection from inflation. Giving up the *scala mobile* also implies a reversal of their egalitarian policies and a recognition of wage inequalities for differentially skilled workers. At the same time, by agreeing to participate in trilateral negotiations over wage increases, the unions are committing themselves to working with organized business and the government on containing wage growth and thus (they hope) restimulating demand for Italian goods on world markets.

It is ironic that at a time when incomes policies are being abandoned in their Scandinavian homeland, they are being revived in Italy, a country with none of the institutional supports or legacies once deemed essential for such arrangements to succeed. But stranger things have been known to happen in Italy and only time will tell whether or not these new arrangements will work as planned. If they do, we will be forced to rethink our (often) outdated views of what is and is not possible in Italy.

Notes

1. The Italian union movement is divided into three national union confederations : the Communist and Socialist-dominated *Confederazione Generale Italiana del Lavoro* (CGIL), the Catholic-inspired *Confederazione Italiana dei Sindacati Lavoratori* (CISL), and the *Unione Italiana dei Lavoratori* (UIL) made up of Republican, Socialist, and Social-Democratic trade unionists. In addition, several so-called "autonomous" unions organize workers in specific sectors (e.g., transportation, health care, secondary schools).

2. Indexation consisted in automatic wage increases related to changes in a union-controlled price index. Increases, however, were not based on a worker's existing wage rate; instead all workers received equal lump-sum increases (the so-called *punto unico di contingenza*). As Italy experienced double-digit inflation rates in the late 1970s and early 1980s, these "egalitarian" adjustments provided full protection of wages for workers in the lower job classifications but eroded the real wages of higher skilled workers. As a result, wage differentials based on skill were drastically reduced.

3. For more on the *scala mobile* and Italian union strategy in these years, see Peter Lange and Maurizio Vannicelli, "Strategy Under Stress : The Italian Union Movement and the Italian Crisis in Developmental Perspective," in Peter Lange, George Ross and Maurizio Vannicelli, *Unions, Change and Crisis* (Boston : Allen and Unwin, 1982).

4. On the importance of egalitarianism in the Italian union movement, see Aris Accornero, *La parabola del sindacato* (Bologna: Il Mulino, 1992). For more on the "Hot Autumn", see Alessandro Pizzorno, Emilio Reyneri, Marino Regini, and Ida Regalia, *Lotte operaie e sindacato: Il ciclo 1968-1972 in Italia* (Bologna: Il Mulino, 1978); and Charles F. Sabel, *Work and Politics* (New York : Cambridge University Press, 1982).

5. According to Flanagan, Soskice and Ulman:

The objective of Agnelli's [CEO of Fiat and then head of *Confindustria*] exercise appears to have been the transfer of resources to the industrial sector and away from the public sector, which would be accomplished under conditions of rapid inflation as long as inflation was offset by depreciation of exchange rates and as long as 100 percent indexation was confined to the industrial sector. While real wages of industrial workers in relation to consumer prices were safeguarded, consumer prices, reflecting smaller economywide increases, would fall in relation to industrial prices, and the real cost of industrial labor, in relation to industrial prices, would fall.

Rovert J. Flanagan, David W. Soskice, and Lloyd Ulman, *Unionism, Economic Stabilization and Incomes Policies: European Experience* (Washington, D.C.: The Brookings Institution, 1983), pp. 543-546.

6. See Stefano Patriarca, "Caratteristiche e risultati della politica dei redditi 1983-1984," in Mimmo Carrieri and Paolo Perulli, eds., *Il Teorema sindacale : Flessibilità e competizione nelle relazioni industriali* (Bologna: Il Mulino, 1985), especially pp. 77-84.

7. See Lorenzo Bordogna, "The COBAS: Fragmentation of Trade-Union Representation and Conflict," in Robert Leonardi and Piergiorgio Corbetta, eds., *Italian Politics : A Review*, Vol. 3 (London: Pinter, 1989), pp. 50-65.

8. See Marino Regini, "The Conditions for Political Exchange : How Concertation Emerged and Collapsed in Italy and Great Britain," in John H. Goldthorpe, ed., *Order and Conflict in Contemporary Capitalism* (Oxford: Clarendon Press, 1984).

9. On the details of the agreement, see Miriam Golden, *Labor Divided : Austerity and Working Class Politics in Contemporary Italy* (Ithaca, NY: Cornell University Press, 1988), pp. 82-84.

10. For further analysis of these events, see Peter Lange, "The End of an Era : The Wage Indexation Referendum of 1985," in Robert Leonardi and Raffaela Y. Nanetti, eds., *Italian Politics : a Review*, Vol. 1 (London: Pinter, 1986), pp. 29-46.

11. On the 1991 congress and *Essere Sindacato*, see Carol A. Mershon, "The Crisis of the CGIL: Open Division in the 12th National Congress," in Stephen Hellman and Gianfranco Pasquino, eds., *Italian Politics*, Vol. 7 (New York and London: Pinter, 1992).

10

The Italian Intervention in Somalia: A New Italian Foreign Policy After the Cold War?

Osvaldo Croci

Introduction

On July 2, 1993, while on a weapons search mission in Mogadishu, a detachment of the Italian military contingent assigned to the United Nations forces in Somalia was attacked by a group of armed Somalis. Three soldiers were killed and twenty-two others were wounded. This incident shocked the Italian public, particularly as these were the first Italian soldiers to die in combat since the end of World War II. It also led Italian decision makers to take a closer look at the goals and methods of the U.N. initiative in Somalia, which they had hurriedly decided to join six months earlier.

Until then, both the Italian government and the press had fully supported the U.N. mission, even though they had manifested some displeasure for not having been invited to occupy a position of responsibility in its military command structure.

This desire to become part of the command team was not a simple matter of prestige. Rather, it sprang from increasing misgivings about the turn the mission seemed to have taken after June 5, 1993. On that day twenty-three Pakistani soldiers were killed in what U.N. officials later described as an "ambush" masterminded by the forces of General Aidid, leader of one of the factions in the Somali civil war. The U.N. command reacted by launching a series of air strikes against various objectives in Mogadishu, which resulted in hundreds of Somali deaths.

As Somali public outrage mounted, the situation in the city became increasingly dangerous both for relief workers, whose protection had been the main reason for the U.N. military intervention in the first place, and for U.N. peacekeepers themselves. It was in this tense atmosphere that the July 2 attack on the Italian contingent occurred. When, on July 12, four foreign journalists were killed by an angry crowd in the wake of another air attack that killed yet more Somali civilians, disagreement between Italy and the U.N. became public.

The same day Defense Minister Fabio Fabbri, following a meeting with Prime Minister Carlo Azeglio Ciampi and Foreign Minister Beniamino Andreatta, officially requested the United Nations to put a halt to military actions in Somalia. The U.N. Secretariat dismissed such a request and told the Italians to "either get on the team or get off." It then announced that the commander of the Italian forces in Somalia, General Bruno Loi, would be sent back home for insubordination. The response of the Italian government was immediate and brusque. Andreatta pointed out that "only the Italian government ha[d] the competence to decide who should lead [Italian] soldiers," while Ciampi accused the U.N. of having transformed a peace mission into "a military intervention almost as an end in itself, against the wishes of those who [were] carrying it out." He then called for the U.N. to re-examine the goals of its mission and define the role of the troops, adding that such a clarification was "essential for [Italy's] presence in Somalia."[1]

Although Italy had had differences with its allies in the past, this was the first time that a disagreement produced such a harsh and open exchange of accusations and remonstrances. After a brief account of the genesis of, and reasons for, the U.N. intervention in Somalia, this study examines the evolution of this intervention as well as the dynamics of the disagreement among Italy, the U.S. and the U.N. It concludes by assessing whether such an episode signals a new, more assertive foreign policy to be pursued by Italy after the Cold War.

The Somali Problem
and the Origins of U.N. Intervention

The U.N. intervened in Somalia in 1992 to try to bring relief to a population devastated by famine and civil war.

The roots of the Somali tragedy go back to 1978, when President Siad Barre played the card of irredentism but lost in his attempt to take the Somali-inhabited region of Ogaden from Ethiopia.[2] Although almost all Somalis belong to the same ethnic group, a small Bantu minority being the only exception, clans exert a strong claim on individuals' loyalties and thus constitute the most important social and political cleavage in Somali society. If the war over Ogaden represented "the high point of Somali nationalist fervour,"[3] defeat by Ethiopia dealt a blow to Barre's regime and led to increasing antagonism among different clans, thereby starting the process of national disintegration. By the late 1980s the country was in the midst of a ruthless civil war. When Barre fled Mogadishu in January 1991, the clan-based opposition forces, which had uneasily cooperated to defeat him, turned against each other.

The struggle was particularly fierce in Mogadishu, where two main contenders, Ali Mahdi and Mohammed Farah Aidid, battled each other and tried to forge a multi-clan alliance as each attempted to emerge as the predominant "national" leader.[4]

As the situation in the country worsened, a few relief organizations tried, without much success, to raise Western public awareness about the plight of the Somalis. In January 1992, the U.N. began making some efforts to deliver humanitarian assistance and promote national reconciliation. Its initiatives were coordinated by Mohammed Sahnoun, an Algerian diplomat whom U.N. Secretary General Boutros Boutros-Ghali appointed as his Special Representative to Somalia. Sahnoun devoted much effort to, and made some progress in, carrying out these tasks, but in October 1992, he resigned in protest, criticizing the U.N. for bureaucratic delays and obfuscation.[5]

In April 1992, the Security Council authorized the establishment of a small peacekeeping force (UNOSOM) to protect the activities of relief organizations in Mogadishu and surrounding areas, first and foremost the delivery of food. UNOSOM, which consisted of 500 Pakistani soldiers, was not deployed until October, and immediately proved to be too small for the task assigned it. Boutros-Ghali then sought to convince the Security Council that the Somali situation required the deployment of a larger military force. It was at this point that the United States volunteered to help. If authorized by the Security Council, President Bush offered to put at the disposal of the U.N. a large American contingent to do the job UNOSOM could not do. Boutros-Ghali preferred a force under direct U.N. command, but since this would take some time to put together, he accepted the American offer. Thus, on December 3, 1992, Security Council Resolution 794 authorized the deployment in Somalia of a U.S.-led international force (UNITAF), giving it the task of establishing "a secure environment for humanitarian relief operations."

The Italian government immediately announced its intention to take part in the mission. The Italian offer was met at first with some reluctance on the part of both the U.S. and the U.N., the official explanation being that Italy's past ties with Somalia could represent a liability for the success of the mission.[6] This reluctance, however, was soon overcome, and on December 9, the same day the American marines landed in Mogadishu, the Italian Parliament approved Italian participation in the U.N. operation. The first Italian soldiers left from Brindisi that same night.

The Reasons for the Intervention

Why did the U.N. and the U.S. move to intervene so decisively in
Somalia at the end of 1992 when until then they had paid relatively
little attention to events there? The U.N. decision can be explained quite
easily. Some observers contend that the end of the Cold War has provided
an opportunity for the U.N. to begin to play a much more active role in
the maintenance of international peace and security.[7] It is not surprising
that the organization itself should seek ways in which its role could be
enhanced. Boutros-Ghali's ideas about the ways and means needed to
achieve this goal were set forth in a report he submitted to the Security Council in June 1992. He suggested the expansion of traditional
peacekeeping activities to "peace operations," i.e. military intervention by
the U.N. aimed at resolving conflicts even in the absence of a request from
the belligerents. To conduct these operations he called for major member
countries to put at the permanent disposal of the U.N. some special units
he called "peace enforcement units," to be deployed to trouble spots
around the world on short notice.[8] There is hardly any doubt that by the
end of 1992, Boutros-Ghali came to regard Somalia as providing the
perfect field in which to test his ideas about the U.N.'s new, more
interventionist role. It seems, in fact, that the main reason for Sahnoun's
resignation was his opposition to Boutros-Ghali's intention of sending
a large military force to Somalia without first obtaining the agreement
of Somali faction leaders and clan elders.[9] UNITAF represented a
novelty from several points of view. It was the first time the U.N.
authorized a military intervention in a country without an explicit
invitation from its government (the justification advanced by Boutros-
Ghali was that "no government existed in Somalia that could request and
allow" intervention). Although presented as a humanitarian intervention,
UNITAF was established within the legal context of a response to a "threat
to peace" (art. 39, Chap. VII of the U.N. Charter) said to result from the
"repercussions of the Somali conflict on the entire region." Finally,
UNITAF was authorized to use force not only in self-defence but also to
ensure the accomplishment of its task.[10]

Some analysts have interpreted the American decision to intervene
militarily in Somalia as a step in a process of "recolonization" aimed at
protecting the strategic interests the U.S. has in the region.[11] Throughout
1992, however, the State Department, while willing to contribute to a
humanitarian intervention, argued that the U.S. had no reason to become
politically involved in what it regarded as a "clan-based quagmire destined to last for years if not decades."[12] With the end of the Cold War,
Somalia does seem to have lost most of its strategic military importance.
Somali bases, for instance, were not utilized at all during the Gulf War. The

U.S. ambassador to Kenya, Smith Hempstone Jr., criticized Bush's decision to intervene in Somalia because "aside from the humanitarian issue," which although compelling was no more so than in many other countries, he "fail[ed] to see where any vital interest [was] involved."[13] Indeed, it would appear that more than from strategic considerations, Bush's decision to mount "Operation Restore Hope" resulted primarily from a desire to end his term with a "demonstrative humanitarian intervention" that would give a benign face to his much touted concept of "new world order" and assure his being remembered as "a decisive leader."[14] Such an intervention could have been organized in a range of countries. Somalia seems to have been picked simply because, unlike Sudan, it can be accessed by the sea, because a mission there, unlike one in Bosnia, promised to be swift and successful and, last but not least, because by December 1992, its sufferings "were much publicized on TV."[15] This analysis is supported both by the theatrics of the landing and the fact that it was Bush's stated intention to have most, if not all, of the American forces back by the end of January 1993.

Why did Italy insist on contributing forces to UNITAF given the initial reluctance of the U.N. to accept them? It would be difficult—and indeed nobody has even tried—to explain the Italian decision in terms of strategic interests or as a result of pressures from economic groups, such as banana growers, which in the past influenced Italian policies toward Somalia. Senator Gian Giacomo Migone, vice-president of the Senate Committee on Foreign Affairs, has attributed the decision of the Italian government to *presenzialismo*. For him, the imperative of being there, as part of the deciding team, has been a traditional "obsession" of Italian foreign policy and it fully explains the Italian government's decision to intervene in Somalia.[16] Migone's explanation may indeed capture part of what drove Italy to contribute to UNITAF. Given the delicate phase the domestic political situation had entered by the end of 1992, the Italian government did not have much time to make a considered decision on the Somali question. Yet, to equate the Italian decision with little more than an instinctive response seems a bit reductionist, especially since such an analysis fails to take into account Italy's ties with Somalia. Besides the colonial and trusteeship experience, one must not forget that Italy was the only Western country to have maintained ties with Somalia during the years of Soviet presence there and the last one to abandon it after the fall of Barre. Therefore, in the case of Somalia, *presenzialismo* has at least a tradition, if not a justification. Undoubtedly, Italy's *presenza* has not been free of controversy and scandal. Most of the funds made available to Somalia through the Ministry of Foreign Affairs' foreign aid branch (*Cooperazione allo Sviluppo*), for instance, hardly contributed to the country's economic development but went to finance questionable projects and ended up in kickbacks to political parties and in the coffers of Barre and his clan. Although this might be little more than an *ex post facto* rationalization, the Italian decision to intervene in Somalia has also been explained by some Italian government officials as an attempt to make up for these past mistakes.[17] Last, it should be pointed out that, with the end of the Cold War, both Italian diplomats and the military have begun to feel that the time has come for Italy to take a more active part in the creation of a new international security system. As put by then Minister of Defense, Salvo Andò:

> We have until recently been a security consuming country; we have con-
> sumed the security produced and offered to us by our allies. ... This has ...
> meant ... a renunciation, almost an inability, on the part of politicians and the
> country in general, to think fully of our security, of the military instrument,
> its preparation, its possible use. In the future, and Somalia represents one of
> the choices we have made on this new road, we will have to become more
> and more a security producing country.[18]

Not surprisingly, the major pressures to convince the government to participate in the mission came from high officials within the Foreign Affairs and Defence Ministries, which regarded Somalia as the testing ground for this new, more active foreign policy.

From Humanitarianism to Militarism

No sooner had the American soldiers arrived in Mogadishu than a disagreement developed between the UNITAF commander and the U.N. Secretariat regarding the disarming of Somali factions. Technically, Resolution 794 did not require UNITAF to disarm Somali factions but Boutros-Ghali argued that the creation of a "secure environment" mentioned in the resolution presupposed doing exactly that. The UNITAF commander and the Pentagon did not share that opinion. As the Americans saw it, UNITAF's mission was to secure the port and the airport and open up supply routes so that food could be delivered. In this narrow sense, the UNITAF mission was, officially at least, considered a success.[19] Although UNITAF occasionally confronted groups of armed Somalis and proceeded to disarm them, such operations were not conducted in any systematic or organized fashion.

On March 26, 1993, Security Council Resolution 814 set up a multinational force under U.N. command (UNOSOM II) that replaced UNITAF. The Security Council also approved a request made by Boutros-Ghali that UNOSOM II, like UNITAF before it, be authorized to use force to carry out its mission. The mandate given to UNOSOM II went beyond that of UNITAF or, at least, beyond the narrow interpretation the U.S. had given it. The UNOSOM II mandate included, among other things, the tasks of disarming factions that did not voluntarily hand over their weaponry and taking action against those breaking the cease-fire agreement that fourteen Somali factions had signed at a U.N.-sponsored meeting in Addis Ababa the previous January. UNOSOM II, the largest peacekeeping force in U.N. history, was made up of combat units from most of the countries that had already supplied troops to UNITAF, including an American logistics contingent. The U.S. also agreed to leave behind a "Quick Reaction Force" outside UNOSOM II command but ready to intervene to assist U.N. forces if the need arose.[20]

The expanded but imprecise mandate given to UNOSOM II, in conjunction with the authorization to use force, increased the chances that confrontations with Somali factions over disarmament and cease-fire violations would turn violent. The first serious incident occurred on June 5, when a contingent of Pakistani soldiers was attacked by members of the Somali National Alliance (S.N.A.), a faction headed by General Aidid. The Somalis argued that they had acted to defend their radio station (Radio Mogadishu), which the "blue helmets" intended to destroy. The UNOSOM II command, on the other hand, claimed that the objective of the Pakistani contingent had been an arms depot and that the S.N.A. attack had been a "calculated and premeditated" one. The following day, the Security Council passed Resolution 837, which authorized UNOSOM II to take "all necessary measures against all those responsible for the armed attack."[21] Thereafter, the situation rapidly worsened. Starting that same night and throughout the rest of the month, the American "Quick Reaction Force" staged a series of air strikes that destroyed a number of buildings reputed to be Aidid's arms deposits or command centres, killing many Somali civilians in the process. More Somalis were killed by UNOSOM II forces conducting arms search missions. Over two hundred people reputed to be S.N.A. members were arrested. It was during one of these ground missions that the Italian contingent was attacked.[22] This "month of fire" culminated in the July 12 air strike on a villa in southern Mogadishu. According to newspaper reports 17 American helicopters fired 16 missiles and more than 2,000 cannon rounds into the building, killing 54 Somalis and wounding 174. The U.N. argued that the villa was "Aidid's command and control centre" and was hit "during a meeting of General Aidid's senior military and political staff." It described the action as "a clean, surgical attack" and a "very successful operation with no collateral damage." According to S.N.A. members, however, the villa was a "conference centre" and was hit while a group of clan elders was holding a meeting that was part of Somali efforts towards national reconciliation.[23]

The Italian-U.N. Disagreement

The first six months of "Operation Ibis"— the code name given to the Italian mission in Somalia—passed without major problems. The Italian press treated Somalia like a replay of Lebanon and praised the "professional behaviour" of Italian soldiers, which was supposedly gaining them the trust of Somalis and the grudging esteem of the U.S. Criticism was reserved for past governments and their scandalous misuse of economic aid and support for Barre's regime.[24]

The Italian government began to develop some misgivings about UNOSOM II operations only at the beginning of June, in the wake of reports from General Bruno Loi, the commander of the Italian contingent, and Enrico Augelli, the diplomatic envoy in Mogadishu. Both were concerned that the military operations against Aidid's faction were fast becoming the central, if not the only, objective of the U.N. in Somalia, complained that the UNOSOM II command paid no attention to their views and advice, and asked the government for instructions.[25] The Italian government continued to express public support for the conduct of UNOSOM II but decided to solicit Italian representation on the U.N. policy making team in Mogadishu. On June 12, after an American raid destroyed "Radio Mogadishu," Foreign Minister Andreatta dryly commented that "one could not expect to be able to reconstruct a state only with music and flowers and without the use of force." At the same time, however, Defence Minister Fabbri left for Somalia to convince U.N. Special Representative Jonathan Howe that: "the growing responsibilities of the Italian contingent ... require[d] that its commander become a full member of the team planning UNOSOM II operations."[26] The Italians thought that such a request was not unreasonable given that Italy had contributed the third largest national contingent after those of the U.S. and Pakistan and could claim a more profound knowledge of Somali society than any of the other countries present.

After the death of the three Italian soldiers, the Italian press became more critical of UNOSOM II.[27] The position of the government, instead, did not change. At the Tokyo Summit of July 7, Prime Minister Ciampi tried to convince President Clinton that "every nation with a substantial military presence [in Somalia] should at least have its views heard in some organized way," but admitted that "political action [there] of course [was to] be supported by military action."[28] The only reservation about events in Mogadishu expressed by the Italian government was that the conduct of UNOSOM II was perhaps a bit "too Prussian." The question of the permanence of the Italian forces in Somalia was raised in a debate in the Senate but all political parties, albeit with different motivations and to different degrees, agreed that the Italian contingent should not be withdrawn.[29] It was only after the July 12 attack on the purported command centre of Aidid that the Italian government publicly criticized the U.N. for having turned a humanitarian mission into a war.

Such criticism certainly did not stem from some peculiar Italian revulsion towards the use of force. Both the Italian government and its representatives in Mogadishu recognized that the Italian contingent might have to use force in order to carry out its mission and were willing to accept such a risk. As Defence Minister Fabbri later put it: "Italy has never denied that the U.N. mandate includes the possible use of force. We know that we did not go to Somalia simply to distribute bread and chocolate."[30] The disagreement between Italy and the U.N., therefore, did not concern the use of force *per se*. Rather, it was a question of what role force should play in the search for a political solution to the Somali problem, and, of how, when, and against whom force was appropriately used. The Italians understood that U.N. policy in Somalia would employ a two-track approach. In the Italian view, the primary task was to engage in a dialogue with all Somali factions in an effort to convince them to lay down weapons and promote the process of social reconciliation. Only if this approach did not yield results, would the use of force be justified. In this case the task of disarming Somalis would have to be carried out in an organized and systematic manner and, even more important, would have to treat all factions equally, that is, attempt to disarm all of them.

By the beginning of July, it seemed clear that the U.N. had abandoned this two-track policy and had embraced force as its only instrument. Even worse, the U.N. was using force exclusively against one faction, thus giving the impression of partisanship. The Italians felt that the methods used against Aidid and the S.N.A. amounted to a change of policy that was both unjustifiable and unacceptable since it nullified, at one blow, all the efforts spent on establishing a relationship of trust with the Somali population. Even worse, it did so precisely when these efforts were finally starting to pay off. Loi reported, for instance, that just before the air strikes began, the Italian contingent had collected many weapons voluntarily surrendered by Somalis. According to Augelli, this had been possible because the Italian contingent "had shown a position of neutrality that had allowed it to develop good relations with all the factions." The attacks against Aidid, however, "were being interpreted by Somalis as support given by the international community to one of the two factions facing each other [in Mogadishu]." The results, besides being deleterious for the U.N. mission as a whole, put the Italians in a delicate predicament. As Augelli saw it:

Ali Mahdi accuses us of being reluctant to eliminate the 'threat to peace' represented by Aidid, while the latter, after having praised our efforts towards a peaceful solution, now views Italian participation in UNOSOM II attacks against his faction as a betrayal.[31]

The military campaign against Aidid posed another problem. As Loi pointed out while asking for instructions from Rome: "If one wants to capture Aidid, one must be willing to engage in guerrilla warfare." Loi left this decision to the government but observed that the Italian contingent was not trained for that kind of mission.[32]

The Italian government had avoided facing this issue for over a month, in the hope that the disagreement could be solved once Italy obtained representation on the UNOSOM II command. This temporizing attitude was facilitated by what might be defined as "the Lebanon syndrome," that is, the belief that Italian soldiers, unlike those of other U.N. contingents, would not become the target of Somali attacks.[33] By July 12, however, this position had become untenable. First, the July 2 incident had dramatically ended the feeling of invulnerability brought to Somalia from Lebanon. Second, the U.S. and the U.N., while not openly turning down the Italian request, had sent clear signals that they did not intend to change the command structure of UNOSOM II. Third, it was evident that the policy of military confrontation with the S.N.A. faction was not about to be changed, as demonstrated by UNOSOM II's decision to put a $ 25,000 bounty on Aidid's head and by Howe's comments that "the important thing was to persevere in what [UNOSOM was] doing ... and get Aidid behind bars."[34] At this point, the Italian government felt it had no choice but to criticize publicly the conduct of UNOSOM II. By so doing, the Italian government was not taking a bold initiative but simply bringing up the rear of an increasingly larger group. In Italy, by mid-July, the press and public opinion were both openly critical of events in Somalia and pressed the government to clarify its position.[35] Other critics of UNOSOM II included peacekeeping forces from other countries, international, non-governmental relief groups, former U.N. special representative Sahnoun as well as other U.N. officials and agencies, the Organization of African Unity, the Western European Union, and even Amnesty International.[36]

The U.N. responded to Italian criticism with a diplomatic *faux pas*. On July 14, Kofi Annan, head of the U.N.'s peacekeeping operations, announced at a press conference—*before* the issue had been raised with the Italian government—that General Loi would be recalled to Rome for insubordination. Boutros-Ghali did immediately and publicly express his "profound regrets" to Rome but by then Italy had already threatened to withdraw its troops unless differences over the conduct of the mission were resolved.[37]

After this exchange, the public diatribe rapidly escalated, in part because of personal tensions between Admiral Howe, on the one side, and

General Loi and the Italian diplomatic envoy Enrico Augelli, on the other. Loi, a veteran of the Italian mission in Lebanon, had replaced General Giampiero Rossi, commander of the Italian contingent in UNITAF, in May 1993. Unlike Rossi, who had unobtrusively carried out his mission under American command, Loi had a more independent character and tended to look to Rome for verification whenever he personally disagreed with the courses of actions chosen by UNOSOM II.[38] Augelli was a career diplomat with a long experience in the Third World, and Somalia in particular, having headed, for some time, the technical section of *Cooperazione allo Sviluppo*. After being removed from this post by Foreign Minister Gianni De Michelis, apparently because of his outspoken opposition to the most questionable projects financed by the Ministry, Augelli spent one year as a visiting fellow at Harvard University, where he coauthored a study very critical of American policies towards the Third World. In late 1992, the Italian government sent him as a special envoy to Somalia with the task of promoting the process of social and political reconciliation. When he saw all his efforts being nullified by UNOSOM's military campaign against Aidid, Augelli blamed Admiral Howe and his very rudimentary and simplistic understanding of Somali politics.[39]

Before he was appointed U.N. special representative to Somalia, Admiral Howe had occupied various positions in the U.S. national security apparatus. A born-again Christian who was rumoured to begin all UNOSOM II meetings with a prayer, he might be viewed as a strange choice to head a humanitarian mission in a Muslim country. Howe reacted to Augelli's criticism by sending the U.N. headquarters a virulent report on the two Italian officials.[40] He accused Loi of refusing to carry out UNOSOM II orders and requested his recall. The accusation, as later revealed by *Newsweek*, referred to the June 2 incident when the Italian contingent supposedly waited seven hours before answering the call for help of the Pakistanis because Loi insisted on receiving clearance from Rome before moving his troops. Loi explained that clearance was required because he was called to intervene outside the sector assigned to his troops. He pointed out that the delay had lasted only two hours and that, in any case, his soldiers had arrived on the scene even before those of the American "Quick Reaction Force." He also complained that American forces, more than once, had come hunting for Aidid in his sector without first informing him. His troops were then left to face the anger of Somali crowds.[41] Howe also accused the Italians of siding with Aidid and, even worse, of sabotaging UNOSOM II efforts to capture the general by warning him of operations against his forces and sheltering him in their embassy building in Mogadishu. The Italians emphatically denied these accusations. The main objective of the mission was political, they contended, and it required keeping channels of communications open with all Somali clans, including

Aidid's. If Howe accused them of siding with Aidid, it was simply because he had become obsessed with the capture of the general and had lost sight of the main objective of the mission.[42]

The Failure of Peace Enforcement

The withdrawal of Italian troops as a protest against the conduct of UNOSOM II would have represented a dramatic break with the U.N. and the Italian government was not prepared to go this far. Thus, while these accusations and counter-accusations were being flung back and forth in the press, the Ciampi government took steps to ease the strained relations. After a debate in Parliament and consultations with its European partners, the government decided that even if its requests were not fully met, it would not withdraw from Somalia but instead simply redeploy the troops it had in Mogadishu to the north of the capital, where the rest of the Italian contingent had been sent in December 1992. The U.N., for its part, decided to appoint an Italian military official to the Secretariat's peacekeeping operations in New York. It was "a small step in the right direction," as Defence Minister Fabbri put it, but not big enough to satisfy the Italians. Hence, on August 13, the Italian government announced that it would withdraw from Mogadishu at the next scheduled rotation of troops. On that occasion, General Loi would be replaced by General Carmine Fiore.[43] This compromise solution put an end to the disagreement over the question of Italian participation in the UNOSOM II command. The controversy over the more fundamental issue of the role of military operations, however, was far from being solved.

The U.N. continued to stress that the capture of Aidid took precedence over other initiatives and Admiral Howe repeatedly asked the U.S. administration for elite troops to help UNOSOM II carry out this task. The U.S. had until then fully backed Admiral Howe. By late August, however, both Congress and the American public began to manifest some reservations about his "Wild West style." Aware that the American presence in Somalia would not retain public support for long unless it could show some concrete results, President Clinton chose at first a two-track policy. On the one hand, he sent Howe a small contingent of elite troops to help in the hunt for Aidid. On the other, he began to press the U.N. to resume its work towards a political solution.[44]

During an official visit to Washington on September 16 and 17, Prime Minister Ciampi reiterated to President Clinton the importance of abandoning force in favour of political and diplomatic means. Ciampi's appeal derived additional urgency from the fact that two more Italian soldiers had recently died and, as a result, at least four opposition parties in the Italian Parliament (the Northern League, *Rifondazione Comunista*, the Greens and *La Rete*) now pressed the government for a complete withdrawal. Clinton, however, was still hesitant and only assured Ciampi of his intention of submitting to the U.N. a proposal for the relaunching of political initiatives.[45] Yet, in the next few weeks, much to Boutros-Ghali's dismay, Clinton was pushed to embrace the Italian position by UNOSOM II's embarrassing blunders in its hunt for Aidid, by mounting international criticism, and, most important of all, by the pressures of Congress following the death of three American soldiers on September 25 and of twelve more on October 4. On October 7, with the Vietnam experience being mentioned ever more often in the press and Congress threatening to cut funds, President Clinton decided that all American troops would be withdrawn from Somalia by March 31, 1994. He also appointed Ambassador Robert Oakley as presidential envoy to Somalia and charged him with the task of convincing all Somali factions to convene around a conference table in Addis Ababa.[46]

Having lost the support of the U.S., Boutros-Ghali had to admit that the U.N.'s first experiment in peace enforcement had failed. In late October, Mahdi and Aidid's factions clashed again in Mogadishu but U.N. troops did not intervene because, as a U.N. spokesperson explained: "It is not our business to impose peace."[47] On November 19, the Security Council decided to prolong the life of UNOSOM II until May 3, 1994. After the American decision to withdraw, however, all the other Western countries, including Italy, announced their plan to withdraw their forces from Somalia at the latest by the date set by the U.S. The continuation of UNOSOM II after March 31, 1994, therefore, will depend on Boutros-Ghali's ability to persuade some countries to remain involved.[48]

On the political front, Oakley was able to convince representatives of Somali factions to meet again in Addis Ababa at the end of November. Although symbolically important, the meeting yielded no agreement. As for Aidid, on November 17, the Security Council revoked his arrest warrant and a few days later a U.S. Army plane flew him to Addis Ababa to attend the U.N. meeting. This would have been an ironic close to the story, had it not been for the fact that clashes between Somalis and UNOSOM II caused between 6,000 and 10,000 casualties.[49]

Conclusions: Lessons and Prospects for Italian Foreign Policy

The 1985 *Achille Lauro* affair, which ruffled Italian-American relations for a time, led at least one observer to conclude that there was "a trend of growing assertiveness in Italian foreign policy".[50] To what extent can the Somali episode be considered a continuation of this trend? The end of the Cold War has opened up possibilities for middle powers and former junior allies to play a more significant role not only on issues of immediate interest to them, but also on questions affecting the international system as a whole. Some political observers doubt Italy's ability to conduct a more assertive foreign policy, especially at a time when the domestic political scene is undergoing such dramatic change. Thus, it has been suggested that although the Italian government might have decided to go to Somalia to contribute to the construction of a new international security system, it soon found itself in a dead end because it lacked clear political goals of its own and lost heart in pursuing those of the U.S. and the U.N.[51] This analysis is unduly harsh, especially since it assumes a clarity of political goals on the part of the U.S. and the U.N. that simply did not exist. Granted, Italy may not have fully defined the goals it sought and the means needed to achieve them when it decided to intervene in Somalia; but once there it certainly developed at least a rudimentary vision of its aims and strategy. Furthermore, the Italian approach emerged as the winning one, in the sense that both the U.S. and the U.N. eventually embraced it.

So far, however, this new assertiveness has been a trait more of the Italian military and diplomatic corps than of the government, which has merely responded to the solicitations of the former.[52] Foreign policy, first and foremost the question of the future of Italian foreign policy, has recently gained unprecedented attention from Italian scholars, journalists and the public in general.[53] The still somewhat hesitant attitude of the Italian government, therefore, is bound to disappear as soon as the domestic political situation settles.

The lesson of Somalia, then, is not that Italy has yet to acquire the ability to conduct a more assertive foreign policy. Rather, it is that with the end of the Cold War, the increase in opportunities for middle powers to play a more significant role on the international scene has not yet been accompanied by a corresponding evolution in decision making, that is, mechanisms do not yet exist to integrate former junior partners into international policy making at the planning stage. Hence open protest is the only avenue open to them when they disagree with initiatives taken, inspired, or simply approved by the U.S.

To move towards decision sharing, Italian diplomats and politicians have explicitly urged the modification of some multilateral institutions as well as the creation of some new mechanisms. Ambassador Roberto Gaja called more than two years ago for a new "concert of powers" as the forum where the content of Bush's "new world order" should be defined and decided.[54] Prime Minister Ciampi, during his September 1993 visit to Washington, suggested to President Clinton that in the future the direction of such operations as UNOSOM II should be entrusted to a committee rather than to one person. A few days later, in a speech to the U.N., Foreign

Minister Andreatta argued in favour of creating a new layer of semi-permanent members in the Security Council. These would include Italy as well as other "countries capable of making important contributions to the U.N."[55]

The Italian request for new mechanisms of participation cannot be simply dismissed as a new form of *presenzialismo*. Rather, it is an aspiration shared by other middle powers and recognized as legitimate by some influential American scholars.[56] It reflects the belief that the construction of the post-Cold War world order is not the exclusive prerogative of the remaining superpower. This request for more participatory mechanisms does not imply, however, any dramatic shift in the content of Italian foreign policy. As Ciampi reassuringly put it to Clinton: "Italy is changing at a very rapid pace but one thing that will not change is its foreign policy."[57] The "emergent consensus" on Italian foreign policy that one scholar noted some fifteen years ago has in fact become a stronger "multipartisan consensus" among both citizens and policy makers.[58]

Notes

I would like to thank the Laurentian University Research Fund Committee for awarding me a grant to finance this research.

1. All quotations in this paragraph from *New York Times*, July 14 and 16, 1993.

2. It is not possible here to treat in detail the domestic aspects of the Somali problem. An essential bibliography would include: Said S. Samatar, *Somalia: A Nation in Turmoil* (London: Minority Rights Group, 1991); Ian M. Lewis, "Nazionalismo frammentato e collasso del regime somalo," *Politica Internazionale*, 4, July-August 1992, pp. 35-51; Hussein A. Adam, "Somalia: Militarism, Warlordism or Democracy?," *Review of African Political Economy*, 54, 1992, pp. 11-26; Samuel Makinda, *Seeking Peace from Chaos: Humanitarian Intervention in Somalia* (Boulder: Lynne Rienner, 1993), and Ahmed I. Samatar (ed.), *The Somali Challenge: From Catastrophe to Renewal* (Boulder: Lynne Rienner, 1994). For developments since August 1992, see *Somalia News Update*, an electronic newsletter compiled by Dr. Bernhard Helander of the Scandinavian Institute of African Studies of the University of Uppsala. Copies of this newsletter can be obtained by sending a request to Bernhard.Helander @ antro.uu.se or Antbh @ strix.udac.uu.se.

3. Ian M. Lewis, "The Ogaden and the Fragility of Somali Segmentary Nationalism," *African Affairs*, 88, 354, October 1989, p. 573.

4. For a discussion of the different anti-Barre groups see Daniel Compagnon, "The Somali Opposition Fronts," *Horn of Africa Bulletin*, 13, 1-2, April-June, 1990, pp. 29-54.

5. *The Economist*, November 7, 1992, p. 48. U.N. initiatives and Sahnoun's efforts in this period are recounted in Makinda, *Seeking Peace from Chaos*, pp. 59-69.

6. *Panorama*, January 3, 1993.

7. See, for instance, James N. Rosenau, *The United Nations in a Turbulent World* (Boulder: Lynne Rienner, 1992).

8. Boutros Boutros-Ghali, *Agenda for Peace* (New York: United Nations, 1992) and "Empowering the United Nations," *Foreign Affairs*, 72, 5, Winter 1992/93, pp. 89-102. See also his interview with David Frost of Skynews reprinted in "Dossier Somalia," *Guerre & Pace*, 1, 3/4, July-September 1993, pp. 20-24 and Brian Urquhart, "Needed—a U.N. Military Force," *New York Review of Books*, June 10, 1993.

9. See Jean Daniel, "Clinton e la Somalia," *La Repubblica*, October 23, 1993; *Africa Confidential*, 33, 24, December 4, 1992, p. 1 and Jonathan Stevenson, "Hope Restored in Somalia?" *Foreign Policy*, 91, Summer 1993, pp. 147-148.

10. *UN Chronicle*, March 1993, pp. 13-16. On the evolution of U.N. peacekeeping see Adam Roberts, "Humanitarian War: Military Intervention and Human Rights" and Marrack Goulding, "The Evolution of United Nations Peacekeeping," *International Affairs*, 69, 3, 1993, pp. 429-449 and 451-464. Quotations are at p. 440.

11. See, for instance, "Dossier Somalia", *Guerre & Pace*, which contains an interview with Professor Mohammed Usuf Hassan of the University of Mogadishu as well as articles by Michel Chossudovsky and Stefano Chiarini reprinted from *Le Monde Diplomatique*, July 1993 and *Il Manifesto*, July 13, 1993. These analyses regard Somalia as a forward base from which the U.S. can control the oil routes to the Mediterranean, and mount military operations in Africa and the Middle East.

12. Quoted in Peter J. Schraeder, "U.S. Intervention in the Horn of Africa Amidst the End of the Cold War," *Africa Today*, 40, 2, 1993, p. 14.

13. Hempstone's remarks are reported in *New York Times*, December 6, 1992. On the decreasing value of U.S. military bases in Somalia see Jeffrey A. Lefebvre, *Arms for the Horn: U.S. Security Policy in Ethiopia and Somalia, 1953-1991* (Pittsburgh: University of Pittsburgh Press, 1991).

14. Quotations from Edward N. Luttwak, "Wrong Time, Wrong Place," *New York Times*, July 22, 1993, and Michael Wines, "Aides Say U.S. Role in Somalia Gives Bush a Way to Exit in Glory," *ibid.*, December 6, 1992.

15. E. Luttwak, "Wrong Time, Wrong Place," and interviews in *La Stampa*, July 16, 1993 and *L'Espresso*, July 18, 1993; Jean Daniel, "Clinton e la Somalia,".

16. Migone's remarks were made at a round table on "La crisi della Somalia" held in Rome on January 15, 1993. The proceedings can be found in *Politica Internazionale*, 1, January-March 1993, pp. 213-236.

17. See the remarks of Defence Minister Salvo Andò in *Panorama*, December 13, 1992, p. 43 and those of former ambassador Sergio Romano in *Epoca*, July 27, 1993, pp. 6-7. On Italy's long history of involvement in Somalia see A. Del Boca, *Una sconfitta dell'intelligenza: Italia e Somalia* (Bari: Laterza, 1993). On the misuse of economic aid, see *L'Espresso*, September 6, 1992, pp. 36-39.

18. Quoted in Vincenzo Nigro, "In Somalia una 'guerra' dell'ONU," *Affari Esteri*, XXV, 100, Autumn 1993, pp. 697-705. See also Franco Angioni, "Operazioni di peace-keeping e peace-enforcing: Il ruolo dell'Italia" in Carlo M. Santoro (ed.), *L'Elmo di scipio. Studi sul modello di difesa italiano* (Bologna: Il Mulino, 1992), p. 70.

19. For a contrasting view see, Mark Huband, "When the Yankee Goes Home," *Africa Report*, March-April 1993, pp. 20-23.

20. Makinda, *Seeking Peace from Chaos*, pp. 61-66, 71-72 and 76-77; *Africa Confidential*, 34, 6, March 19, 1993, pp. 1-3 and *Somalia News Update*, 2, 10, March 11, 1993.

21. *UN Chronicle*, September 1993, p. 4.

22. *Africa Research Bulletin*, June 1-30 and July 1-31, 1993, pp. 11053-11055 and 11095-11096. For a report on the dynamics of the attack on the Italian contingent see *Epoca*, July 13, 1993.

23. *Globe and Mail* (Toronto), July 13, 1993 and *New York Times*, July 14, 1993. See also *Africa Confidential*, 34, 14, July 16, 1993, p. 8.

24. See *Epoca* and *Il Giornale* for praise of soldiers and *L'Espresso* for criticism of past governments. The major scoop was the publication by *Epoca*, June 15, 1993, of photographs of Italian soldiers who appeared to be using brutal methods to arrest some Somalis. The publication led to an official inquiry by the Ministry of Defence, which concluded that the soldiers had followed "NATO approved procedures", *ibid.*, July 6, 1993.

25. *L'Espresso*, July 25, 1993.

26. Both quotations from *Il Giornale*, June 13, 1993. The UNOSOM II command team was composed almost entirely of American nationals. Howe was a retired American admiral; General Cevik Bir, the military commander, was from Turkey but had been chosen by the U.S.; and Bir's deputy was another American, the commander of the "Quick Reaction Force," Major-General Thomas Montgomery.

27. For a review of the change of attitude in the press see Alessandro Boscaro, "I soldati Italiani più duri dei marines" in "Dossier Somalia," *Guerre & Pace*, pp. 20-23.

28. *Somalia News Update*, 2, 16, July 9, 1993.

29. "Dossier Somalia," *Guerre & Pace*, p. 19. On the Senate debate see *Il Giornale*, July 4, 1993.

30. *Il Giorno*, July 21, 1993.

31. Quotations in Giovanni Porzio and Gabriella Simoni, *Inferno Somalia: quando muore la speranza* (Milan: Mursia, 1993), p. 175.

32. *Corriere della Sera*, August 15, 1993.

33. For some evidence of the "Lebanon syndrome" see G. Porzio and G. Simoni, *Inferno Somalia*, p. 17 and *Panorama*, June 27, 1993, p. 90.

34. *New York Times*, July 14, 1993.

35. An opinion poll reported in *L'Espresso*, July 25, 1993, p. 54, shows, for instance, that after the July 12 strike, 66.3% of Italians were critical of UNOSOM II actions, 72% favoured dialogue over the use of force and only 12% supported the idea of leaving Italian forces in Mogadishu even if the Italian position did not prevail or if Italy continued to be denied a position of responsibility on the UNOSOM II command team.

36. *Globe and Mail*, July 12, 13 and 15, 1993; *Times Magazine*, July 26, 1993; *New York Times*, July 14, 1993; *Africa Research Bulletin*, July 1-31, 1993, p. 11096; *Africa Confidential*, 34, 15, July 30, 1993, pp. 1-2 and 34, 19, September 24, 1993, p. 1; Hilary Naylor, "Somalia: Amnesty International concerned about detention and killing

by United Nations Troops," Africa-N @ UToronto.Bitnet, October 31, 1993. Articles in Africa-N (Africa News & Information Service) can be retrieved by sending an "Index Africa-N" command to Listserv @ UToronto.Bitnet.

37. *New York Times*, July 16, 1993.

38. For a portrait of Loi, see *Epoca*, July 6 and 27, 1993 and *L'Espresso*, August 29, 1993.

39. *L'Espresso*, December 27, 1992 and August 29, 1993, and *Panorama*, June 27, 1993. Enrico Augelli and Craig Murphy, *America's Quest for Supremacy and the Third World. A Gramscian Analysis* (London: Pinter Publishers, 1988).

40. *L'Espresso*, August 29, 1993, p. 62. For a portrait of Howe, see *Somalia News Update*, 2, 25, September 20, 1993.

41. *Newsweek*, July 26, 1993 and *L'Espresso*, August 1, 1993; G. Porzio and G. Simoni, *Inferno Somalia*, p. 177.

42. *Corriere della Sera*, August 15, 1993; *Panorama*, October 3, 1993; *La Repubblica*, September 19/20, 1993. Howe, it appears, was particularly furious at the fact that the Italian contingent retook a checkpoint lost on July 2, by negotiating with, and perhaps bribing, local elders of the Aidid clan, rather than fighting. The admiral seems to have preferred to use force in order to teach Aidid a lesson. Loi pointed out that he saw no need to use force when the same objective could be achieved by negotiations. See *Africa Confidential*, 34, 15, July 30, 1993, p. 2 and Frances Kennedy, "In Somalia, Machiavelli Vs. Rambo," *New York Times*, July 22, 1993.

43. *Il Giorno*, July 21, 1993 and *Corriere della Sera*, August 15, 1993.

44. *Newsweek*, October 18, 1993.

45. *La Repubblica*, September 17 and 18, 1993; *Somalia News Update*, 2, 24, September 18, 1993.

46. On Clinton's slow conversion see *La Repubblica*, September 26/27, October 2, 5-12, 1993 and *Newsweek*, October 18, 1993. For the mounting criticism of Howe, see *Somalia News Update*, 2, 21, September 1, 1993, and 2, 29, October 20, 1993.

47. Reported in *Toronto Star*, October 31, 1993. See also *The Globe and Mail* (Toronto), and *La Repubblica* of October 26, 1993. The reasons for the failure of UNOSOM II have been well illustrated by a U.N. official in an essay on peacekeeping, published just before the Somali experiment was launched: "The nonviolent nature of United Nations peacekeeping operations is at the same time their most important and their least understood characteristic. It is the characteristic that makes peacekeeping forces acceptable both to the governments and parties engaged in conflict, and to the governments that contribute the troops", Brian Urquhart, "Introduction" to F. T. Liu, *United Nations Peacekeeping and the Non-Use of Force* (Boulder: Lynne Rienner, 1992), p. 7. It seems logical to conclude that peace-enforcement operations become unacceptable both to the parties engaged in conflict and to the governments that contribute soldiers as soon as the soldiers resort to force and begin to die in combat.

48. *La Repubblica*, November 18 and 20, December 23, 1993; *Corriere della Sera*, December 14, 1993; *Somalia News Update*, 2, 34, November 27, 1993.

49. *Somalia News Update*, 2, 32, November 1, 1993; 34, November 27, 1993; and 35, December 7, 1993).

50. Frank J. Piason, "Italian Foreign Policy: The *Achille Lauro* Affair" in Robert

Leonardi and Raffaella Y. Nanetti, eds., *Italian Politics: A Review*, Vol. 1 (London: Frances Pinter, 1986), p. 162.

51. V. Nigro, "In Somalia una 'guerra' dell'ONU", p. 704.

52. Note, for instance, that the most vocal support for the line taken by the Italian government after June 1993 came from General Luigi Caligaris and former ambassador Sergio Romano. See their columns in *Epoca*, especially those of June 22 and July 27, 1993.

53. The last few years have seen the publication of an unusual number of historical studies of Italian foreign and defence policies [see, for instance, Richard J.B. Bosworth and Sergio Romano, eds., *La politica estera italiana—1860-1985* (Bologna: Il Mulino, 1991); Carlo M. Santoro, *La politica estera di una media potenza. L'Italia dall'Unità ad oggi* (Bologna: Il Mulino, 1991)], critical commentaries on current debates and initiatives [e.g. Carlo M. Santoro, ed., *L'Elmo di scipio*] as well as new periodicals devoted to foreign policy (e.g. *Limes*). For the most recent debates in the press, see Leopoldo Fabiani, "L'Italia è condannata a diventare protagonista" and "Un paese senza politica estera," *La Repubblica*, December 19 and 23, 1993 and Dino Frescobaldi, "Un 'forum' per la Farnesina," *ibid.*, December 28, 1993. For the attitude of the Italian public, see Pierangelo Isernia, "Opinione pubblica e politica internazionale in Italia" in Carlo M. Santoro, ed., *L'Elmo di scipio*, pp. 219-261.

54. Roberto Gaja, "Alcune note su mezzo secolo di politica estera italiana," *Affari Esteri*, 23, 92, October 1991, pp. 882-834.

55. *La Repubblica*, September 18 and October 1, 1993.

56. See, for instance, Janice Gross Stein, "Living with Uncertainty: Canada and the Architecture of the New World Order," *International Journal*, 47, Summer 1992, pp. 614-629; Robert O. Keohane, "The Diplomacy of Structural Change: Multilateral Institutions and State Strategies" and Joseph S. Nye, Jr., "Patrons and Clients: New Roles in the Post-Cold War Order" in Helga Haftendorn and Christian Tuschhoff, eds., *America and Europe in an Era of Change* (Boulder: Westview Press, 1993), pp. 43-59 and 87-104.

57. *La Repubblica*, September 17, 1993.

58. Robert D. Putnam, "Italian Foreign Policy. The Emergent Consensus" in H. R. Penniman ed., *Italy at the Polls. The Parliamentary Elections of 1976* (Washington D.C.: American Enterprise Institute, 1977), pp. 287-326; Pierangelo Isernia talks of "bipartisan consensus", "Opinione pubblica e politica internazionale in Italia", p. 251, but in the Italian case the label "multipartisan consensus" seems more appropriate.

Documentary Appendix

compiled by Rosalba Salvato

This documentary appendix is divided into three sections: background data, electoral results, and local governments.

The first section (Tables A1-A6) furnishes data for the 1983-1992 period on the Italian population, the labor force, crime, and the economy and public finance.

The second section (Tables B1-20) summarizes the results of elections held during 1993. In particular, the section reports data, disaggregated by region, for the eight referendum items submitted to voters on April 18, as well as the results of regional, provincial, and muncipal elections held in June and November. The section also presents, for several major cities, the results of the first direct mayoral elections, held under the new law for municipal and provincial elections (Law No. 81, March 25, 1993).

The third section (Tables C1 and C2) provides statistics gathered by the Ministry of the Interior on the political composition of municipal governments. The data are current up to April 1993, since information on the administrations formed after the municipal elections of June and November (held under the new legislation) are not yet available.

218

TABLE A1 Resident Population by Age Group and by Sex (in Thousands)

	Age Groups			
	0-14	15-64	65 and over	Total population
Both sexes				
1982	12,054	37,005	7,476	56,536
1983	11,777	37,568	7,396	56,742
1984	11,497	38,159	7,272	56,929
1985	11,177	38,632	7,270	57,080
1986	10,877	38,854	7,470	57,202
1987	10,541	39,085	7,664	57,290
1988	10,218	39,293	7,887	57,399
1989	9,924	39,467	8,112	57,504
1990	9,620	39,620	8,335	57,576
1991	9,385	39,804	8,558	57,746
Men only				
1982	6,178	18,253	3,061	27,493
1983	6,039	18,538	3,011	27,589
1984	5,896	18,837	2,941	27,674
1985	5,732	19,080	2,927	27,740
1986	5,578	19,209	3,003	27,791
1987	5,408	19,348	3,076	27,833
1988	5,245	19,482	3,162	27,889
1989	5,096	19,586	3,255	27,938
1990	4,941	19,678	3,349	27,968
1991[a]	4,925	19,802	3,445	28,072

[a] Data 1992 not available.

Source: ISTAT, *Popolazione e movimento anagrafico dei comuni*, (Rome 1982-1992).

TABLE A2 Present Population by Position on the Labor Market (in Thousands)

	Labor Forces				
	Employed	Seeking Job			Total
		Unemployed	Seeking First Job	Other Persons seeking Job	
			Both sexes		
1983	20,557	343	1,257	563	22,720
1984	20,647	466	1,136	703	22,952
1985	20,742	468	1,215	698	23,123
1986	20,856	501	1,296	814	23,467
1987	20,836	547	1,354	932	23,669
1988	21,103	537	1,412	937	23,989
1989	21,004	507	1,405	954	23,870
1990	21,396	483	1,357	912	24,148
1991	21,592	469	1,285	898	24,244
1992	21,459	551	1,370	878	24,258
			Men only		
1983	13,960	186	594	168	14,908
1984	13,972	267	533	187	14,959
1985	13,986	269	580	174	15,009
1986	13,953	289	617	209	15,068
1987	13,845	313	665	251	15,074
1988	13,990	305	687	248	15,230
1989	13,851	286	676	257	15,070
1990	14,015	264	667	246	15,192
1991	14,102	256	645	241	15,244
1992	13,945	297	692	238	15,172

Source: ISTAT, «Annuario statistico italiano», (Rome 1984-1993).

TABLE A3 Labor Conflicts: Number and Impact of Contractual and Non-Contractual Disputes (i.e. Political) (in Thousands)

	Conflicts	Participants	Number of Hours Lost
		Contractual Disputes	
1983	1,550	4,625	82,626
1984	1,759	3,540	31,786
1985	1,166	1,224	11,036
1986	1,462	2,940	36,742
1987	1,146	1,473	20,147
1988	1,767	1,609	17,086
1989	1,295	2,108	21,001
1990	1,094	1,634	36,269
1991	784	750	11,573
1992	895	621	5,605
		Non-Contractual Disputes	
1983	15	2,219	15,395
1984	57	3,816	29,137
1985	5	3,619	15,779
1986	7	667	2,764
1987	3	2,800	12,093
1988	2	1,103	6,120
1989	2	2,344	10,052
1990	-	-	-
1991	7	2,202	9,322
1992	8	2,557	13,905

Source: Istat, «Annuario statistico italiano», (Rome, 1984-1993).

TABLE A4 Classification of Officially Recorded Crimes[a]

	Against Persons	Against the Family or Morality	Against Property	Against the Economy or Public Trust	Against the State	Other	Total
1983	135,137	13,877	1,520,499	290,848	32,392	50,017	2,042,770
1984	126,729	12,652	1,457,093	291,409	33,675	56,781	1,978,339
1985	125,940	13,559	1,369,325	385,691	37,831	68,090	2,000,436
1986	125,192	14,118	1,355,507	410,934	41,734	82,688	2,030,173
1987	138,272	14,826	1,507,040	394,360	47,093	103,395	2,204,986
1988	136,685	14,228	1,529,876	416,387	46,158	90,597	2,233,931
1989	125,769	13,073	1,573,805	422,166	41,968	97,314	2,274,095
1990	103,039	7,363	1,575,016	223,740	21,550	67,366	1,998,074
1991	121,881	10,256	2,255,918	326,584	35,590	66,834	2,817,063
1992	202,149	11,552	2,032,579	378,331	43,297	72,983	2,740,891

[a] For 1990 and subsequent years, the data are no longer fully comparable with those for earlier years. For criminal accusations against a person already subjected to investigations, the new Code of Criminal Procedure (Article 405) identifies the start of judicial action as the moment at which the person is formally charged with a crime. Unlike previous years, then, the statistics no longer include cases closed without trial for lack of evidence or other causes. In comparing 1990 and 1991 data, it should be kept in mind that organizational difficulties linked to the implementation of the new Code have caused delays in judicial action and in the transmittal of information to ISTAT. Thus, for most classifications above, the ISTAT data register decreases in 1990 and then increases in 1991.

Source: Istat, «Annuario statistico italiano», (Rome, 1984-1993).

TABLE A5 Gross Domestic Product (in Market Prices) and the Consumer Price Index: Yearly Values and Variations (in Percentages). Over the Previous Year

| | Gross Domestic Product | | | | Consumer Price Index (1990 = 100) | |
	In Current Prices[a]	Variation (in %)	In 1985 Prices	Variation	Index	Variation
1983	633,436	16.20	769,370	0.97	62.70	14.63
1984	725,760	14.58	790,036	2.69	69.50	10.85
1985	810,580	11.69	810,580	2.60	75.90	9.21
1986	899,903	11.02	834,262	2.92	80.30	5.80
1987	983,803	9.32	860,422	3.14	84.10	4.73
1988	1,091,837	10.98	895,397	4.06	88.40	5.11
1989	1,193,462	9.31	921,714	2.94	93.90	6.22
1990	1,311,638	9.90	942,271	2.23	100.00	6.50
1991	1,427,342	8.82	955,817	1.44	106.40	6.40
1992	1,507,190	5.59	962,037	0.65	111.70	4.98

[a] In billions of lire.

Source: Istat-Ministero del Bilancio, *Relazione generale sulla situazione economica del paese*, (Roma, 1992); Istat, «Annuario statistico italiano», (Rome, 1993).

TABLE A6   The National Debt and the Annual Budgetary Deficit, in Absolute Terms and as a Percentage of the Gross Domestic Product

	National Debt			Budget Deficit		
	Absolute Figures[a]	Variation over previous year	% of GDP	Absolute Figures[a]	Variation over previous year	% of GDP
1983	456,031	25.97	71.99	59,117	36.47	9.33
1984	561,489	23.13	77.37	77,100	30.42	10.62
1985	683,044	21.65	84.27	101,702	31.91	12.55
1986	793,583	16.18	88.19	116,826	14.87	12.98
1987	910,542	14.74	92.55	128,226	9.76	13.03
1988	1,035,263	13.70	94.82	124,986	-2.53	11.45
1989	1,167,813	12.80	97.85	119,466	4.42	10.01
1990	1,318,244	12.88	100.50	122,471	2.52	9.34
1991	1,485,141	12.66	104.05	118,620	-3.14	8.31
1992	1,673,574	12.69	111.04	120,501	1.59	8.00

[a] In billions of lire.

Source: Bank of Italy, Relazione annuale, (Rome, 1993).

TABLE B1 Popular Referendum April 18, 1993: "Environmental Responsibilities of Local Health Units (USL)". Regional and National Returns

	Piemonte	V. D'Aosta	Lombardia	Tr.A.A.	Veneto	Friuli V.G.	Liguria	Emilia R.	Toscana	Umbria
Electors	3,668,679	99,211	7,427,807	737,909	3,705,193	1,064,693	1,487,329	3,383,999	3,012,616	698,825
Voters	3,045,996	76,979	6,368,852	597,076	3,237,619	844,788	1,183,350	2,965,463	2,518,254	570,867
% voters	83.0	77.6	85.7	80.9	87.4	79.3	79.6	87.6	83.6	81.7
"Yes" votes	2,424,751	56,609	5,178,959	469,919	2,741,154	696,564	931,535	2,242,994	1,850,537	436,197
%	83.9	79.0	84.5	86.0	87.8	84.5	82.5	78.9	77.6	80.5
"No" votes	464,799	15,008	953,471	76,577	381,260	127,863	197,610	600,676	535,709	105,348
%	16.1	21.0	15.5	14.0	12.2	15.5	17.5	21.1	22.4	19.5
Total valid votes	2,889,550	71,617	6,132,430	546,496	3,122,414	824,427	1,129,145	2,843,670	2,386,246	541,545
Not valid votes	156,134	5,362	233,378	50,559	113,638	20,205	51,230	121,697	127,541	29,322
% of non valid votes/voters	5.1	7.0	3.7	8.5	3.5	2.4	4.3	4.1	5.1	5.1
of which blank ballots	99,458	3,853	162,034	42,669	78,800	13,163	35,864	86,953	91,656	19,288
% of blank ballots/ not valid votes	63.7	71.9	69.4	84.4	69.3	65.1	70.0	71.5	71.9	65.8

	Marche	Lazio	Abruzzi	Molise	Campania	Puglia	Basilicata	Calabria	Sicilia	Sardegna	Tot. Italy
Electors	1,223,393	4,340,285	1,131,910	310,562	4,501,252	3,246,210	509,679	1,733,075	4,263,131	1,344,447	47,890,203
Voters	993,900	3,453,883	803,906	191,220	2,870,763	2,213,810	327,216	949,779	2,656,225	973,650	36,843,596
% voters	81.2	79.6	71.0	61.6	63.8	68.2	64.2	54.8	62.3	72.4	76.9
"Yes" votes	774,584	2,722,274	607,251	137,750	2,110,595	1,651,425	236,205	663,016	1,833,339	801,754	28,567,412
%	83.5	82.8	82.5	80.7	80.2	81.6	81.4	79.8	78.9	86.4	82.5
"No" votes	152,567	565,173	128,741	32,899	522,374	372,931	53,960	168,223	491,606	125,997	6,072,792
%	16.5	17.2	17.5	19.3	19.8	18.4	18.6	20.2	21.1	13.6	17.5
Total valid votes	927,151	3,287,447	735,992	170,649	2,632,969	2,024,356	290,165	831,239	2,324,945	927,751	34,640,204
Not valid votes	65,796	164,520	67,907	20,383	237,614	189,389	37,026	103,441	330,833	45,822	2,171,797
% of non valid votes/voters	6.6	4.8	8.4	10.7	8.3	8.6	11.3	10.9	12.5	4.7	5.9
of which blank ballots	44,818	98,488	41,153	14,209	162,190	124,000	24,425	76,724	151,943	28,619	1,400,307
% of blank ballots/ not valid votes	68.1	59.9	60.6	69.7	68.3	65.5	66.0	74.2	45.9	62.5	64.5

Source: Calculated from data provided by Ministero dell'Interno - Direzione centrale per i servizi elettorali.

TABLE B2   Popular Referendum April 18, 1993: "Personal Use of Drugs". Regional and National Returns

	Piemonte	V. D'Aosta	Lombardia	Tr.A.A.	Veneto	Friuli V.G.	Liguria	Emilia R.	Toscana	Umbria
Electors	3,668,679	99,211	7,427,807	737,909	3,705,193	1,064,691	1,487,329	3,383,999	3,012,616	698,825
Voters	3,048,736	77,030	6,375,258	598,924	3,239,222	856,285	1,184,585	2,968,523	2,523,701	570,894
% voters	83.1	77.6	85.8	81.2	87.4	80.4	79.6	87.7	83.8	81.7
"Yes" votes	1,598,828	44,315	3,202,003	303,996	1,682,332	469,349	591,805	1,723,021	1,438,718	320,616
%	55.4	61.8	52.3	55.3	54.0	56.9	52.3	60.4	59.9	59.0
"No" votes	1,288,346	27,379	2,923,457	245,645	1,433,905	356,076	539,979	1,127,479	962,814	222,672
%	44.6	38.2	47.7	44.7	46.0	43.1	47.7	39.6	40.1	41.0
Total valid votes	2,887,174	71,694	6,125,460	549,641	3,116,237	825,425	1,131,784	2,850,500	2,401,532	543,288
Not valid votes	161,114	5,336	244,939	49,265	120,855	30,840	49,579	117,930	117,670	27,590
% of non valid votes/voters	5.3	6.9	3.8	8.2	3.7	3.6	4.2	4.0	4.7	4.8
of which blank ballots	97,198	3,731	154,719	38,980	78,542	19,147	32,256	79,503	79,704	17,788
% of blank ballots/ not valid votes	60.3	69.9	63.2	79.1	65.0	62.1	65.1	67.4	67.7	64.5

	Marche	Lazio	Abruzzi	Molise	Campania	Puglia	Basilicata	Calabria	Sicilia	Sardegna	Tot. Italy
Electors	1,223,393	4,340,285	1,131,910	310,562	4,501,252	3,246,210	509,679	1,733,075	4,263,131	1,344,447	47,890,203
Voters	993,857	3,459,361	804,124	191,447	2,875,919	2,215,973	327,459	950,093	2,657,419	974,858	36,893,668
% voters	81.2	79.7	71.0	61.6	63.9	68.3	64.2	54.8	62.3	72.5	77.0
"Yes" votes	541,938	1,804,466	428,678	101,960	1,374,759	1,021,385	167,749	486,284	1,389,534	533,902	19,225,638
%	58.3	54.6	58.0	59.7	52.1	50.2	57.6	58.2	58.3	57.5	55.3
"No" votes	387,822	1,498,459	310,013	68,845	1,264,113	1,011,570	123,451	348,866	994,747	395,110	15,530,748
%	41.7	45.4	42.0	40.3	47.9	49.8	42.4	41.8	41.7	42.5	44.7
Total valid votes	929,760	3,302,925	738,691	170,805	2,638,872	2,032,955	291,200	835,150	2,384,281	929,012	34,756,386
Not valid votes	63,753	153,539	65,416	20,526	236,955	182,717	36,250	100,476	272,860	45,777	2,103,387
% of non valid votes/voters	6.4	4.4	8.1	10.7	8.2	8.2	11.1	10.6	10.3	4.7	5.7
of which blank ballots	41,645	87,946	40,431	13,148	146,859	113,064	23,660	73,329	147,924	25,864	1,315,438
% of blank ballots/ not valid votes	65.3	57.3	61.8	64.1	62.0	61.9	65.3	73.0	54.2	56.5	62.5

Source: Calculated from data provided by Ministero dell'Interno - Direzione centrale per i servizi elettorali.

TABLE B3 Popular Referendum April 18, 1993: "Public Financing of Political Parties". Regional and National Returns

	Piemonte	V.D'Aosta	Lombardia	Tr.A.A.	Veneto	Friuli V.G.	Liguria	Emilia R.	Toscana	Umbria
Electors	3,668,679	99,211	7,427,807	737,909	3,705,193	1,064,691	1,487,329	3,383,999	3,012,616	698,825
Voters	3,048,215	77,047	6,373,284	597,629	3,238,683	856,028	1,184,389	2,967,074	2,520,949	571,214
% voters	83.1	77.7	85.8	81.0	87.4	80.4	79.6	87.7	83.7	81.7
"Yes" votes	2,682,413	68,219	5,721,607	506,251	2,950,245	769,209	1,047,880	2,658,049	2,193,602	493,737
%	92.3	94.0	92.9	91.9	94.2	92.7	92.1	92.9	91.1	90.6
"No" votes	225,322	4,384	438,271	44,501	182,258	60,273	90,131	203,360	215,287	51,091
%	7.7	6.0	7.1	8.1	5.8	7.3	7.9	7.1	8.9	9.4
Total valid votes	2,907,735	72,603	6,159,878	550,752	3,132,503	829,482	1,138,011	2,861,409	2,408,889	544,828
Not valid votes	140,425	4,444	212,333	46,854	104,638	26,523	43,586	105,556	108,801	26,380
% of non valid votes/voters	4.6	5.8	3.3	7.8	3.2	3.1	3.7	3.6	4.3	4.6
of which blank ballots	87,134	3,109	143,422	39,879	72,029	17,357	29,538	74,654	76,135	17,210
% of blank ballots/ not valid votes	62.1	70.0	67.5	85.1	68.8	65.4	67.8	70.7	70.0	65.2

	Marche	Lazio	Abruzzi	Molise	Campania	Puglia	Basilicata	Calabria	Sicilia	Sardegna	Tot. Italy
Electors	1,223,393	4,340,285	1,131,910	310,562	4,501,252	3,246,210	509,679	1,733,075	4,263,131	1,344,447	47,890,203
Voters	993,842	3,457,243	803,730	191,423	2,875,373	2,215,500	327,378	949,633	2,657,067	974,610	36,880,311
% voters	81.2	79.7	71.0	61.6	63.9	68.2	64.2	54.8	62.3	72.5	77.0
"Yes" votes	845,647	2,958,404	654,233	147,814	2,240,330	1,756,462	251,676	709,534	1,987,117	850,379	31,492,808
%	90.7	89.3	88.3	86.2	85.0	86.5	86.5	85.0	83.2	91.2	90.3
"No" votes	86,857	353,083	86,480	23,594	393,891	272,998	39,325	125,538	400,221	82,040	3,378,905
%	9.3	10.7	11.7	13.8	15.0	13.5	13.5	15.0	16.8	8.8	9.7
Total valid votes	932,504	3,311,487	740,713	171,408	2,634,221	2,029,460	291,001	835,072	2,387,338	932,419	34,871,713
Not valid votes	60,970	143,759	62,992	19,867	241,047	185,969	36,371	100,886	269,404	42,133	1,982,938
% of non valid votes/voters	6.1	4.2	7.8	10.4	8.4	8.4	11.1	10.6	10.1	4.3	5.4
of which blank ballots	40,512	85,877	39,944	13,828	152,975	122,018	24,503	74,991	150,830	25,422	1,291,367
% of blank ballots/ not valid votes	66.4	59.7	63.4	69.6	63.5	65.6	67.4	74.3	56.0	60.3	65.1

Source: Calculated from data provided by Ministero dell'Interno - Direzione centrale per i servizi elettorali.

TABLE B4 Popular Referendum April 18, 1993: "Nominations of Directors of Saving Banks". Regional and National Returns

	Piemonte	V.D'Aosta	Lombardia	Tr.A.A.	Veneto	Friuli V.G.	Liguria	Emilia R.	Toscana	Umbria
Electors	3,668,679	99,211	7,427,807	737,909	3,705,193	1,064,691	1,487,329	3,383,999	3,012,616	698,825
Voters	3,046,080	76,989	6,367,982	597,017	3,236,993	855,280	1,183,304	2,964,919	2,517,691	570,821
% voters	83.0	77.6	85.7	80.9	87.4	80.3	79.6	87.6	83.6	81.7
"Yes" votes	2,655,473	67,454	5,692,691	498,040	2,932,585	762,563	1,036,658	2,649,363	2,157,485	485,643
%	92.1	93.9	93.0	91.6	94.1	92.6	92.0	93.3	90.7	90.1
"No" votes	226,323	4,372	425,595	45,938	185,333	60,865	89,899	191,531	221,974	53,390
%	7.9	6.1	7.0	8.4	5.9	7.4	8.0	6.7	9.3	9.9
Total valid votes	2,881,796	71,826	6,118,286	543,978	3,117,918	823,428	1,126,557	2,840,894	2,379,459	539,033
Not valid votes	163,511	5,163	248,723	53,021	117,486	31,825	53,690	123,893	133,699	31,788
% of non valid votes/voters	5.4	6.7	3.9	8.9	3.6	3.7	4.5	4.2	5.3	5.6
of which blank ballots	106,596	3,735	174,277	45,285	82,836	21,706	37,879	91,024	97,400	20,772
% of blank ballots/not valid votes	65.2	72.3	70.1	85.4	70.5	68.2	70.6	73.5	72.9	65.3

	Marche	Lazio	Abruzzi	Molise	Campania	Puglia	Basilicata	Calabria	Sicilia	Sardegna	Tot. Italy
Electors	1,223,393	4,340,285	1,131,910	310,562	4,501,252	3,246,210	509,679	1,733,075	4,263,131	1,344,447	47,890,203
Voters	993,398	3,453,915	803,516	191,291	2,874,179	2,213,709	327,666	949,511	2,655,267	974,125	36,853,653
% voters	81.2	79.6	71.0	61.6	63.9	68.2	64.3	54.8	62.3	72.5	77.0
"Yes" votes	833,521	2,913,572	639,130	143,419	2,185,244	1,706,188	245,515	687,415	1,926,504	839,997	31,058,460
%	90.2	88.9	87.2	84.7	83.5	84.9	85.2	83.3	81.7	90.9	89.8
"No" votes	90,520	365,440	93,731	26,006	432,820	304,618	42,764	138,083	431,562	84,442	3,515,206
%	9.8	11.1	12.8	15.3	16.5	15.1	14.8	16.7	18.3	9.1	10.2
Total valid votes	924,041	3,279,012	732,861	169,425	2,618,064	2,010,806	288,279	825,498	2,358,066	924,439	34,573,666
Not valid votes	69,054	172,985	70,631	21,707	255,984	202,839	39,384	109,565	296,908	49,634	2,251,490
% of non valid votes/voters	7.0	5.0	8.8	11.3	8.9	9.2	12.0	11.5	11.2	5.1	6.1
of which blank ballots	47,362	105,524	45,631	15,263	168,584	136,150	26,377	82,126	169,883	31,496	1,509,906
% of blank ballots/not valid votes	68.6	61.0	64.6	70.3	65.9	67.1	67.0	75.0	57.2	63.5	67.1

Source: Calculated from data provided by Ministero dell'Interno - Direzione centrale per i servizi elettorali.

TABLE B5 Popular Referendum April 18, 1993: "Abolition of the Ministry for State Holdings". Regional and National Returns

	Piemonte	V.D'Aosta	Lombardia	Tr.A.A.	Veneto	Friuli V.G.	Liguria	Emilia R.	Toscana	Umbria
Electors	3,668,679	99,211	7,427,807	737,909	3,705,193	1,064,691	1,487,329	3,383,999	3,012,616	698,825
Voters	3,045,673	76,982	6,367,108	597,025	3,233,766	855,092	1,183,078	2,964,813	2,517,395	570,801
% voters	83.0	77.6	85.7	80.9	87.3	80.3	79.5	87.6	83.6	81.7
"Yes" votes	2,671,947	67,549	5,735,925	514,358	2,957,423	767,358	1,038,511	2,658,375	2,163,973	489,151
%	92.5	93.9	93.5	93.0	94.8	93.0	92.0	93.4	90.7	90.3
"No" votes	217,877	4,408	397,433	38,895	163,789	57,376	90,674	186,532	221,696	52,699
%	7.5	6.1	6.5	7.0	5.2	7.0	8.0	6.6	9.3	9.7
Total valid votes	2,889,824	71,957	6,133,358	553,253	3,121,212	824,734	1,129,185	2,844,907	2,385,669	541,850
Not valid votes	155,816	5,025	223,737	43,742	110,935	30,324	50,751	119,642	127,431	28,951
% of non valid votes/voters	5.1	6.5	3.5	7.3	3.4	3.5	4.3	4.0	5.1	5.1
of which blank ballots	101,266	3,604	159,197	36,591	79,675	20,758	35,764	87,763	92,529	19,423
% of blank ballots/ not valid votes	65.0	71.7	71.2	83.7	71.8	68.5	70.5	73.4	72.6	67.1

	Marche	Lazio	Abruzzi	Molise	Campania	Puglia	Basilicata	Calabria	Sicilia	Sardegna	Tot. Italy
Electors	1,223,393	4,340,168	1,131,910	310,562	4,501,252	3,246,210	509,679	1,733,075	4,263,131	1,344,447	47,890,086
Voters	993,423	3,452,833	803,632	190,928	2,873,718	2,213,780	327,619	949,075	2,655,081	974,006	36,845,828
% voters	81.2	79.6	71.0	61.5	63.8	68.2	64.3	54.8	62.3	72.4	76.9
"Yes" votes	842,873	2,915,713	644,246	139,898	2,193,876	1,723,774	247,450	689,204	1,938,863	842,387	31,242,854
%	90.9	88.7	87.6	82.0	83.5	85.6	85.5	83.3	81.9	90.9	90.1
"No" votes	83,946	372,043	91,206	30,626	432,775	290,519	41,860	138,588	427,887	84,083	3,424,912
%	9.1	11.3	12.4	18.0	16.5	14.4	14.5	16.7	18.1	9.1	9.9
Total valid votes	926,819	3,287,756	735,452	170,524	2,626,651	2,014,293	289,310	827,792	2,366,750	926,470	34,667,766
Not valid votes	66,329	163,160	68,175	20,263	246,961	199,425	38,301	107,799	288,070	47,514	2,142,351
% of non valid votes/voters	6.7	4.7	8.5	10.6	8.6	9.0	11.7	11.4	10.8	4.9	5.8
of which blank ballots	46,102	98,919	44,047	8,347	165,167	135,637	25,693	80,565	165,886	30,258	1,437,191
% of blank ballots/ not valid votes	69.5	60.6	64.6	41.2	66.9	68.0	67.1	74.7	57.6	63.7	67.1

Source: Calculated from data provided by Ministero dell'Interno - Direzione centrale per i servizi elettorali.

TABLE B6 Popular Referendum April 18, 1993: "Electoral Laws for the Senate". Regional and National Returns

	Piemonte	V.D'Aosta	Lombardia	Tr.A.A.	Veneto	Friuli V.G.	Liguria	Emilia R.	Toscana	Umbria
Electors	3,668,679	99,211	7,427,807	737,909	3,705,193	1,064,691	1,487,329	3,383,999	3,012,616	698,825
Voters	3,050,042	77,075	6,379,320	598,069	3,242,624	856,899	1,185,664	2,970,434	2,525,934	571,289
% voters	83.1	77.7	85.9	81.0	87.5	80.5	79.7	87.8	83.8	81.7
"Yes" votes	2,491,034	64,595	5,421,139	466,005	2,800,951	716,984	965,458	2,516,402	2,014,268	454,304
%	85.8	89.3	87.9	83.9	89.4	86.3	84.7	87.7	83.2	83.1
"No" votes	413,496	7,760	744,730	89,446	332,421	113,451	174,540	352,193	407,802	92,376
%	14.2	10.7	12.1	16.1	10.6	13.7	15.3	12.3	16.8	16.9
Total valid votes	2,904,530	72,355	6,165,869	555,451	3,133,372	830,435	1,139,998	2,868,595	2,422,070	546,680
Not valid votes	145,467	4,720	203,806	42,590	107,708	26,423	42,810	101,763	99,861	24,550
% of non valid votes/voters	4.8	6.1	3.2	7.1	3.3	3.1	3.6	3.4	4.0	4.3
of which blank ballots	89,859	3,326	141,455	35,135	71,798	16,714	27,969	70,028	66,233	15,525
% of blank ballots/not valid votes	61.8	70.5	69.4	82.5	66.7	63.3	65.3	68.8	66.3	63.2

	Marche	Lazio	Abruzzi	Molise	Campania	Puglia	Basilicata	Calabria	Sicilia	Sardegna	Tot. Italy
Electors	1,223,393	4,340,168	1,131,910	310,562	4,501,252	3,246,210	509,679	1,733,075	4,263,131	1,344,447	47,890,086
Voters	994,863	3,461,741	804,696	191,546	2,877,235	2,215,514	328,092	950,828	2,657,436	975,325	36,914,626
% voters	81.3	79.8	71.1	61.7	63.9	68.2	64.4	54.9	62.3	72.5	77.1
"Yes" votes	780,895	2,657,073	597,081	135,494	1,981,890	1,590,370	233,357	626,833	1,623,778	799,464	28,937,375
%	83.3	80.1	80.2	78.6	74.7	77.8	79.6	74.5	67.7	85.3	82.7
"No" votes	156,320	659,499	147,089	36,813	670,236	455,109	59,721	214,433	773,474	138,000	6,038,909
%	16.7	19.9	19.8	21.4	25.3	22.2	20.4	25.5	32.3	14.7	17.3
Total valid votes	937,215	3,316,572	744,170	172,307	2,652,126	2,045,479	293,078	841,266	2,397,252	937,464	34,976,284
Not valid votes	57,374	143,606	60,520	19,087	225,051	169,897	35,009	95,300	260,037	37,806	1,903,385
% of non valid votes/voters	5.8	4.1	7.5	10.6	7.8	7.7	10.7	10.0	9.8	3.9	5.2
of which blank ballots	37,570	80,675	36,828	13,159	141,602	107,021	22,425	68,233	137,995	24,165	1,207,715
% of blank ballots/not valid votes	65.5	56.2	60.9	68.9	62.9	63.0	64.1	71.6	53.1	63.9	63.5

Source: Calculated from data provided by Ministero dell'Interno - Direzione centrale per i servizi elettorali.

TABLE B7 Popular Referendum April 18, 1993: "Abolition of the Ministry of Agriculture". Regional and National Returns

	Piemonte	V.D'Aosta	Lombardia	Tr.A.A.	Veneto	Friuli V.G.	Liguria	Emilia R.	Toscana	Umbria
Electors	3,668,679	99,211	7,427,807	737,909	3,705,193	1,064,691	1,487,329	3,383,999	3,012,616	698,825
Voters	3,045,475	76,978	6,367,668	596,967	3,236,746	855,033	1,183,080	2,964,636	2,518,128	570,910
% voters	83.0	77.6	85.7	80.9	87.4	80.3	79.5	87.6	83.6	81.7
"Yes" votes	2,212,705	59,407	4,546,261	417,029	2,405,561	607,371	829,111	2,096,820	1,687,758	359,850
%	76.5	82.4	74.2	75.3	77.1	73.7	73.4	73.7	70.7	66.3
"No" votes	678,326	12,731	1,579,158	136,597	716,335	217,237	300,195	748,722	699,443	182,649
%	23.5	17.6	25.8	24.7	22.9	26.3	26.6	26.3	29.3	33.7
Total valid votes	2,891,031	72,138	6,125,419	553,626	3,121,896	824,608	1,129,306	2,845,542	2,387,201	542,499
Not valid votes	154,407	4,840	232,129	43,321	113,282	30,386	50,957	118,932	126,609	28,380
% of non valid votes/voters	5.1	6.3	3.6	7.3	3.5	3.6	4.3	4.0	5.0	5.0
of which blank ballots	100,066	3,513	167,593	36,142	81,265	20,732	36,325	86,103	93,650	18,717
% of blank ballots/ not valid votes	64.8	72.6	72.2	83.4	71.7	68.2	71.3	72.4	74.0	66.0

	Marche	Lazio	Abruzzi	Molise	Campania	Puglia	Basilicata	Calabria	Sicilia	Sardegna	Tot. Italy
Electors	1,223,393	4,340,168	1,131,910	310,562	4,501,252	3,246,210	509,679	1,733,075	4,263,131	1,344,447	47,890,086
Voters	997,529	3,452,977	803,787	191,769	2,874,020	2,213,674	327,246	949,167	2,655,612	974,050	36,855,452
% voters	81.5	79.6	71.0	61.7	63.8	68.2	64.2	54.8	62.3	72.4	77.0
"Yes" votes	623,139	2,070,843	484,094	107,782	1,634,671	1,224,010	175,506	520,560	1,569,406	702,991	24,334,875
%	67.1	62.9	65.6	62.8	62.1	60.4	60.2	62.5	66.2	75.7	70.1
"No" votes	305,307	1,220,594	253,771	63,787	997,283	801,133	115,876	312,582	800,399	225,373	10,367,498
%	32.9	37.1	34.4	37.2	37.9	39.6	39.8	37.5	33.8	24.3	29.9
Total valid votes	928,446	3,291,437	737,865	171,569	2,631,954	2,025,143	291,382	833,142	2,369,805	928,364	34,702,373
Not valid votes	69,049	159,792	65,918	20,024	242,012	188,254	35,805	102,403	285,547	45,627	2,117,674
% of non valid votes/voters	6.9	4.6	8.2	10.4	8.4	8.5	10.9	10.8	10.8	4.7	5.7
of which blank ballots	44,544	97,049	42,145	14,185	156,735	124,667	24,077	77,245	158,352	28,719	1,411,824
% of blank ballots/ not valid votes	64.5	60.7	63.9	70.8	64.8	66.2	67.2	75.4	55.5	62.9	66.7

Source: Calculated from data provided by Ministero dell'Interno - Direzione centrale per i servizi elettorali.

TABLE B8 Popular Referendum April 18, 1993: "Abolition of the Ministry of Tourism". Regional and National Returns

	Piemonte	V.D'Aosta	Lombardia	T.A.A.	Veneto	Friuli V.G.	Liguria	Emilia R.	Toscana	Umbria
Electors	3,668,679	99,211	7,427,807	737,909	3,705,193	1,064,691	1,487,329	3,383,999	3,012,616	698,825
Voters	3,045,080	76,975	6,365,309	596,908	3,231,905	854,981	1,183,014	2,964,059	2,516,836	570,772
% voters	83.0	77.6	85.7	80.9	87.2	80.3	79.5	87.6	83.5	81.7
"Yes" votes	2,508,849	64,702	5,395,729	487,947	2,800,364	715,393	970,272	2,492,039	1,986,019	437,822
%	86.9	89.8	88.1	87.9	89.8	86.8	86.0	87.7	83.3	80.9
"No" votes	378,267	7,388	726,194	66,983	319,130	109,104	157,738	348,560	399,438	103,647
%	13.1	10.2	11.9	12.1	10.2	13.2	14.0	12.3	16.7	19.1
Total valid votes	2,887,116	72,090	6,121,923	554,930	3,119,494	824,497	1,128,010	2,840,599	2,385,457	541,469
Not valid votes	157,917	4,885	241,282	41,949	110,927	30,449	52,167	123,367	127,117	29,293
% of non valid votes/voters	5.2	6.3	3.8	7.0	3.4	3.6	4.4	4.2	5.1	5.1
of which blank ballots	105,866	3,543	171,724	34,959	78,978	20,973	37,184	91,071	90,316	19,537
% of blank ballots/ not valid votes	67.0	72.5	71.2	83.3	71.2	68.9	71.3	73.8	71.0	66.7

	Marche	Lazio	Abruzzi	Molise	Campania	Puglia	Basilicata	Calabria	Sicilia	Sardegna	Tot. Italy
Electors	1,223,393	4,340,168	1,131,910	310,562	4,501,252	3,246,210	509,679	1,733,075	4,263,131	1,344,447	47,890,086
Voters	993,199	3,452,276	803,733	191,267	2,873,465	2,213,059	327,640	949,056	2,655,356	973,898	36,838,788
% voters	81.2	79.5	71.0	61.6	63.8	68.2	64.3	54.8	62.3	72.4	76.9
"Yes" votes	765,443	2,485,864	575,058	128,255	1,879,011	1,482,007	221,358	609,379	1,723,911	782,746	28,512,168
%	82.6	75.6	78.0	75.0	71.2	73.0	76.1	73.1	72.4	84.3	82.2
"No" votes	161,499	801,811	162,639	42,747	758,687	546,977	69,657	224,379	657,416	145,585	6,187,846
%	17.4	24.4	22.0	25.0	28.8	27.0	23.9	26.9	27.6	15.7	17.8
Total valid votes	926,942	3,287,675	737,697	171,002	2,637,698	2,028,984	291,015	833,758	2,381,327	928,331	34,700,014
Not valid votes	66,179	163,007	66,028	20,265	235,689	184,027	36,622	101,312	273,768	45,517	2,111,767
% of non valid, votes/voters	6.7	4.7	8.2	10.6	8.2	8.3	11.2	10.7	10.3	4.7	5.7
of which blank ballots	45,840	97,238	42,116	14,255	155,870	124,140	24,134	74,971	150,785	28,606	1,412,106
% of blank b,llots/ not valid votes	69.3	59.7	63.8	70.3	66.1	67.5	65.9	74.0	55.1	62.8	66.9

Source: Calculated from data provided by Ministero dell'Interno - Direzione centrale per i servizi elettorali.

TABLE B9   Popular Referendum April 18, 1993: Summary of National Returns

	Environmental Responsibility of Local Health Units (USL)	Personal Use of Drugs	Public Financing of Political Parties	Nominations of Directors of Saving Banks
Electors	47,890,205	47,890,203	47,890,203	47,890,203
Voters	36,843,596	36,893,668	36,880,311	36,853,653
% voters	76.9	77.0	77.0	77.0
"Yes" votes	28,567,412	19,225,638	31,492,808	31,058,460
%	82.5	55.3	90.3	89.8
"No" votes	6,072,792	15,530,748	3,378,905	3,515,206
%	17.5	44.7	9.7	10.2
Total valid votes	34,640,204	34,756,386	34,871,713	34,573,666
Not valid votes	2,171,797	2,103,387	1,982,938	2,251,490
% of non valid votes/voters	5.9	5.7	5.4	6.1
of which blank ballots	1,400,307	1,315,438	1,291,367	1,509,906
% of blank ballots/not valid votes	64.5	62.5	65.1	67.1

	Abolition of the Ministry for State Holdings	Electoral Laws for the Senate	Abolition of the Ministry of Agricolture	Abolition of the Ministry of Tourism
Electors	47,890,086	47,890,086	47,890,086	47,890,086
Voters	36,845,828	36,914,626	36,855,452	36,838,788
% voters	76.9	77.1	77.0	76.9
"Yes" votes	31,242,854	28,937,375	24,334,875	28,512,168
%	90.1	82.7	70.1	82.2
"No" votes	3,424,912	6,038,909	10,367,498	6,187,846
%	9.9	17.3	29.9	17.8
Total valid votes	34,667,766	34,976,284	34,702,373	34,700,014
Not valid votes	2,142,351	1,903,385	2,117,674	2,111,767
% of non valid votes/voters	5.8	5.2	5.7	5.7
of which blank ballots	1,437,191	1,207,715	1,411,824	1,412,106
% of blank ballots/notvalid votes	67.1	63.5	66.7	66.9

Source: Calculated from data provided by Ministero dell'Interno - Direzione centrale per i servizi elettorali.

TABLE B10   Friuli Venezia Giulia: Regional Election June 6, 1993

Lists	Valid votes	%	Seats
Dc	177,857	22.3	15
Pds	78,581	9.9	6
Rifondazione comunista	43,992	5.5	4
Psi	37,652	4.7	3
Msi-Dn	66,321	8.3	5
Pri	13,453	1.7	1
Pli	10,287	1.3	1
Psdi-Verdi Fvg	12,663	1.6	-
Lega Lombarda	212,501	26.7	18
All. verde-Fvg	43,022	5.4	3
Lega autonomia Friuli	37,419	4.7	2
La Rete-Mov. dem.	14,044	1.8	-
Lista per Trieste	26,294	3.3	2
Unione slovena	9,635	1.2	-
Movimento Friuli	12,364	1.6	-
Total	796,085	100.0	60

Electors	1,065,598
Voters	853,762
% voters	80.1
Not valid votes	57,677
% non valid votes/voters	6.8
of which blank ballots	22,620
% of blank ballots/not valid votes	39.2

Source: Calculated from data provided by Ministero dell'Interno - Direzione centrale per i servizi elettorali.

TABLE B11   Trentino Alto Adige: Regional Elections November 21, 1993

Lists	Valid votes	%	Seats
Dc	87,851	14.3	11
Pds	28,418	4.6	3
Rifondazione comunista	7,827	1.3	1
Psi	3,847	0.6	-
Msi-Dn	45,266	7.4	5
Pri	3,365	0.5	-
Psdi	5,274	0.9	1
Patt	62,132	10.1	7
Other Green Lists	21,188	3.4	2
Lega Nord	59,194	9.6	7
Other Leagues	15,524	2.5	1
La Rete-Mov. Dem.	32,195	5.2	4
Svp	160,206	26.0	19
Alleanza-Patto	16,678	2.7	2
Autonomist Lists	39,518	6.4	5
Left mixed	3,271	0.5	-
Centre mixed	8,388	1.4	1
P. Dem.	506	0.1	-
Other Lists	15,526	2.5	1
Total	616,174	100.0	70

Electors	729,627
Voters	646,227
% voters	88.6
Not valid votes	30,053
% of non valid votes/voters	4.7
of which blank ballots	9,877
% of blank ballots/not valid votes	32.9

Source: Calculated from data provided by Ministero dell'Interno - Direzione centrale per i servizi elettorali.

TABLE B12 Communal Elections June 6, 1993: 1070 Communes up to 15,000 Inhabitants (10,000 for Sicily) Summary of National Returns

Lists	Valid votes	%	Seats
Dc	482,054	18.7	3,031
Pds	57,548	2.2	375
Rifondazione comunista	42,375	1.6	74
Psi	26,023	1.0	165
Msi-Dn	44,747	1.7	73
Pri	1,256	0.1	8
Pli	2,223	0.1	16
Psdi	2,521	0.1	6
Green Federation	2,160	0.1	2
Other Green Lists	269	-	-
Lega lombarda	172,722	6.7	651
Lega aut. veneta	4,026	0.2	15
Other Leagues	36,936	1.4	157
La Rete-Mov. Dem.	3,574	0.1	6
Alleanze democratiche	89,449	3.5	465
Coalition gov. area	154,346	6.0	1,039
Coalition gov. area-Others	60,914	2.4	268
Center mixed	7,994	0.3	39
Left mixed	187,938	7.3	1,075
Right mixed	1,827	0.1	3
Uv	1,031	-	16
Autonomist Lists	28	-	-
Partito sardo d'azione	709	-	8
Mixed	555,805	21.5	3,285
Indipendents	129,708	5.0	886
Civic Lists	481,675	18.6	3,070
Other Lists	33,397	1.3	162
Total	2,583,255	100.0	14,895

Electors	3,312,032
Voters	2,717,331
% voters	82.0
Not valid votes	130,576
% of non valid votes/voters	4.8
of which blank ballots	53,123
% of blank ballots/not valid votes	40.7

Source: Calculated from data provisional provided by Ministero dell'Interno - Direzione centrale per i servizi elettorali.

TABLE B13 Communal Elections June 6, 1993: 122 Communes over 15,000 Inhabitants (10,000 for Sicily)

Lists	Valid votes	%	Seats
Dc	684,517	18.8	654
Pds	422,121	11.6	501
Rifondazione comunista	274,939	7.5	87
Pds-Rifond. comun.	1,918	0.1	9
Pds-Psi	1,179	-	-
Psi	132,095	3.6	148
Msi-Dn	202,689	5.6	106
Pri	44,329	1.2	40
Pli	9,847	0.3	7
Psdi	49,387	1.4	30
Lista Pannella	919	-	1
Green Federation	62,088	1.7	14
Verdi federalisti	901	-	-
Other Green Lists	18,230	0.5	1
Psdi-Verdi Fvg	1,765	0.1	1
Lega lombarda	557,312	15.3	287
Lega aut. veneta	962	-	-
Lega alpina lumbarda	8,677	0.2	-
Other Legues	36,394	1.0	32
Lega autonom. Friuli	1,895	0.1	-
La Rete-Mov. Dem.	118,378	3.3	53
Alleanze democratiche	34,858	1.0	48
Autonomist Lists	15,916	0.4	-
Coalition gov. area	48,405	1.3	82
Coalition gov. area-Others	6,931	0.2	3
Left mixed	27,407	0.8	53
Partito sardo d'azione	3,966	0.1	7
Partito pensionati	11,940	0.3	-
Mixed	110,100	3.0	191
Indipendents	84,508	2.3	127
Civic Lists	260,293	7.1	314
Other Lists	408,173	11.2	176
Total	3,643,039	100.0	2,972

Electors	5,490,922	
Voters	4,351,757	
% voters	79.3	
Not valid votes	276,980	
of non valid votes/voters	6.4	
of which blank ballots	100,993	
% of blank ballots/not valid votes	36.5	

Source: Calculated from data provisional provided by Ministero dell'Interno - Direzione centrale per i servizi elettorali.

TABLE B14 Communal Elections November 21, 1993: 325 Communes up to 15,000 Inhabitants

Lists	Valid votes	%	Seats
Dc	94,868	8.2	409
Pds	38,445	3.3	162
Rifondazione comunista	12,025	1.0	14
Psi	9,696	0.8	33
Msi-Dn	18,128	1.6	21
Pri	587	-	1
Fed. dei verdi	747	0.1	1
Lega Nord	66,821	5.8	278
Lega Italia federale	250	-	-
Piemont-Lega Nord	7,325	0.6	13
Liga Veneta-Lega Nord	22,650	2.0	95
Lega autonom. Friuli	1,220	0.1	2
La Rete-Mov. Dem.	1,990	0.2	1
Alleanza-Patto	20,530	1.8	70
Unione di centro	2,977	0.3	13
Left mixed	227,786	19.7	999
Centre mixed	289,431	25.1	1,241
Right mixed	2,063	0.2	12
Mixed	172,449	15.0	758
Indipendents	67,002	5.8	270
Civic Green Lists	916	0.1	1
Civic Lists	93,336	8.1	391
Other Lists	2,050	0.2	13
Total	1,153,292	100.0	4,798

Electors	1,484,264
Voters	1,171,124
% Voters	78.9
Not valid votes	59,751
% of non valid votes/voters	5.1
of which blank ballots	23,125
% of blank ballots/not valid votes	38.7

Source: Calculated from data provisional provided by Ministero dell'Interno - Direzione centrale per i servizi elettorali.

238

TABLE B15 Communal Elections November 21, 1993: 99 Communes over 15,000 Inhabitants

Lists	Valid votes	%	Seats
Dc	563,560	11.2	289
Pds	706,433	14.1	435
Rifondazione comunista	311,685	6.2	92
Psi	66,117	1.3	38
Msi-Dn	719,438	14.4	150
Pri	13,669	0.3	5
Pli	8,509	0.2	-
Psdi	52,538	1.0	20
Lista Pannella	55,669	1.1	4
Federazione dei verdi	213,177	4.3	38
Verdi federalisti	10,627	0.2	-
Other green lists	1,670	-	-
Lega Nord	312,976	6.2	281
Lega Italia federale	25,441	0.5	-
Piemont-Lega Nord	48,359	1.0	58
Liga Veneta-Lega Nord	84,774	1.7	78
Lega autonomia veneta	12,032	0.2	1
Lega alpina lumbarda	2,716	0.1	-
Other Leagues	44,074	0,9	24
La Rete-Mov. Dem.	189,203	3.8	74
Alleanza-Patto	340,318	6.8	165
Unione di centro	64,794	1.3	3
Autonomist Lists	8,200	0.2	1
Lista per Trieste	15,284	0.3	3
Left mixed	353,887	7.1	228
Centre mixed	321,365	6.4	191
Partito sardo d'azione	1,048	-	1
Partito pensionati	7,305	0.1	1
Right mixed	87,691	1.8	43
Mixed	46,066	0.9	66
Indipendents	41,656	0.8	27
Civic Lists	122,685	2.4	116
Other Lists	158,364	3.2	30
Total	5,011,330	100.0	2,262

Electors	8,033,495
Voters	6,266,127
% Voters	78.0
Not valid votes	392,781
% non valid votes/voters	6.3
of which blank ballots	117,248
% of blank ballots/not valid votes	29.9

Source: Calculated from data provisional provided by Ministero dell'Interno - Direzione centrale per i servizi elettorali.

TABLE B16 Mayor Elections - June 1993: Torino, Milano e Catania

	First Round - 6 June			Second Round - 20 June		
	Candidates	%	Lists	Candidates	%	Lists
Torino	**Novelli Diego**	**36.1**	Rif. com., All. verde Torino, La Rete-Mov.Dem., Partito pensionati	**Castellani Valentino**	**57.3**	Pds,Fed. dei verdi, Alleanza per Torino
	Castellani Valentino	**20.3**	Pds, Fed. dei verdi, Alleanza per Torino	Novelli Diego	42.7	Rif. com., All. verde Torino, La Rete-Mov. Dem., Partito pensionati
	Comino Domenico	19.5	Lega lombarda			
	Zanetti Giovanni	13.1	Dc, Torino liberale			
	Martinat Ugo	4.6	Msi-Dn			
	Lupi Maurizio	1.9	Verdi-Verdi, Lista autonomista, Pensionati uniti, Lista delle donne			
	Marzano Marziano	1.8	Psi-Psdi			
	Pioli Claudio	1.7	Lega Torino			
	Zingaro Giacomo	0.6	Lega pensionati insieme			
	Vittucci Righini di S.Albino R.	0.4	Monarchic List			

(continues)

TABLE B16 (continued)

	First Round - 6 June			Second Round - 20 June		
	Candidates	%	Lists	Candidates	%	Lists
Milano	**Formentini Marco**	**38.8**	Lega lombarda	**Formentini Marco**	**57.1**	Lega lombarda
	Dalla Chiesa Fernando	30.4	Pds, Rif. com., Fed. dei verdi, La Rete-Mov.Dem., Per Milano	Dalla Chiesa Fernando	42.9	Pds, Rif. com., Fed. dei verdi, La Rete-Mov.Dem., Per Milano
	Bassetti Piero	10.9	Dc, PSsdi Federalismo, Con le donne			
	Teso Adriano	6.7	Patto con Milano			
	Borghini Gianpietro	6.2	PSI, Fiducia in Milano			
	De Corato Riccardo	2.9	MSI-DN			
	Prosperini Pier Gianni	1.1	Lega alpina lumbarda			
	Bossi Angela	0.9	All. lom. aut.			
	Maiolo Tiziana	0.8	Giust. ecol. libertà			
	Armand Arman	0.5	Lega pens.-L. lomb.			
	Stroppa Claudio	0.5	Part. pens.			
	Fatuzzo Carlo	0.3	Pensionati di Milano			
Catania	**Bianco Vincenzo**	**40.4**	Patto per Catania	**Bianco Vincenzo**	**52.1**	Patto per Catania
	Fava Giovanni	27.5	Civic List	Fava Giovanni	47.9	Civic List
	Trantino Vincenzo	17.3	Civic List			
	Scavone Antonio	12.3	Dc			
	Petrina Mario	2.5	Civic List			

First round candidates who advanced to the second round and the second round winner are in boldface.

Source: Calculated from data provided by Ministero dell'Interno - Direzione centrale per i servizi elettorali.

TABLE B16 *(continued)*

	First round - 6 June		Second round - 20 June	
Torino	Electors	829,491	Electors	829,491
	Voters	639,386	Voters	514,762
	% voters	77.1	% voters	62.1
	Not valid votes	38,345	Not valid votes	26,091
	% of non valid votes/voters	6.0	% of non valid votes/voters	5.1
	of which blank ballots	11,950	of which blank ballots	6,648
	% of blank ballots/not valid votes	31.2	% of blank ballots/not valid votes	25.5
Milano	Electors	1,195,257	Electors	1,195,257
	Voters	934,060	Voters	828,152
	% voters	78.1	% voters	69.3
	Not valid votes	42,259	Not valid votes	34,731
	% of non valid votes/voters	4.5	% of non valid votes/voters	4.2
	of which blank ballots	13,242	of which blank ballots	16,965
	% of blank ballots/not valid votes	31.3	% of blank ballots/not valid votes	48.8
Catania	Electors	280,517	Electors	280,517
	Voters	203,777	Voters	162,970
	% voters	72.6	% voters	58.1
	Not valid votes	21,216	Not valid votes	6,900
	% of non valid votes/voters	10.4	% of non valid votes/voters	4.2
	of which blank ballots	21,060	of which blank ballots	1,475
	% of blank ballots/not valid votes	99.3	% of blank ballots/not valid votes	21.4

Source: Calculated from data provided by Ministero dell'Interno - Direzione centrale per i servizi elettorali.

TABLE B17 Mayor Elections, November 1993: Venezia, Genova, Roma, Napoli e Palermo

	First Round - 21 November			Second Round - 5 December		
	Candidates	%	Lists	Candidates	%	Lists
Venezia	Cacciari Massimo	42.3	Pds, Rif.com., Fed. dei verdi, La Rete-Mov.dem., All. Venezia e Mestre, Progresso socialista	Cacciari Massimo	55.4	Pds, Rif. com., Fed. dei verdi, La Rete-Mov.dem., All. Venezia e Mestre, Progresso socialista
	Mariconda Aldo	26.5	Liga veneta-Lega nord	Mariconda Aldo	44.6	Liga veneta-Lega nord
	Castellani Giovanni	23.4	Lega aut. veneta, Patto Venezia Mestre, Progr. autonomia, Verso part. pop.			
	Canella Bruno	2.9	Msi-Dn			
	Salvadori Augusto	2.6	Unione dei cittadini			
	Merlo Francesco	1.2	L. Ven. autonomo			
	Minchillo Paolo	1.1	Il gruppo			
Genova	Sansa Adriano	42.9	Pds, L.Pannella, Fed. dei verdi, La Rete-Mov.Dem., All. per Genova, Patto solidarietà	Sansa Adriano	59.2	Pds, L. Pannella, Fed. dei verdi, La Rete-Mov.Dem., All. per Genova, Patto solidarietà
	Serra Enrico	26.5	Lega nord	Serra Enrico	40.8	Lega nord
	Signorini Ugo	15.0	Un. di centro, Rin. soc., Popolari Genova			
	Boffardi Giuliano	7.4	Rifondazione comunista			
	Plinio Vincenzo	6.2	Msi-Dn, Part. pens.			
	Di Rella Fabrizio	0.8	Giovani per Genova			
	Genta Giovanni	0.3	Pens. U.V.-Lega ligure			
	Romeo Pasquale	0.3	Mov. lav. autonomi			

(continues)

TABLE B17 *(continued)*

	First Round - 21 November			Second Round - 5 December		
	Candidates	%	Lists	Candidates	%	Lists
Roma	Rutelli Francesco	39.6	Pds, L. Pannella, Fed. dei verdi, All. Roma	Rutelli Francesco	53.1	Pds, L. Pannella Fed. dei verdi, All. Roma
	Fini Gianfranco	35.8	Msi-Dn, Insieme per Roma	Fini Gianfranco	46.9	Msi-Dn, Insieme per Roma
	Caruso Carmelo	11.4	Dc, Psdi, Un. di centro, Civiltà e progresso			
	Nicolini Renato	8.3	Rifond. comun., Liberare Roma			
	Ripa di Meana Vittorio	1.5	All. laica riformista			
	Germontani Maria Ida	0.7	Lega Italia federale			
	Pappalardo Antonio	0.6	Solidarietà democratica			
	Scalabrini Laura	0.5	Verdi federalisti			
	Pozzi Anna Moana	0.5	Partito amore			
	Savelli Giulio	0.2	Movimento ind. Roma			
	Rossi Federica	0.2	Nuova Italia			
	Pasquali Gabriella	0.2	Partito crist. democrazia			
	Cece Mirella	0.1	Mov. eur. lib. crist.			
	Caccamo Rosario	0.1	Mov. pop. crist. uomo amb.			
	Olivieri Carlo	0.1	Alleanza umanista			
	Fiorelli Pier Vittorio	0.1	Diritti e doveri			
	Bartolomei Rosanna	0.1	Dem. cor. libertà			

(continues)

TABLE B17 *(continued)*

	First Round - 21 November			Second Round - 5 December		
	Candidates	%	Lists	Candidates	%	Lists
Napoli	**Bassolino Antonio**	**41.6**	Pds, Rif. com., Fed. dei verdi, La Rete-Mov.Dem., Rinascita socialista, Alternativa Napoli	**Bassolino Antonio**	**55.6**	Pds, Rif. com., Fed. dei verdi, La Rete-Mov.Dem., Rinascita socialista, Alternativa Napoli
	Mussolini Alessandra	31.1	Msi-Dn	Mussolini Alessandra	44.4	Msi-Dn
	Caprara Massimo	14.1	Dc, Psi, Pli, Psdi			
	Santangelo Sabatino	8.6	Alleanza Napoli			
	Garofalo Alberto	1.2	Servire Napoli			
	D'Acunto Antonio	1.1	Lista arcobaleno			
	Sommella Fortunato	0.9	Progetto Napoli nuova			
	Saggese Giuseppe	0.7	Noi per Napoli			
	Dufour Donatella	0.7	Unione civica			
Palermo	**Orlando Leoluca**	75.2	La Rete-Mov.Dem.			
	Pucci Elda	16.3	Forum			
	Giordano Alfonso	6.1	Unione di centro			
	Ranelli Salvatore	1.4	Movimento democratico siciliano			
	La Barbera Giuseppe	1.0	Unione lega Italia federale			

First round candidates who advanced to the second round and the second round winner are in boldface.
* Elected mayor of the first round.

Source: Calculated from data provided by Ministero dell'Interno - Direzione centrale per i servizi elettorali.

TABLE B17 *(continued)*

	First round - 21 November		Second round - 5 December	
Venezia	Electors	270,305	Electors	270,305
	Voters	224,180	Voters	205,517
	% voters	82.9	% voters	76.0
	Not valid votes	13,628	Not valid votes	17,195
	% of non valid votes/voters	6.1	% of non valid votes/voters	8.4
	of which blank ballots	4,677	of which blank ballots	6,877
	%of blank ballots/not valid votes	34.3	%of blank ballots/not valid votes	40.0
Genova	Electors	642,300	Electors	642,300
	Voters	472,436	Voters	472,782
	% voters	73.6	% voters	73.6
	Not valid votes	30,043	Not valid votes	21,423
	% of non valid votes/voters	6.4	% of non valid votes/voters	4.5
	of which blank ballots	11,054	of which blank ballots	9,288
	%of blank ballots/not valid votes	36.8	%of blank ballots/not valid votes	43.4
Roma	Electors	2,317,077	Electors	2,317,077
	Voters	1,814,684	Voters	1,850,290
	% voters	78.3	% voters	79.9
	Not valid votes	100,015	Not valid votes	50,401
	% of non valid votes/voters	5.5	% of non valid votes/voters	2.7
	of which blank ballots	25,717	of which blank ballots	14,614
	%of blank ballots/not valid votes	25.7	%of blank ballots/not valid votes	29.0
Napoli	Electors	879,237	Electors	879,237
	Voters	589,063	Voters	559,696
	% voters	67.0	% voters	63.7
	Not valid votes	37,698	Not valid votes	18,865
	% of non valid votes/voters	6.4	% of non valid votes/voters	3.4
	of which blank ballots	8,974	of which blank ballots	3,838
	%of blank ballots/not valid votes	23.8	%of blank ballots/not valid votes	20.3
Palermo	Electors	565,579		
	Voters	414,471		
	% voters	73.3		
	Not valid votes	42,702		
	% of non valid votes/voters	10.3		
	of which blank ballots	17,032		
	%of blank ballots/not valid votes	39.9		

Source: Calculated from data provided by Ministero dell'Interno - Direzione centrale per i servizi elettorali.

TABLE C1 Communal Administrations by Political Composition (April 1993)

	All Communes				
	No.	Population	Prov. Capitals	Over 5,000 inhabitants*	Under 5,000 inhabitants
Dc	1,987	6,145,864	3	284	1,703
Pds	138	1,194,276	1	81	57
Psi	117	280,946		6	111
Pci	33	116,708		4	29
Pri	5	11,604			5
Pli	4	5,551			4
Psdi	14	26,437			14
Msi-Dn	3	5,650			3
Ind.	265	325,181			265
Ppst	75	160,774		75	
P.S. d'az.	4	4,230			4
UV	11	8,329			11
Civic Lists	4	14,735			4
Lega lombarda	4	29,572		1	3
Dc-Pri	41	340,260	1	21	20
Dc-Pri-Pci	8	183,784	1	7	1
Dc-Pri-Pci-Pli	1	5,162		1	
Dc-Pri-Pci-Ind.-Psi	1	1,747			1
Dc-Pri-Pci-Psi	8	46,190		2	6
Dc-Pri-Pci-Psi-Msi-Dn	2	3,051			2
Dc-Pri-Pci-Psdi	2	35,332		1	1
Dc-Pri-Pli	5	27,546		3	2
Dc-Pri-Pli-Ind.	2	1,895			2
Dc-Pri-Pli-Ind.-Psi	2	17,984		1	1
Dc-Pri-Pli-Ind.-Psi-Psdi	1	104,509	1	1	
Dc-Pri-Pli-Ind.-Psdi	1	10,547		1	
Dc-Pri-Pli-Ppst-Psi	1	105,180	1	1	
Dc-Pri-Pli-Psi	13	715,347	3	9	4
Dc-Pri-Pli-Psi-Psdi	5	367,878	2	5	
Dc-Pri-Pli-Psi-Psdi-Pds	1	15,562		1	
Dc-Pri-Pli-Psi-Pds	1	17,438		1	
Dc-Pri-Pli-Psdi	8	290,819	1	8	
Dc-Pri-Pli-Msi-Dn	1	999			1
Dc-Pri-Pli-Pds	4	131,606		4	
Dc-Pri-Ind.	19	163,061		5	14
Dc-Pri-Ind.-UV	1	3,897			1
Dc-PRI-Ind.-Psi	14	2,845,486	1	3	11
Dc-Pri-Ind.-Psi-Psdi	4	22,523		1	3
Dc-Pri-Ind.-Psi-Psdi-Pds	1	6,914		1	
Dc-Pri-Ind.-Psi-Msi-Dn	1	2,675			1
Dc-Pri-Ind.-Psi-Pds	4	15,701		2	2
Dc-Pri-Ind.-Psdi	1	1,202			1
Dc-Pri-Ind.-Psdi-Lega lomb.	1	11,494		1	
Dc-Pri-Ind.-Psdi-L.verde Verdi arc.	1	13,233		1	
Dc-Pri-Ind.-Psdi-Pds	1	40,135		1	
Dc-Pri-Ind.-Pds	2	25,102		2	
Dc-Pri-Ppst-Psi	1	12,577		1	

(continues)

TABLE C1 *(continued)*

	All Communes		Prov. Capitals	Over 5,000 inhabitants[a]	Under 5,000 inhabitants
	No.	Population			
Dc-Pri-P.S. d'az.	2	6,481			2
Dc-Pri-P.S. d'az.-Psi-Pds	1	2,531			1
Dc-Pri-Uds-Psi	1	102,086	1	1	
Dc-Pri-Psi	74	729,493		56	18
Dc-Pri-Psi-Psdi	28	593,124	3	22	6
Dc-Pri-Psi-Psdi-Verdi	1	80,757		1	
Dc-Pri-Psi-Psdi-Verdi-Pds	1	371,022	1	1	
Dc-Pri-Psi-Psdi-Pds	9	89,736		7	2
Dc-Pri-Psi-Msi-Dn	1	3,049			1
Dc-Pri-Psi-Msi-Dn-Pds	2	12,498		1	1
Dc-Pri-Psi-Dem.prol.					
L.verde Verdi arc.	1	2,303		1	
Dc-Pri-Psi-L.verde-Pds	1	31,367		1	
Dc-Pri-Psi-Verdi	2	11,488		2	
Dc-Pri-Psi-Verdi-Pds	1	114,598	1	1	
Dc-Pri-Psi-Patt	1	7,924		1	
Dc-Pri-Psi-L. verde-Pds	1	99,179	1	1	
Dc-Pri-Psi-Pds	18	216,157		13	5
Dc-Pri-Psdi	11	85,325		8	3
Dc-Pri-Psdi-L. civica	1	12,390		1	
Dc-Pri-Psdi-Verdi	1	22,809		1	
Dc-Pri-Psdi-L. verde-Pds	1	52,440		1	
Dc-Pri-Psdi-Pds	8	134,796		7	1
Dc-Pri-Msi-Dn-Pds-Rif.com.	1	1,493			1
Dc-Pri-Verdi	1	379			1
Dc-Pri-Verdi-Pds	1	15,992		1	
Dc-Pri-Patt	1	519			1
Dc-Pri-Verdi arc.-Pds	1	24,440		1	
Dc-Pri-Pds	30	340,152		24	6
Dc-Pci	62	323,016		22	40
Dc-Pci-Pli	3	25,224		1	2
Dc-Pci-Pli-Ind.	2	3,201			2
Dc-Pci-Pli-Psi	4	13,250		1	3
Dc-Pci-Ind.	24	54,046		3	21
Dc-Pci-Ind.-Mov.Friuli-Psi	1	3,084			1
Dc-Pci-Ind.-Psi	13	20,950			13
Dc-Pci-Ind.-Psdi	4	7,522			4
Dc-Pci-Ind.-Msi-Dn	1	721			1
Dc-Pci-Ind.-Pds	2	1,642			2
Dc-Pci-P.rad.	1	1,781			1
Dc-Pci-P.S. d'az.	2	1,553			2
Dc-Pci-P.S. d'az.-Psi	1	3,043			1
Dc-Pci-Psi	45	145,229		11	34
Dc-Pci-Psi-Psdi	5	17,260		1	4
Dc-Pci-Psi-Msi-Dn	4	15,471		1	3
Dc-Pci-Psi-Dem.prol.	1	104			1
Dc-Pci-Psi-Dem.prol.-Patt	1	3,002		1	
Dc-Pci-Psi-Verdi	1	1,725			1

(continues)

TABLE C1 *(continued)*

	All Communes				
	No.	Population	Prov. Capitals	Over 5,000 inhabitants[a]	Under 5,000 inhabitants
Dc-Pci-Psi-Pds	3	2,551			3
Dc-Pci-Psdi	7	17,968		2	5
Dc-Pci-Psdi-Pds	2	9,102		1	1
Dc-Pci-Msi-Dn	4	9,649			4
Dc-Pci-Dem.prol.	1	1,740		1	
Dc-Pci-L.verde	1	80,929	1	1	
Dc-Pci-Verdi	3	37,385		2	1
Dc-Pci-Patt	1	199			1
Dc-Pci-Pds	5	46,409		3	2
Dc-Pli	23	195,446		10	13
Dc-Pli-Ind.	12	37,672		2	10
Dc-Pli-Ind.-Psi	7	26,438		1	6
Dc-Pli-Ind.-Psi-Psdi	2	9,431		1	1
Dc-Pli-Ind.-Psi-Msi-Dn-Pds	1	9,319		1	
Dc-Pli-Ind.-Psi-Democratico pop.	1	1,125			1
Dc-Pli-Ind.-Psdi	1	16,913		1	
Dc-Pli-Ind.-Msi-Dn	1	120			1
Dc-Pli-Ind.-Pds	1	9,046		1	
Dc-Pli-Psi	27	290,642		16	11
Dc-Pli-Psi-Psdi	14	547,681	2	12	2
Dc-Pli-Psi-Psdi-Pds	3	54,379		3	
Dc-Pli-Psi-Msi-Dn	1	1,766			1
Dc-Pli-Psi-Liga ven.-L. verde-Pds	1	18,105		1	
Dc-Pli-Psi-Verdi-Verdi arc.	1	265,932	1	1	
Dc-Pli-Psi-Verdi-Pds	1	13,663		1	
Dc-Pli-Psi-Pds	3	172,594	2	3	
Dc-Pli-Psdi	8	305,177	2	5	3
Dc-Pli-Psdi-Pds	2	128,125	1	2	
Dc-Pli-Msi-Dn	2	6,091			2
Dc-Pli-Msi-Dn-Pds	1	7,906		1	
Dc-Pli-Patt	1	597			1
Dc-Pli-L. verde-Pds	1	234,678	1	1	
Dc-Pli-Pds	1	27,931		1	
Dc-Ind.	318	631,307		21	297
Dc-Ind.-P.rad.-Psi	1	2,196			1
Dc-Ind.-P.S. d'az.	5	18,741		1	4
Dc-Ind.-P.S. d'az.-Psi	4	4,904			4
Dc-Ind.-P.S. d'az.-Psi-Pds	1	8,033		1	
Dc-Ind.-P.S.d'az.-Psi-Rif.com.	1	5,670		1	
Dc-Ind.-P.S. d'az.-Pds	3	7,767		1	2
Dc-Ind.-Uv	5	4,935			5
Dc-Ind.-Uv-Adp	2	6,028			2
Dc-Ind.-Psi	190	502,067		24	166
Dc-Ind.-Psi-Psdi	27	151,862		4	23
Dc-Ind.-Psi-Psdi-Msi-Dn	1	4,125			1
Dc-Ind.-Psi-Psdi-Pds	5	69,126		3	2
Dc-Ind.-Psi-Msi-Dn	6	7,923			6
Dc-Ind.-Psi-Msi-Dn-Pds	1	1,984			1

(continues)

TABLE C1 *(continued)*

	All Communes				
	No.	Population	Prov. Capitals	Over 5,000 inhabitants[a]	Under 5,000 inhabitants
Dc-Ind.-Psi-Dem.prol.-Pds	1	3,971			1
Dc-Ind.-Psi-L. verde-Pds-Rif.com.	1	4,276			1
Dc-Ind.-Psi-Caccia pesca	1	7,075		1	
Dc-Ind.-Psi-Verdi-Pds	1	95,571	1	1	
Dc-Ind.-Psi-Verdi arc.	1	5,570		1	
Dc-Ind.-Psi-Pds	27	314,345	1	7	20
Dc-Ind.-Psdi	36	115,305		4	32
Dc-Ind.-Psdi-Msi-Dn	1	6,670		1	
Dc-Ind.-Psdi-Pds	3	19,380		2	1
Dc-Ind.-Msi-Dn	6	13,027			6
Dc-Ind.-Sin.indip.-Verdi arc.	1	2,460			1
Dc-Ind.-L. verde-Pds	1	15,317		1	
Dc-Ind.-Adp	1	2,704			1
Dc-Ind.-L.civica verde	1	3,875			1
Dc-Ind.-Lega lomb.-L.aut.ven.-Lega ven.aut.	1	35,834		1	
Dc-Ind.-Verdi	2	4,646			2
Dc-Ind.-Verdi-Pds	1	1,850			1
Dc-Ind.-Patt	1	1,193		1	
Dc-Ind.-Verdi Fvg	1	830			1
Dc-Ind.-Pds	49	232,778		17	32
Dc-Ind.-Pds-Rif.com.	2	10,446		1	1
Dc-Ind.-Rif.com.	1	5,479		1	
Dc-Ind. di sinistra-Pds	1	2,001			1
Dc-Part.cattolico-Psi-Psdi	1	1,778			1
Dc-Ppst	23	93,104		23	
Dc-Ppst-Psi	3	6,501		3	
Dc-Ppst-Psi-Psdi	2	34,271		2	
Dc-Ppst-Verdi alt.	1	477		1	
Dc-P.rad.-Psi	1	1,064			1
Dc-P.S. d'az.	7	19,917		1	6
Dc-P.S. d'az.-Psi	14	74,041		7	7
Dc-P.S. d'az.-Psi-Psdi	1	3,598			1
Dc-P.S. d'az.-Psi-Psdi-Pds	2	10,461		1	1
Dc-P.S. d'az.-Psi-Pds	5	6,691		1	4
Dc-P.S. d'az.-Pds	4	18,171		2	2
Dc-Un.sl.-Psi	1	8,255		1	
Dc-Uv	2	3,273			2
Dc-Uv-Adp	3	7,150			3
Dc-Uv-Adp-Pds	1	4,675			1
Dc-Psi	574	3,590,469	6	260	314
Dc-Psi-Psdi	132	2,526,319	6	68	64
Dc-Psi-Psdi-Msi-Dn	2	18,880		2	
Dc-Psi-Psdi-Msi-Dn-Pds	2	71,347		2	
Dc-Psi-Psdi-Democratico pop.	1	1,121			1
Dc-Psi-Psdi-Dem.prol.-Pds	1	68,521		1	
Dc-Psi-Psdi-Verdi	2	55,745		2	
Dc-Psi-Psdi-Verdi arc.-Pds	1	32,349		1	

(continues)

TABLE C1 *(continued)*

	All Communes		Prov. Capitals	Over 5,000 inhabitants[a]	Under 5,000 inhabitants
	No.	Population			
Dc-Psi-Psdi-Pds	32	620,021	1	24	8
Dc-Psi-Msi-Dn	4	15,509		1	3
Dc-Psi-Msi-Dn-Pds	6	39,763		3	3
Dc-Psi-Sin.in.-Pds	1	2,624			1
Dc-Psi-Per Trieste	1	252,369	1	1	
Dc-Psi-L. civica	1	32,650		1	
Dc-Psi-L. verde	3	12,588		3	
Dc-Psi-Caccia pesca	1	11,701		1	
Dc-Psi-Verdi	3	24,639		3	
Dc-Psi-Verdi-Patt	1	3,981		1	
Dc-Psi-Verdi-Pds	1	12,065		1	
Dc-Psi-Patt	3	3,720		2	1
Dc-Psi-Patt-L. verde	1	3,634		1	
Dc-Psi-Patt-Pds	2	1,978		1	1
Dc-Psi-L. verde-Pds	1	1,151		1	
Dc-Psi-Uds	1	19,457		1	
Dc-Psi-L.verde verdi arc.	3	20,081		3	
Dc-Psi-Pds	119	1,077,833	1	69	50
Dc-Psi-Pds-Rif.com.	2	16,124		2	
Dc-Psi-Rif.com.	3	25,702		2	1
Dc-Psi-La Rete-Mov.dem.	1	790			1
Dc-Psdi	97	709,609	3	33	64
Dc-Psdi-Msi-Dn	2	2,310			2
Dc-Psdi-Cattolici democratici	1	18,202		1	
Dc-Psdi-L. verde-Pds	1	85,029	1	1	
Dc-Psdi-Patt	1	854			1
Dc-Psdi-L.verde verdi arc.-Pds	1	52,218	1	1	
Dc-Psdi-Pds	34	503,025		28	6
Dc-Msi-Dn	16	52,886		4	12
Dc-Msi-Dn-L. verde	1	3,482			1
Dc-Msi-Dn-Pds	4	28,751		2	2
Dc-Dem.prol.	1	1,304			1
Dc-Dem.prol.-Patt	1	1,019		1	
Dc-L.verde	2	5,247		1	1
Dc-Caccia pesca	1	17,788		1	
Dc-Lega lomb.	3	13,864		2	1
Dc-Verdi	2	10,556		1	1
Dc-Verdi-Pds	7	110,722		7	
Dc-Patt	19	21,658		9	10
Dc-L. verde-Pds	2	57,852		2	
Dc-Pds	150	1,224,428		105	45
Dc-Pds-Rif.com.	5	35,851		3	2
Dc-Rif.com.	1	1,014			1
Pri-Pci	2	6,663			2
Pri-Pci-Pli-Psi	1	30,507		1	
Pri-Pci-Pli-Psi-Verdi	1	37,807		1	
Pri-Pci-Ind.	4	8,016			4
Pri-Pci-Ind.-Psi	5	10,421			5

(continues)

TABLE C1 *(continued)*

	No.	Population	Prov. Capitals	Over 5,000 inhabitants[a]	Under 5,000 inhabitants
Pri-Pci-Ind.-Psdi	1	3,972			1
Pri-Pci-Ind.-Psdi-L. verde	1	3,003			1
Pri-Pci-Ind.-Msi-Dn-Pds	1	3,696			1
Pri-Pci-Psi	7	87,999		4	3
Pri-Pci-Psi-Psdi	1	10,839		1	
Pri-Pci-Psi-Pds	2	3,772			2
Pri-Pli-Ind.	1	1,774			1
Pri-Pli-Ind.-Psi	1	1,673			1
Pri-Pli-Ind.-Psi-Pds	1	4,415			1
Pri-Pli-Ind.-Psdi-Pds	1	3,107			1
Pri-Pli-Psi-Psdi-Pds	1	16,081		1	
Pri-Pli-Psi-Psdi-Rif.com.	1	6,458		1	
Pri-Pli-Psi-Pds	2	97,615	1	2	
Pri-Pli-Pds	1	2,196			1
Pri-Ind.	2	1,309			2
Pri-Ind.-Psi	4	30,922		2	2
Pri-Ind.-Psi-Psdi	4	17,290		1	3
Pri-Ind.-Psi-Psdi-Pds	4	41,015		2	2
Pri-Ind.-Psi-L. verde	1	1,611			1
Pri-Ind.-Psi-Pds	15	99,497		5	10
Pri-Ind.-Psi-Pds-Rif.com.	1	3,427			1
Pri-Ind.-Mao	1	1,088			1
Pri-Ind.-Pds	6	198,342	1	1	5
Pri-P.S. d'az.-Psi-Psdi-Pds	2	129,714	1	2	
Pri-P.S. d'az.-Pds	1	1,347			1
Pri-Uv-Psi-Adp-Pds	1	37,194	1	1	
Pri-Psi	1	413			1
Pri-Psi-Psdi	3	40,264		1	2
Pri-Psi-Psdi-L. civica-L. verde-Pds	1	35,440		1	
Pri-Psi-Psdi-Pds	20	459,856	2	13	
Pri-Psi-Psdi-Pds-Rif.com.	1	10,119		1	
Pri-Psi-Msi-Dn-Pds	2	52,013		1	1
Pri-Psi-Msi-Dn-Pds-Rif.com.	1	12,637		1	
Pri-Psi-Dem.prol.	1	894			1
Pri-Psi-L.civica-Pds	1	30,229		1	
Pri-Psi-Verdi-Pds	3	64,747		3	
Pri-Psi-Verdi arc.	1	3,577		1	
Pri-Psi-L. verde-Pds	1	42,469		1	
Pri-Psi-Pds	46	1,018,210	4	27	19
Pri-Psi-Rif.com.	2	15,178		1	1
Pri-Psdi-Pds	4	19,450		1	3
Pri-Sin.in.-Pds	1	1,840			1
Pri-Lega lomb.	1	14,752		1	
Pri-Verdi-Pds-Rif.com.	1	11,826		1	
Pri-Verdi arc.-L. verde-Pds	1	10,850		1	
Pri-Lega lomb.-Lega nord	1	90,527	1	1	
Pri-Pds	4	4,934			4
Pri-Pds-Rif.com.	1	1,790			1

(continues)

TABLE C1 *(continued)*

	All Communes		Prov. Capitals	Over 5,000 inhabitants[a]	Under 5,000 inhabitants
	No.	Population			
Pci-Pli-Ind.-Psi	3	3,823			3
Pci-Pli-Ind.-Psi-Psdi	1	113			1
Pci-Pli-Ind.-Psi-Pds	1	4,932			1
Pci-Pli-Ind.-Pds	1	4,359			1
Pci-Pli-P.S. d'az.-Psi	1	1,177			1
Pci-Pli-Psi	1	5,148		1	
Pci-Ind.	46	94,388		2	44
Pci-Ind.-P.rad.-P.S. d'az.	1	1,307			1
Pci-Ind.-P.rad.-Psi	1	3,251			1
Pci-Ind.-P.S. d'az.-Psi	3	6,706			3
Pci-Ind.-P.S. d'az.-Psdi	1	1,807			1
Pci-Ind.-P.S. d'az.-Psdi-Pds	1	3,862			1
Pci-Ind.-Psi	94	226,335		3	91
Pci-Ind.-Psi-Psdi	9	20,218		1	8
Pci-Ind.-Psi-Psdi-Pds	1	4,621			1
Pci-Ind.-Psi-Msi-Dn	1	1,993			1
Pci-Ind.-Psi-Msi-Dn-Dem.prol.	1	1,511			1
Pci-Ind.-Psi-Democratico pop.	1	4,072			1
Pci-Ind.-Psi-Pds	12	26,397		1	11
Pci-Ind.-Psdi	4	8,349			4
Pci-Ind.-Dem.prol.	1	1,448			1
Pci-Ind.-Sin.in.	1	834			1
Pci-Ind.-Verdi	1	1,343			1
Pci-Ind.-Pds	8	12,132			8
Pci-P.S. d'az.	2	7,422			2
Pci-P.S. d'az.-Psi	2	1,960			2
Pci-P.S. d'az.-Psi-Msi-Dn-Pds	1	3,973			1
Pci-P.S. d'az.-Psi-Pds	2	7,480			2
Pci-P.S. d'az.-Pds	1	1,406			1
Pci-Psi	84	340,995		14	70
Pci-Psi-Psdi	8	26,944		2	6
Pci-Psi-Psdi-Dem.prol.	1	2,765			1
Pci-Psi-Psdi-L. verde	1	9,085		1	
Pci-Psi-Psdi-Pds	3	23,028		3	
Pci-Psi-Msi-Dn	1	456			1
Pci-Psi-Dem.prol.	1	2,324			1
Pci-Psi-L. civica	1	7,851		1	
Pci-Psi-Verdi	1	3,617			1
Pci-Psi-Pds	25	69,116		2	23
Pci-Psdi	5	45,766		1	4
Pci-Msi-Dn-Pds	1	826			1
Pci-Dem.prol.	1	2,711			1
Pci-Patt-Verdi arc.	1	1,506		1	
Pci-Pds	12	28,170			12
Pci-Pds-Rif.com.	2	6,689			2
Pci-Rif.com.	1	1,852			1
Pli-Ind.	4	3,148			4
Pli-Ind.-Uv	1	142			1

(continues)

TABLE C1 *(continued)*

	All Communes		Prov. Capitals	Over 5,000 inhabitants[a]	Under 5,000 inhabitants
	No.	Population			
Pli-Ind.-Uv-Adp	1	550			1
Pli-Ind.-Psi	4	13,609		1	3
Pli-Ind.-Psi-Psdi-L. verde	1	11,591		1	
Pli-Ind.-Psi-Sin.in.-Pds	1	1,537			1
Pli-Ind.-Psi-Pds	2	15,871		1	1
Pli-Ind.-Psdi	1	1,455			1
Pli-Ind.-Psdi-Pds	1	16,461		1	
Pli-Ind.-Msi-Dn-Pds	1	8,535		1	
Pli-Ind. di sinistra-Psi-Psdi	1	2,830			1
Pli-Psi	1	1,222			1
Pli-Psi-Psdi-L. verde-Pds	1	89,786	1	1	
Pli-Psi-Psdi-Pds	1	2,331			1
Pli-Psi-Pds	6	40,039		4	2
Pli-Pds	1	694			1
Ind.-Ind. di sinistra-Psi-Pds	1	2,436			1
Ind.-Ppst	2	3,619		2	
Ind.-Ppst-Union fur sud tirol	1	1,648		1	
Ind.-P.rad.-Psi-Psdi	1	914			1
Ind.-P.S. d'az.	1	2,162			1
Ind.-P.S. d'az.-Psi-Psdi-Pds	1	3,620			1
Ind.-P.S. d'az.-Psi-Pds	7	16,054		1	6
Ind.-P.S. d'az.-Psi-Pds-Rif.com.	1	13,539		1	
Ind.-P.S. d'az.-Pds	6	15,304			6
Ind.-Uv	20	17,512			20
Ind.-Uv-Adp	3	1,630			3
Ind.-Mov.Friuli-Psi-Verdi Fvg-Pds	1	4,942			1
Ind.-Psi	117	166,029		1	116
Ind.-Psi-Psdi	7	49,780		2	5
Ind.-Psi-Psdi-Pds	24	211,602	1	5	19
Ind.-Psi-Msi-Dn-Pds	2	6,587			2
Ind.-Psi-Democratico pop.	1	753			1
Ind.-Psi-Democratico pop.-Pds	1	3,513			1
Ind.-Psi-Dem.prol.-Pds	2	3,096			2
Ind.-Psi-L. civica	1	4,180			1
Ind.-Psi-Rad.ind.-Pds	1	3,879			1
Ind.-Psi-L.civica-Pds	1	8,605		1	
Ind.-Psi-Alleanza verde Fvg-Pds	1	10,460		1	
Ind.-Psi-Verdi	1	7,841		1	
Ind.-Psi-Verdi-Pds	1	8,148		1	
Ind.-Psi-Verdi arc.-Pds	3	12,393		1	2
Ind.-Psi-L. verde	1	883			1
Ind.-Psi-Pds	208	918,357	1	39	169
Ind.-Psi-Pds-Rif.com.	7	28,208		1	6
Ind.-Psi-Rif.com.	5	9,499			5
Ind.-Psdi	11	14,365		1	10
Ind.-Psdi-Verdi	1	9,596		1	
Ind.-Psdi-Pds	23	67,408		1	22

(continues)

TABLE C1 *(continued)*

	All Communes				
	No.	Population	Prov. Capitals	Over 5,000 inhabitants[a]	Under 5,000 inhabitants
Ind.-Msi-Dn	2	4,581			2
Ind.-Democratici pop.-Pds	1	4,331			1
Ind.-Dem.prol.	1	1,081			1
Ind.-Sin.in.-Pds	1	4,561			1
Ind.-P.dem.	1	2,951			1
Ind.-Adp	4	1,521			4
Ind.-Adp-Pds	2	2,594			2
Ind.-Caccia pesca-Pds	1	137,375	1	1	
Ind.-Verdi-Pds	3	53,289		3	
Ind.-Verdi-Rif.com.	1	1,630			1
Ind.-Verdi arc.	1	1,193			1
Ind.-Lega lomb.-Lega nord	1	5,731		1	
Ind.-Pds	173	681,182		38	135
Ind.-Pds-Rif.com.	11	56,680		3	8
Ind.-Rif.com.	2	2,683			2
Ind. di sinistra-Pds	1	3,956			1
Ppst-Psi	3	3,667		3	
Ppst-Verdi alt.	1	715		1	
P.S. d'az.-Psi	1	1,366			1
P.S. d'az.-Psi-Psdi	1	364			1
P.S. d'az.-Psi-Psdi-Pds	5	77,083		3	2
P.S. d'az.-Psi-Pds	7	19,018		2	5
P.S. d'az.-Msi-Dn-Pds	1	1,589			1
P.S. d'az.-Pds	2	3,843			2
Un.sl.-Psi-Pds	1	6,159		1	
Uv-Adp	3	1,701			3
Mov.Friuli-Psi-Psdi-Verdi Fvg-Pds	1	6,568		1	
Psi-Psdi	12	30,269		2	10
Psi-Psdi-Msi-Dn	1	2,499			1
Psi-Psdi-Dem.prol.	1	438			1
Psi-Psdi-Dem.prol.-Verdi	1	7,516		1	
Psi-Psdi-Verdi-Pds	3	133,780		3	
Psi-Psdi-Verdi Fvg-Pds	1	10,323		1	
Psi-Psdi-Pds	53	1,969,888	4	26	27
Psi-Psdi-Pds-Rif.com.	3	63,015		3	
Psi-Msi-Dn-Pds	4	38,114		1	3
Psi-Democratico pop.-Pds	1	2,038			1
Psi-Dem.prol.	1	2,037		1	
Psi-Dem.prol.-Pds	1	4,054			1
Psi-Sin.in.-Verdi-Pds	1	7,541		1	
Psi-Sin.in.-Pds	1	1,138			1
Psi-Dc-Ind.-Pds	1	11,166		1	
Psi-L. civica-Pds	1	9,011		1	
Psi-L. verde	2	5,938			2
Psi-L. verde-Pds	3	30,402		2	1
Psi-Verdi-Pds	3	107,088	1	3	
Psi-Verdi alt.-Pds	1	14,646		1	
Psi-Pds	258	1,829,643	1	101	157

(continues)

TABLE C1 *(continued)*

	All Communes		Prov. Capitals	Over 5,000 inhabitants*	Under 5,000 inhabitants
	No.	Population			
Psi-Pds-Rif.com.	5	71,243		4	1
Psi-Rif.com.	1	2,344			1
Psdi-Msi-Dn-Pds	1	211			1
Psdi-Unione ossolana per l'aut.	1	483			1
Psdi-Verdi-Pds	1	15,937		1	
Psdi-Pds	7	22,416		1	6
Msi-Dn-Pds	1	2,479			1
Sin.in.-Pds-Rif.com.	1	611			1
L. civica-Lega lomb.-Lega nord	1	5,438		1	
L. verde-Pds-Rif.com.	1	13,695		1	
Verdi	1	694			1
Verdi-Lega lomb.-Lega nord	1	123,145		1	
Verdi-Pds	2	12,992		1	1
Verdi-Pds-Rif.com.	1	7,365		1	
Patt-L. verde	1	865			1
L. verde-Pds	1	14,685		1	
Pds-Rif.com.	12	73,590		6	6
Other Mixed	729	2,158,505	6	82	647
External, prefectoral Administration	276	6,579,669	9	176	100
Information missing	70	1,908,120	5	50	20
TOTAL	8,102	56,556,911	95	2,317	5,785

* Includes provincial capitals, all Communes in Bolzano prov. and over 1,000 inhabitants communes in Trento prov.

Source: Calculated from data provided by Ministero dell'Interno - Direzione centrale per i servizi elettorali.

TABLE C2   Political Affiliation of Communal Administrators (April 1993)

	Mayor	Aldermen	Councillors	Total
Dc	3,933	16,569	39,649	60,151
Pds	1,066	4,359	11,343	16,768
Psi	1,047	5,755	14,636	21,438
Rif.com.	9	108	587	704
Psdi	105	998	2,061	3,164
Pri	64	638	1,535	2,237
Pci	263	1,256	5,090	6,609
Pli	51	243	679	973
Msi-Dn	17	129	1,174	1,320
Partito Popolare Sud				
Tirolese	111	452	1,026	1,589
Partito sardo d'azione	15	158	368	541
Uv	35	131	254	420
Dem.prol.	4	22	128	154
Indipendents	643	4,471	12,694	17,808
Green Lists	9	147	1,061	1,217
P.Rad.	1	8	26	35
Civic Lists	9	39	438	486
Lega lombarda	10	55	683	748
Liga veneta		1	38	39
Partito Autonomista				
Trentino Tirolese	7	43	171	221
Cattolici democratici	1	3	14	18
La Rete-Mov.dem.		1	12	13
Caccia pesca e ambiente		4	66	70
Dc D. *	22	105	379	506
Dc T. **	183	919	2,358	3,460
Pds D. *			1	1
Pds T. **	1	41	107	149
Psi D. *	2	5	46	53
Psi T. **	57	366	833	1,256
Psdi D. *		3	5	8
Psdi T. **	16	64	158	238
Pri D. *		2	6	8
Pri T. **	9	39	90	138
Pci D. *		4	6	10
Pci T. **	24	120	361	505
Msi-Dn D. *		3	4	7
Msi-Dn T. **	2	16	44	62
Pli D. *		1		1
Pli T. **	16	31	84	131
Ppst D. *		3	25	28

(continues)

TABLE C2 *(continued)*

	Mayor	Aldermen	Councillors	Total
P.S. d'az. D. *			2	2
P.S. d'az. T. **		3	5	8
Rif. com. T. **	1	2	11	14
Dem.prol. T. **		3	5	8
Other Lists	13	70	460	543
Total	7,746	37,390	98,723	143,859
Non-councillor Aldermen ***	315			
Vacant positions				
on city councils	8,117			
in city governments	2,946			
Prefectoral commissions	276			

* Considered a dissident within the indicated party.
** Considered of the indicated party, even if not a member.
*** Technical person without any party affiliation.

Source: Calculated from data provided by Ministero dell'Interno - Direzione centrale per i servizi elettorali.

About the Editors
and Contributors

Piergiorgio Corbetta is professor of analysis of classes and social groups in the Faculty of Sociology at the University of Trento.

Osvaldo Croci is assistant professor of political science in the Department of Political Science at the Laurentian University, Canada.

Donatella della Porta is associate professor of local government in the Faculty of Political Science at the University of Florence.

Richard S. Katz is professor of political science in the Department of Political Science at the Johns Hopkins University, Maryland.

Richard Locke is associate professor of industrial relations and political science in the Massachusetts Institute of Technology, Cambridge, Mass.

Gianpietro Mazzoleni is associate professor of sociology of communication in the Faculty of Humanities at the University of Salerno.

Carol Mershon is assistant professor of political science in the Department of Government and Foreign Affairs at the University of Virginia.

Arturo M. L. Parisi is professor of sociology of political phenomena in the Department of Education at the University of Bologna.

Gianfranco Pasquino is professor of political science in the Faculty of Political Science at the University of Bologna.

Martin Rhodes is a lecturer in the Department of Government at the University of Manchester, UK.

Rosalba Salvato is an employee in the Electoral Bureau at the Italian Ministry of the Interior.

Alberto Vannucci has finished his PhD in political science at the Scuola superiore di studi universitari e di perfezionamento "S. Anna" in Pisa where he is now a researcher.

Salvatore Vassallo is a PhD student in political science at the University of Florence.

Douglas Wertman is a resource analyst at the United States Information Agency, Washington, DC.

Index